RELIGION AS COMMUNICATION

Why do Gods persist in contemporary society? Religious revival and vitality all over the world contradict the vision of continuing declining of belief. This linear process of eclipse of the sacred in modern society has been proved wrong. Religion indeed is an expert system competent in ultimate meanings of human being and social order.

Enzo Pace argues that religion persists as a symbol because of its intrinsic power of communication, in its will to wield the power to dominate the event of death, and to build a bridge between the visible and the invisible. The crucial passage from living word to holy scripture is a fundamental device in the construction of a system of religious belief. This book provides an insight on a new approach to religious studies, drawing from systems theory to consider religion as a means of communication, and offering a critical alternative to the secularization theory to explain why religion persists in modernity.

Religion as Communication
God's Talk

ENZO PACE
University of Padova, Italy

ASHGATE

Published by
Ashgate Publishing Limited
Wey Court East
Union Road
Farnham
Surrey, GU9 7PT
England

Ashgate Publishing Company
Suite 420
101 Cherry Street
Burlington
VT 05401-4405
USA

www.ashgate.com

British Library Cataloguing in Publication Data
Pace, Enzo.
  Religion as communication : God's talk. 1. Religion and sociology.
  I. Title
  306.6–dc22

Library of Congress Cataloging-in-Publication Data
Pace, Enzo.
  Religion as communication : God's talk / Enzo Pace.
    p. cm.
  Includes bibliographical references and index.
  ISBN 978-1-4094-3523-5 (hardcover : alk. paper) — ISBN 978-1-4094-3524-2
  (ebook) 1. Religion—Philosophy. 2. Communication—Religious aspects. I. Title. II.
  Title: God's talk.
  BL51.P24 2011
  306.6—dc23

2011021375

ISBN 9781409435235 (hbk)
ISBN 9781409435242 (ebk)

Printed and bound in Great Britain by the
MPG Books Group, UK

Contents

List of Figures and Tables   *vii*

Introduction   1

1   Religion as Communication   21

2   Religion and Sense   47

3   From the Capacity for Improvisation to Belief System   65

4   Spirit and Order   97

Conclusion   135

Bibliography   *147*
Index   *155*

List of Figures and Tables

Figures

3.1   The differentiation of the Japanese religious system   77
3.2   The matrix and differentiation in the Chinese religious system   79

4.1   Memory, narrative, and social order   108
4.2   Conception of the deity, according to the Sioux   126
4.3   Conception of the deity among the Bambara populations
        of the African savannah   126

Tables

3.1   The differentiation of the Hindu religious system   71
3.2   Brahman—the perennial impersonal principle   72

Introduction

Secularization Theory and its Limits

The idea that religion would undergo an inexorable decline and that all things holy would progressively lose their plausibility was born of a blunder. The assumption was that the more we became modernized, the less we would need religion, in a linear process of eclipse of the sacred predicted by the generation of sociologists of religion coming soon after World War Two, between 1960 and 1970, and based on empirical data emerging from their preliminary investigations: there were fewer people going to church, fewer vocations for the priesthood, a tendency to use personal judgment (instead of consulting religious authorities) in decisions concerning moral issues, a declining sense of membership, and faith had become a private concern. The sociologists' convictions were sometimes translated into ideological reasonings, particularly when religion was openly challenged as the enemy of modernity and of a secularism imposed by a political power.

For many years, secularization as an ideology (Acquaviva and Stella 1989; Martelli, 1990) clearly became the conceptual horizon of the first generation of sociologists of some of the East European countries dominated at the time by the Soviet Communist model. Now, several years on, when we reread the research conducted in Poland between 1960 and 1980, we see how strongly the sociological analysis of the phenomenon of religion was influenced by different ideological affiliations. On the one hand, there were those who—based on orthodox Marxist premises—believed that the processes of change then underway in Polish society showed all the symptoms of a decline in the force of religion; on the other, the sociologists and intellectuals of Catholic inspiration were demonstrating that the Polish people's devotion, participation, and religious vitality were not only not declining, they were showing signs of a reawakening. Such a striking diversity of interpretation obviously had to do with the authors' different political and ideological preferences. There was clearly a rift dividing those who were in favor of the political regime from those who were against it.

In the case of Poland, the Catholic Church was on the side of the opposition and, through the language of religion, it interpreted the needs and hopes of social and political freedom of millions of people, who were not necessarily all Catholics or practicing believers (Pace 1984; Michel 1989, 1994). When you visited Poland between 1979 and 1985, it was not unusual to meet what were then called "devout Catholic atheists," people who were struggling against the Communist regime and saw the Catholic Church as the only moral entity capable of opposing the dominant power. In the initial throes of the Polish Revolution (between 1980 and 1988), religion enabled people to imagine another society, it became a way for people to speak about the chances of another social and economic model. More importantly, it invented a present that still does not exist even today. What was noticeable then, for instance, if you happened to be in Warsaw or Krakow, or Gdansk, on any Sunday in winter, was the silence that reigned over the roads towards evening, a silence that was suddenly interrupted by enormous crowds spilling out of the churches at the end of Mass. This was not just the spontaneous confusion typically seen when the doors of a church are opened, with people milling about and exchanging greetings, chatting in the churchyard with friends and acquaintances. What tended to happen was that the crowd would soon be transformed into a genuine organized protest march, complete with national flags and slogans against the regime in power. This happened increasingly often, as the Poles progressively became convinced that they could change the course of their history, and as the reaction of the political regime became increasingly repressive. The organization of the marches even contained a hint of *mockery*: as soon as the police showed up, this parade of churchgoers that had emerged from Mass and turned into a protest march rapidly dispersed and little groups silently formed around the bus and tram stops, pretending they were waiting for transport—an ironic reaction in the face of which the police no longer knew what to do or who to hit. It is by no means easy to be ironic when faced with a policeman and, in the Polish case, this behavior can be explained in two ways: the power of the multitude and the power of faith. All these individuals felt that they were not alone, that they could count on an ample, widespread, and reassuring solidarity. Whether they were really believers or not, they were aware that they knew the right *words* in contrast with the regime. Along with many other people like themselves, they understood the power of religion in that particular historical situation. It was certainly not by chance that the collective movement that ultimately succeeded in pooling all the forces of opposition (secular and Catholic, post-Marxist and reformist left-wing, Jews and Orthodox Christians) was to go by the name of *Solidarność* (Bova 2003) and that the charismatic figure of a "Polish" Pope, in the person of John Paul II, was to carry a considerable weight.

The long movie being enacted during those years in the squares and stadiums of Poland, under the directorship of the Catholic Church, frequently showed footage involving two leading actors: on the one hand, there was a leader, with his people joined in prayer around him; on the other, there was a charismatic interaction, where what counted was not only the words that were spoken, but also the silences, and even more the pure image of a merging of hopes, the hopes of a Polish Pope convinced of the need to put an end to the Communist regime (and not only in Poland) and the hopes of the majority of the people who had had enough of mass poverty and ideological totalitarianism (Guizzardi 1983).

In this case, by means of a public rituality that the government forces were unable to contain, religion helped people imagine a new social order—a new solidarity, to use a term dear to Durkheim—by providing a language that made it possible to translate people's deepest feelings into words, linking the words to *things*, to life experiences that people had in common. Linking words to things helps individuals to recognize that they have the same problems and that, by taking action together, they can find a solution. This recognition creates social links.

In the years when the Polish situation was making the world news, something similar was going on far away from Warsaw, in the squares of Teheran. A mass revolution was casting out a political regime there as well, because it was considered oppressive and excessively pro-Western (Guolo 2007). There too, the spark that started the social revolution owed a great deal to religion. In Iran, the religion of the majority is Shi'a, which is a minority branch of Islam that developed in the aftermath of the Battle of Karbala in the year 680 of our era. For historical reasons, Shi'a became a collective *forma mentis* in the land of the ancient Persians, the source of their national identity, as Catholicism is for the Polish people.

In the changes taking place in Iran in 1978–79, Shi'a was consequently the language used to express the desire for change by people who really had very different ideas in many ways, but who nonetheless found it appropriate to take cover under the same umbrella in order to cope with shared adversities and to combat shared social and political adversaries. To understand why Shi'ite Islam became a part of the Iranians' sense of nationality, we need to consider not only the origins of the future State of Iran, but also the specificity of the religious rituals typical of Shi'a, which have no counterpart in the Sunni world (which is still the largest branch of Islam today). The process of territorial unification and national identification of what was to become the modern State of Iran began with the Safavid dynasty in the sixteenth century, under whose rule (begun with Shah Isma'il, 1499–1524) Shi'ite Islam was adopted as the national religion, partly with an anti-Ottoman intent. The dynasty reached its climax under the reign of Abbas the Great (1587–1628), who paved the way to a period of economic prosperity and administrative solidity. The phase of expansion of the Safavid reign came to an end in 1736, but the fortunes of the country's national identity had by this time become tied to the Shi'ite belief system.

The symbolic universe of Shi'ism is dominated by the figure of the martyr: the leaders of the Shi'a—'Ali and his son Husayn—are seen as martyrs who died to defend the true Islam. Their sacrifice—and that of Husayn, in particular, who was defeated and killed by the Sunnite army in 680 AD—is remembered during a sort of Holy Week when the story of the Shi'ite leader's passion and death is retold every evening for ten days (in the month of *muharram*) in a collective mourning process (Canetti 1962; Nesti 2003) that, over the centuries, has created a profound sense of solidarity amongst the Shi'ites and become attached to their national consciousness.

This collective rite is celebrated according to a precise schedule. It is divided into two clearly distinct parts which involve a community prayer and a shared meal. The places where all this happens are called *husayniyya*, from the name of Husayn, and they are usually buildings on two floors: there is a prayer hall on the first floor, while there is a kitchen with a dining room in the basement. The story of Husayn's martyrdom, narrating the end of his life, up to the final battle when he was killed by the Sunnite enemy, is retold one evening after the other, in a rising tide of sorrow for the passion and death of the people's leader. Every evening, a preacher in the prayer halls reads and chants, his voice broken with emotion, about Husayn's experience, accompanied by the faithful singing ritual songs, slowly at first and then with increasing vehemence, beating their breasts as a sign of penitence and woe. The collective emotion grows stronger and stronger as everyone identifies with Husayn's suffering. Everyone beats their breast with their fists with increasing violence. When the excitement reaches a climax, driven by the choked chanting of the prayer reader, who is often in tears and shows sings of intense emotion, the spectators form a sort of ring and begin to dance, every man symbolically embracing all the others in a pact of suffering and solidarity, and exclaiming in one voice their willingness to sacrifice their own lives for Husayn. Before the practice of self-flagellation was outlawed in Iran, a whip with sharp barbs would be used during the procession that followed after the prayers, in a collective ritual representation of the "spilling of blood" in Husayn's honor.

What interests us here is to highlight the symbolic efficacy of such rituals. At least two themes are used, one strictly religious (recollecting the martyrdom of Husayn), the other ethical-political. In other words, the story of the passion and death of the Shi'ite leader is told in order to relive what he suffered, so that everyone can share the pain. At the same time, express a social solidarity is expressed, an exchange of words and gestures that enables everyone to recognize themselves in each other, in the same public passion.

Religious recollection forges a collective identity, giving the impression of a unity between different individuals that would otherwise be unimaginable. Religion becomes pure word, enabling people to *speak* to one another, because it provides them with a shared grammar and language. It is impossible to fully understand the Iranian Revolution of 1978–79 without bearing in mind the symbolic codes that the Shi'ite religion has always provided for the Iranian people's collective consciousness. Although it reflected different interests and hopes (Foucault 1998; Khosrokhawar and Vieille 1990), the revolutionary passion shown by enormous crowds of people in the months leading up to and after the revolution was the projection of another passion, that had been nourished by the cults of the month of *muharram* for generations. Canetti neatly explained the situation that we have described above in the following terms:

> … the breast-beaters could be defined as the rhythmic orchestra of mourning, as effective as mass crystal. Their self-inflicted pain is Hussein's pain, and by showing it they transform it into the suffering of the whole community. This repeated breast beating by the spectators gives rise to a *rhythmic crowd*, sustained by the emotion of the lament. Hussein has been torn away from all of them, and belongs to all of them together. (Canetti 1962: 182)

The rhythm is contagious, affecting body and mind, and it is translated into a collective *habitus* that can be spent equally well in the space of the great religious celebrations and in social and political emergencies. Whether it is a matter of opposing an oppressive regime (like the Pahlevi dynasty) or countering a threat from abroad (as in the difficult relations with the US) is neither here nor there for the purposes of our present discussion. What we wish to emphasize is religion's capacity to direct energies accumulated in the liturgical setting into other spheres of social life, and into political action. During the same period of time, Poland and Iran have provided examples (among many others) of religion's return to the public stage (Casanova 1994), putting to the test and exposing the partiality of those secularization theories that had predicted a progressive withdrawal of religion into the private sphere and a consequent loss of its social plausibility.

These considerations only hold true in part, however. If we take a closer look at what happened in Poland and Iran after the shockwave of the mass revolt (which had produced a far-reaching change of regime) had died down, we find that—despite the role of religion on the public stage—the behavior and attitudes of individuals, be they Polish or Iranian, have not been remodeled *ex novo* and based entirely on religious principles and standards. Iranian society shows clear signs of separation between a government defending the reasoning of an integralist Islamic state and the vast majority of the people who have little sympathy for the regime in power, whose attitude is critical even in relation to their own religious faith. Polish society, meanwhile, has undergone a growing socio-religious differentiation, reflected in a decline in religious practices and a part of the population taking secularized attitudes on issues such as sexual morals, or economic and political decisions. The Polish Catholic Church is well aware that it can no longer play a decisive part in a society that has become pluralist since the end of the Communist regime. In the two cases considered (Poland and Iran), it is as if the people had first identified themselves completely with the respective religions of their birth (Catholicism and Shi'a Islam) in order to subvert the established order, but then directed their desire for freedom and a better individual and social life *elsewhere*, once the new social and political order had become established. That is, the populations of both countries were aware that such freedom and well-being would not arrive like manna from heaven, but had to be assured by the new political regimes that they had helped to establish through the revolutionary process.

All this probably has less to do with any *cyclic nature* of religion, a sort of coming and going of its symbolic power in human societies, and more with the ongoing interaction between the longer and shorter terms of history in a given society. Religion is involved in both cases: acting as a storehouse for collective memory (Hervieu-Léger 1993), it is cyclically capable of *rising again*, providing symbolic repertoires capable of mobilizing people to social and political action; but it is also subject to historical contingencies, suffering the lash and backlash of human vicissitudes. Basically, it never disappears (and therefore can never return) if our gaze encompasses the longer historical period.

Nothing Comes Into Being Nor Perishes

Straining the point a little, I might say that nothing comes into being nor perishes: everything remains under the holy vaults of religion. Nothing comes into being in the sense that it is hard to find *pure* religions, that have not absorbed other religions during the course of their evolution—that is, other religions that have been lost in one way, while in another they have actually managed to survive (and flourish in disguise). Nothing perishes either, in the sense that the boundaries that every religion tries to erect in order to claim its place in the pantheon of history never succeed in protecting it against the invasion of other beliefs and competition from other faiths, that may ultimately prevail. However, it is also true that symbols and concepts released when these boundaries are trampled down go on to infiltrate other religions.

Thus, for religions, the law of accumulation applies: they can be represented as great belief systems consisting of various layers, some deeper down than others, some considered more authentic than others, in a hierarchy that is established over time by those in authority, or by those who control the circulation of the beliefs within the system. This stratification of different beliefs, some from far away, has generally been classified by historians as syncretism. We are told that every religion is intrinsically syncretic, and this is true if we place every religion's claim to be absolute under the magnifying glass, as historians of religions do. If we view the matter from a different angle, however, the syncretism characteristic of religions is really a *code of complexity* that is useful for defining and delimiting purposes, that is, for defining the boundaries of its own identity and for delimiting what is *true* from what is false in terms of its beliefs.

Who am I, and why is it me that is in the right, and not the others who do not believe in what I believe in? Translated into the impersonal form, the answer to these two questions means that every religion is intrinsically complex, in the sense that it is born and continues to live and withstand time in a constant exchange within a wider *environment* where there are also other forms of religious belief, other faiths, or simply the multiplicities or multiple individual facets of believing.

I can use an example to clarify the above statement. The African-American religions are usually considered syncretic *par excellence*. Candomblé, Umbanda, Voodoo, Santeria, and the like are seen as examples of religious concepts that have succumbed to the domination of Catholic religion and that, in doing so, they have come to mix African spirits with Christian saints (Balandier 1955; Bastide 1960; Cròs 1997; Ortiz 1943). During the times of slavery, traditional African deities were concealed behind the masks of the saints, and when slavery was finally abolished, this world of beliefs resurfaced and regained its independence, albeit without entirely abandoning the syncretism accumulated in the times of sorrow of so many men and women torn from their homeland and forcibly transferred to the Americas.

The historical sources on the colonization of the Americas and the mass deportation of black Africans frequently mention, for instance, how amazed the

Catholic missionaries were to see the slaves incessantly striving to somehow gain possession of the Catholic funeral rites, whereas the settlers and missionaries tended to offer the slaves much simpler rites. This is particularly true of the followers of Voodoo, which was widespread from Haiti to what is now the Dominican Republic, including Cuba, ingrained in the traditional religion of the ancient Dahomey (now Benin). They continued to request a Catholic funeral even after slavery was abolished, and they continue to do so even today. According to scholars of this cult, the reason lies in the fact that certain African cultures (or ones that originated in Africa) see death as a crucial passage—and not only for the soul of the deceased. The loss of this person is also an essentially negative event that can undermine the social solidarity of the clan and the family, so it is important to accompany the dead on their journey towards the kingdom of the spirit in the best possible way, to ensure that they bear the members of the community they leave behind no ill will. In Voodoo, therefore, funeral ceremonies are all the more appreciated, the more they assure that the deceased's passage will come under the best possible auspices, with a ritual apparatus that can be relied upon to be powerful and effective. The enslaved Negroes of Africa considered the Catholic rites a powerful instrument, administered by people that they saw as being the holders of a superior holy power. So the Catholic rites were more suitable for celebrating their own dead too, who had suffered the degradation of subhuman conditions but, when they died, could somehow attain redemption through the ceremony. In their eyes, a Catholic funeral worked rather like an insurance policy, since the community could no longer protect the deceased by means of Voodoo rites, which had been outlawed by the colonial authorities (Hurbon 1972, 1993, 2000).

This was no indication of any conversion to Catholicism, but merely of the intention to gain possession of a means of religious and ritual communication not only foreign to their culture, but even emblematic of colonial domination, so as to continue to *speak* to the dead and be able to manipulate the meaning of death in tune with their view of the world, that they had no intention of abandoning. In a sense, the means of communication typical of Catholicism—the Catholic funeral as a code for interpreting the event of death—became separated from its meaning in the Christian view of a transition and reinterpreted under different cultural and spiritual categories, that came closer to Voodoo.

We might appear to be talking about a syncretic process, but in point of fact the issue is rather more complicated: faced with the overwhelming power of a dominating religion such as Catholicism, the religion of those who are dominated resists, only formally adapting to the foreign rites, while in essence it makes them change in sign and sense. There are border wars over the power of communication that one religion claims to wield over the other, in a lengthy, latent conflict that emerges clearly when the balance of power changes and a religion regains its independence. Having learned to *draw sense* from the other religion, however, something of the latter ultimately remains glued to it, as it were.

Religion as Power of Communication

The above example is very useful for illustrating the idea of religion as *power of communication*. Religion relies on complex semantics that establish meanings by using words and gestures in orderly, repetitive, public, and private sequences. The boundaries between the public and private settings are constantly changing, because the death of a loved one is not a matter for the relatives alone, but for the whole community, which tries to repair the negative effects of the event, as we have seen in the Voodoo rites. Moreover, the fact that gestures and words circulating in Voodoo, and in other traditional African religions, can be found in other settings too—for example, in the religions of ancient Rome, or in the early stages of Christianity—should give us food for thought. After the ceremony of separation, the followers of Voodoo are in the habit of periodically offering a meal to the dead (the *manje-lèmô*), attended by the relatives and friends of the deceased.

In all these cases, religion expresses its power of communication in its will to wield the power to dominate the event of death and build a bridge between the visible and the invisible. We could say that questioning the dead is a tradition that has survived in modern spiritism, which has partially secularized the religious aspects of ancient beliefs. If they are treated kindly by the living, the dead may be kind to the latter in return: in dreams or séances they may reveal to the living what they should or should not do, give them gambling tips, or help them succeed in life. They are basically assumed to have understood the secret of life by now, and they possess its codes. After all, the medium in a séance is simply a good communicator with the dead, and this gives him or her a power that not all mortals possess. Besides, the cult of the dead is a fundamental aspect of human cultures.

The Labile Boundaries Between Religions

Some religions have always known the interdependence of symbolic languages (and this is especially so in the modern world), that is, there is a sort of globalization *ante litteram* as a result of which the boundaries between one religion and another are not so impassable and impenetrable as we might be led to believe. Even those religions that have proudly laid claim to the purity and the original and originating authenticity of their message, by *becoming a part of history* (and human history), they have in fact failed to thoroughly control the symbolic frontiers that they built with a view to defining the true and right belief once and for all. They have often allowed beliefs, ritual practices, and symbolisms from far away, and from other regions of the spirit, to slip in through their gates. The spirit of conquest later played in favor not of their presumed purity, but rather of their ongoing contamination by local religious cultures and practices, as their conquest went ahead and appeared to meet with success. In the wide-open spaces stretching before the gaze of the Catholic missionaries—like a mythical frontier that could be shifted further and beyond—Christian preaching had to represent the definitive triumph of the truth.

But time has since shown that, although Christianity has effectively spread to every continent, it has failed to eradicate the antagonist beliefs it has encountered along the way, which have either resisted, masked behind Christian symbols, or have ultimately gained ground again. We shall see this when we take a look at the new African, Asian, or Latin American Pentecostal churches, where the Church may seem, from its words, to be waging war against the ancient traditional religions, when in point of fact it is absorbing the latter's rites and symbolisms.

One religion gains the advantage over another when it steals the secrets of the latter's code, when it identifies its weaknesses, in which case the battle takes place on the plane of communication. A religion is victorious because, at some point, it is not only capable of *speaking to the heart of the people*, but it also succeeds in dominating the other, subdued religion's communication code. According to Todorov (1982), this is basically what happened when the Aztecs and their gods were defeated. In a very enlightening passage on this issue, the anthropologist wrote that Cortés understood relatively well the Aztec world being unveiled before his eyes, certainly much better than Montezuma understood the Spanish world. But this greater degree of understanding did not prevent the *conquistadores* from destroying the Mexican civilization and society; quite the reverse, we have the impression that it was this very ability to understand that made the destruction possible.

Cortés won not just because he used force, but because he also penetrated the symbolic language of the Aztecs; by doing so, he gained possession of the code that the Central American Indian populations used to interpret their world and social order. By taking their cultural code, Cortés was able to demonstrate the superiority of the Christian religion and civilization over those of the Aztecs. At some point, Montezuma succumbed because the Aztec religion's system of signs proved totally inadequate in explaining what was actually happening when the *conquistadores* moved in. The fact that the Aztec emperor continued to consider the Spanish as gods come down from the sky who could have ultimately become integrated in the Aztec pantheon is significant: by overestimating his enemy, he succumbed on the plane of communication even before he was defeated in battle. As a means of communication between human beings and their world, in the case in point, the Aztec religion became less and less plausible as the Spanish imposed their own communication model, which saw the Aztecs as inferior beings to be saved from their savage or barbaric conditions by means of the Christian religion. So religion as a power of communication becomes a weapon that defeats and convinces.

If we take a look at what has happened over the centuries and arrive at the present day, we see that the substrate of the traditional religions of the Central and South American Indians has not really been eradicated. They have continued to survive, grafted onto the main trunk of the religion of the victors (that is, the Christian religion), or remaining on the sidelines of the official religious field controlled by the Catholic Church in Latin America, only to regain ground as soon as this control became less effective, and ultimately re-emerging, bursting with life by means of the expansion of the new Pentecostal churches that have been meeting with favor for some time now and—by no accident—especially in the Latin American countries.

Much the same could be said about sub-Saharan Africa or South-east Asia, where—for at least the past thirty years—new churches of a Christian matrix but with strong links with the traditional religious cultures have been establishing themselves (Augé 1982; Mary 1999, 2000; Mary and Laurent 2001). In all these cases, syncretism is not something to be taken for granted, but is a process for the construction of belief systems that recur, resurfacing after a period of time, or that are newly born and strive to gain a place in the market of contemporary beliefs. This is a communication process, in the sense that every system of belief enters into a relationship with an environment where there are far more beliefs than any system is capable of containing within its symbolic boundaries. It is in this surplus of beliefs, outside the system, that we must seek the communication strategy typically used by every religion to stand apart and reduce the complexity that surrounds it. Syncretism is not only a structural operating principle of religions, it is also a dynamic process of communication between the system and the environment. Following up the fundamental works by Bastide (1960, 1972) on the African-Brazilian religions, and by Balandier (1955) on the traditional African religions, this would explain how syncretism is basically a term which indicates a battle, a sort of wrestling match between the deities of different religions that find themselves competing in the same social space and historical period. In this wrestling match, close contact and contagion are frequent phenomena, even though the parties involved may strive to defend their own religion from the other's. It is inevitable that communication should reawaken analogies, recall associations of ideas and recurrent mythological refrains, and exchanges of symbols and rituals. It is worth mentioning the work done by a scholar of Indo-European myths such as Dumézil (1952, 1958, 1995) to provide support for this theory.

We are indebted to Emile Durkheim for the idea according to which socio-cultural phenomena (and particularly those in the area of the sacred and religion) cannot be explained exclusively as an expression of individual choice or a natural predisposition of humankind. These phenomena are ways of representing society. A social group, be it large or small, defines itself and, in doing so, it *believes* in itself: individuals believe, but it is always as if their belief were an articulation of the collective conscience that governs and influences them. The fundamental concepts of religion—for example, God, the soul, the spirit or totem (that to Durkheim exemplified the *elementary form* of religious life)—originate from the experience through which people become aware of the force and majesty of the social group to which they belong.

Along this line of research, Durkheim's pupil—Marcel Mauss (1923–24)—analyzed the structure of the gift in ancient societies and reconstructed the symbolic code of the gift, which functions according to a normative scheme of the human mind. Giving something in order to receive something else in exchange is not a spontaneous or gratuitous action, it is governed by a principle according to which, if I am to receive something, *I must give something in exchange ...* where the key word is *must*. This indicates a morally binding principle of reciprocity; the principle that obliges individuals and groups of individuals to support one another represents the genesis of social representations that are readily consecrated or legitimated in a religious sense.

Drawing from all these studies, the French anthropologist Lévi-Strauss extended the horizon of the analysis and introduced the new linguistic perspectives opened up by Ferdinand de Saussure, who (according to Lévi-Strauss) inaugurated the great Copernican revolution in the area of human studies. Lévi-Strauss's fundamental work, *The Elementary Structures of Kinship* (1969), deals particularly with the topic of whether and how we can identify the common logic lying behind all systems of kinship, despite their variety, that is, whether and how we can find an invariant structure in relation to which the various forms of kinship are mere adjustments and adaptations, or particular transformations. The author sees the incest taboo as the fundamental principle governing relationships and social representations: by restricting sexual relations within a family, this taboo enables the exchange of a prized commodity (women) between different families, supporting the need of human groups to weave social relationships founded on a reciprocity and solidarity functional to their very survival. It is no accident that many cultures permit marriages between cousins, or that marriage is often not a public act to sanction a link of affection between two people, but merely a contract between families, where one offers the bride and the other pays the "right price" in exchange. Having identified the invariant structure of the social links, Lévi-Strauss can study how different systems of kinship are configured in two main forms: those governed by a principle of limited exchange and those based on a generalized exchange, the former being much more prescriptive than the latter. In either case, exchange governs the flow of the potential relations and communications between human groups. We thus succeed in reconstructing the living grammar of social relations and studying them as systems used by individuals and groups to communicate with one another.

An empirical analysis of the phenomena that we want to observe is not enough to understand these profound, invariant structures behind social actions. We need to adopt abstract models characterized by the ability to reproduce the logical relationships guiding the behavior of individuals and social groups, relationships that are taken for granted, not the object of negotiation, and consequently not easy to see at first glance. So, rather like Max Weber's ideal types, our models never correspond exactly to what we see in reality. They serve instead as the *socio-logic* syntax applicable to the conventions governing relationships of kinship, the lively and living grammar of society in its most elementary aspects. They reveal the logical fabric of reality, the fundamental structure of society, the basic content of social relations seen as they come about, in a congruent arrangement of parts that form a structure. According to Lévi-Strauss, this can be defined as a system containing a functional principle that guarantees the coherence and cohesion of the elements comprising the structure.

We can see that Lévi-Strauss does not use linguistics merely as a metaphor to adopt when studying social phenomena. To define a structure, we need to analyze the grammar and syntax of the social phenomena, not to content ourselves with a list of words. Here lies the difference between the empirical or positivist approach and the structuralist stance. Observable empirical phenomena do not speak per se: we need to reconstruct the global system in which the phenomena observed engage and acquire meaning. What is more, this is the only way to proceed if we want to draw comparisons between apparently different phenomena. What interests Lévi-Strauss is to see how "myths *are thought* in men," that is, how they acquire a relative autonomy as systems of symbols capable of explaining the world. The myth system, accompanied by the fantastic representations that it produces, creates a link between nature and society, between the visible and the invisible, between eros and fear, between life and death, ultimately acting as a socio-linguistic code to which we can refer in order to make sense of the environment in which we live.

Hardly surprisingly, myths generate an infinite number of stories, and the mythological story is a literary genre with its own grammar and syntax. It is also a social story that gives a systematic account, in its own way and *juxta propria principia*, of the relationships between humans and the cosmos, between divine order and social order. In traditional African religions, mythological stories have often even provided (or rather they used to provide, before the intensive urbanization of vast areas of the African continent) the outline to follow in order to place the houses in a village in an *orderly*, non-random manner within the space available. Some cultures have ritual masks that reflect the topographical layout of the village, creating a powerful circle of symbols enclosing the mind, the social group, and the mythological representation of reality. Myths generate images that can be combined to produce other images. Moving according to the logic of binary opposition, stories enable us to go from one mythological nucleus to another, like a code that opens, rather than closes, the doors between belief systems. The classification or hierarchy of animals and plants that we often find in the stories of Yoruba or Dogon mythology, for instance, are not only functional to practical demands, relating to the satisfaction of the need for nourishment, but also an early attempt to arrange the things that are distinguishable from man, and that he cannot always control in a relationship of pure force or domination. That is why Lévi-Strauss fiercely claims, in his famous essay *The Savage Mind* (1966), that even the so-called "primitive thought" is a *thought* because it generates a coherent (albeit relative) and logical explanation of the universe and of humankind's place in it. It is not a pre-logical activity, as Lucien Lévi-Bruhl said (1922), dominated merely by emotionality and an almost mystical sense of participation in the life of nature.

A Comparative Sociology of Systems of Religious Belief

Going along with Lévi-Strauss's idea, we can therefore conduct a comparative study of systems of religious belief as *elaborate communication systems*. No religion seems to be really elementary when we study its rituals and the mythological complexities it is capable of generating. What we aim to do in the following pages is, on the one hand, to treat religion as a system and as power of communication, while on the other, we shall try to reconstruct the links between symbolic-religious worlds and social environments, which change in time and space. To do so, I shall adopt the same method of analysis as Talal Asad (1993) used to compare Islam and Christianity, a method that he described as *genealogical*.

Genealogy is a discipline that studies the lines of descent of families, or of groups of families related to one another by systems of kinship. By analogy, we can consider world religions as *large* families that *know each other*, they are related to one another through spiritual and territorial forms of kinship, as in the case of the three great monotheistic religions of Semitic descent. But, as we saw when we spoke about Voodoo, these religions are also akin to other complex symbolic systems, such as the traditional African religions.

It is not enough to trace the lines of descent to identify the evident resemblances or irreducible differences between different religious traditions, born and consolidated diachronically and in the same or in temporally and spatially remote socio-cultural environments, in order to cover the topic of a comparative sociology of religions, by which we mean a search for the structural components of the relationship between the *founding* process and the process of *constructing* a system of religious belief, between the initial creative experience and the subsequent systematic development of a set of beliefs and ritual practices. In other words, we are interested in analyzing the relationship between the capacity for improvisation that often lies at the origin of a religion and the building of religious belief systems: the former has to do with the power of *communication*, the latter with the construction and reiteration in time and space of a system of *sense*. I am interested here in focusing on the topic of *religion as communication.*

The idea of religion as *communication* offers us a theoretical perspective that may be helpful to avoid us falling into certain common conceptual traps. For a start, we can go beyond the dichotomy between modernity and tradition: if religion is seen as a communication system, it can function as such in different societies, regardless of whether they have reached advanced technological levels or only low degrees of work division. Communication is sometimes confused with the communication market that religions have also joined, demonstrating that they know how to adapt to the logic of supply and demand for symbolic goods or salvation. A sturdy line of research has been developed amongst the sociologists of religion in the United States of America, producing what has been called the paradigm of religious economics. This is not the paradigm that I intend to adopt here. In fact, when it comes to systems of religious belief, communicating has to do with a structural principle of the systems' functioning: combining elements or parts drawn from the world of meanings that a religion acquires right from its act of foundation, and that it continues to develop in the course of time (often under the crossfire of conflict) in order to stand the test of the surrounding social and natural environments, is a very different matter from adapting one's performance to suit the market. The latter may be a contingent issue, whereas we are interested in studying the structural invariants of the relationship and of the communicative practices between religion as a system and the environment.

The second trap that seeing religion as communication enables us to avoid is the simple separation of religion into its various dimensions. Analytically it may be useful, especially for the purposes of empirical research focusing on standardizing the measurement of socio-religious behavior patterns (by means of questionnaires administered to representative samples of a given population), to isolate the elements that are presumably constitutive and characterizing, that is, experience, belief, practice, membership, knowledge. For instance, when we discover in our empirical research that these dimensions are not perfectly interlocked in the individuals interviewed, they enjoy different degrees of relative autonomy (so there may be practicing believers who do not believe entirely in a church's established religious doctrines, or people who say they have an intense religious sentiment but a weak sense of membership, or there may be obvious discrepancies between the rules of moral conduct established by a consolidated religious tradition and an individual's choices). The crucial point that these empirical findings unveil is that, in the end, we have no clear idea of what religion means to the people we interview. We merely find support, or the lack of it, for the analytical approach we have taken to break down religion in order (we believe) to better measure individual attitudes and behavior patterns in society in religious terms. We rarely attempt to understand how the religion's power of communication takes effect in defining an individual's cognitive maps. If, as we shall attempt to demonstrate, the deep-seated structure of religion is dominated by the power of the *pure word*, capable of fixing or shifting the symbolic boundaries of the universes of meaning for individuals and social groups, then we need to study how the force of this word takes effect, depending on the social and historical conditions with which one or more religions have to interact.

In particular, studying the relationship between religion as power of communication on the one hand, and the construction and reproduction in time of an organized system of religious belief on the other, should enable us (and this is the way to escape the third trap) to insist on seeking an *essentialist* definition, that can define the essence of religion once and for all (Lambert 1991). It would be preferable, however, to consider religions as evolving, living systems—they are born, they expand, and they die—depending on whether they are able to translate the external energy into intelligent internal information; that is, whether they succeed in dominating the variety, multiplicity, and unpredictability of the social environments where these systems of religious belief are born, or become engrafted, or uprooted and transplanted, adapting more or less effectively to different environments. In all these cases, for religious belief systems, communication means developing a code capable of converting external differentiation into internal differentiation.

Finally, the last trap that our suggested approach seems able to avoid is the dichotomy between primitive and evolved, or simple and complex, with reference to religions: it is one thing to study, from a historical perspective, how new beliefs or new religions strive to become grafted onto the trunk of previous religious beliefs (often aiming to prevail over their predecessors), while it is quite another to conceive this whole process as a "kill or die" game where a more complex and evolved religion triumphs over another that is more simple and primitive. The stratification of systems of religious belief is really a modality of the *power of communication* adopted by the religions of the "victors" and of the presumed "vanquished" alike. The power of communication is a means for marking the symbolic boundaries between different strata piling up in an environment marked religiously by a plurality of strata of religious belief. It is as if we were standing before a river that carries along all sorts of materials from faraway places and we see floating downriver what appear at first glance to be wrecks, but they are really more like rafts upon which we can ride the waves. As for the power of communication, its exercise in religions has a structural dimension in the conflict that takes place according to a binary, true/false logic that enables true beliefs to be defined in a straightforward and consequently acceptable manner, as distinct from the beliefs that are untrue, or merely tolerable because they resemble the true beliefs due to some analogy that is established in various hierarchical formulas by the religious authorities (which may be more or less tolerant). Even when we deal with spiritual philosophies that strive to consider the two poles—good and evil—as a pair that should be supplanted in order to grasp the vacuity of all things, starting from the consistency of the self and of the gods (as in Buddhism), the rules governing the conflict are influenced more by ascetic practices than by cold reasoning—and the body of an ascetic can communicate a powerful message.

I shall therefore discuss the idea of religion as communication by considering the centrality of the *power of the word* in the great world religions, both when they imagine a God that is revealed to us and when they do not necessarily assume that such a deity is concerned with revealing itself to humankind. We shall do so by taking a comparative approach, drawing on the language and analytical tools of sociology. This is not an attempt to conduct a comparative-historical study of religions, because we lack the competence for such a task. *Comparative religion*, or the comparative history of religions, is a field that was popular in the latter half of the nineteenth century, driven by the impulse coming from various disciplines (from Indo-European comparative linguistics to anthropology, to evolutionist sociology) that aimed to dismantle the historical superstructures of the various religions and identify their original, elemental form: the constitutive germ of religion itself. The weakness of this approach stemmed from the marriage between the search for the origins of the religious phenomenon and the evolutionist paradigm that numerous scholars adopted. They saw elementary form as coinciding with primitive mentality (from Spencer to Durkheim, and including Tylor's anthropology), identified by means of *keywords* belonging to the socio-linguistic universe of societies that were considered primitive (from the Melanesian to that of the Australian aborigines, and so on). These were sometimes interpreted as forces that could be explained, sometimes as an original power that cannot be traced back to any physical and material conditions of living, and sometimes as a pure social force (as in the Durkheim school), inevitably exposing this approach to contradictions. Once the primitive societies had disappeared or been overcome, we would have expected the primitive mentality to be swallowed up in the whirlpool of history too (Filoramo, 2004). In point of fact, research on socio-religious attitudes and behavior conducted in the last thirty years by social scientists has shown that, despite the modernization of customs and lifestyles, so-called *primitive* mentality persists and continues to influence ways of thinking and acting. Magic has not disappeared, it coexists perfectly well both with and within modernity. The truth is that studies in the field of *comparative religion* all too often used a binary type of interpretative approach (primitive–evolved, simple–complex, superstition–science, traditional–modern).

The approach that I intend to take departs from the beaten track of comparative religion and moves closer to Max Weber's way of thinking in his treatise, *The Sociology of Religion* (1993), and it also owes a great deal to the method that the German sociologist called *comprehending*. This method follows a circular analytical course: it starts with a body of information, it seeks to construct models that are, by definition, abstract, and that Weber called "ideal types," then it returns to reorder the baseline information, interpreting it in the light of these models. The difference between the methods of historiography and sociology lies in the different weights that they attribute to typologies and theoretical models.

In other words, our interest lies in focusing dynamically on an aspect that seems crucial to our understanding of the religious phenomenon, without falling back on the binary reasoning approach. We have chosen to start from the hub of the relationship between the original formation of a religious belief and the related *system-building* process—the construction of a system of belief—while keeping an eye on the relationship between these two processes and the social and socio-religious environment with which a system constantly interacts, from its birth until it perishes (maybe). We shall therefore use the huge mass of information that the historians of religion have accumulated with an ever greater degree of philological precision, reconstructing the scriptures and further detailing the relationships between a religion and the various worlds of individual and social life, as if it were a documentation to submit to a *secondary analysis* in a sociological key. The examples that we shall use in the course of the discussion are therefore not, nor could they be, anything more than a necessary, material aid to sustain the validity of a theoretical approach. They simply exemplify what we are discussing and help to support our demonstration of the validity of our chosen sociological theory. So they are combined together like a mosaic, constantly referring to one religion or another, in a deliberate attempt to show how, over and above the objective historical and social differences that have dug (sometimes deep) trenches between different socio-religious civilizations, our theoretical model *also* enables us to grasp elective affinities between different universes of religious belief vis-à-vis the core issue from where we started, that is, the relationship between the *incipit* of a religion and its subsequent establishment as a system.

From the methodological standpoint, we have chosen to observe just one of the many aspects of the religious phenomenon, and from a particular observation point, that is, to see how a *religion sees itself*. By adopting this formula, we mean to allude primarily to the need to *comprehend* (in the literal sense used by Weber of *encompassing*), bearing two fundamental dimensions in mind: first, how religions are originally formed and transformed into belief systems, and secondly, how the relationship works between a religion that has become a system and the environment, or rather the numerous, different and differentiated environments, that interact with it. Using two elliptical formulas, the object of our attention is, on the one hand, the *religion before the religion* and, on the other, how *a religion views itself* once it has become a system. So, with a play on words, a sociology of systems of religious belief is a *view of the view* (if it looks into how a religion sees itself in relation to its social environment).

Every religion tends to represent itself not only as different from any other, but also (on the strength of a legitimate expectation to have the truth on its side) superior, more complete, more genuine than any of the others. In point of fact, religions have difficulty in acknowledging that there are many correlations that make them less different from each another than they seem to believe, correlations that are sometimes historically documented and explicit, sometimes written between the lines, but that historians or anthropologists have nonetheless brought to light (Trentin 1991). Each religion is convinced that it is pure and consistent, clear and distinct from the others, which are seen as being impure, contradictory, confused, and primitive.

This is a dialectic that historically has often generated the identification of a religion with a civilization, with far-reaching social effects. For centuries, the boundaries traced by religions in the past have come to mark latitudes and longitudes in the cognitive maps of entire generations of human beings. Even today, these frontiers are seen as rifts that give rise to friction, conflicts, and wars—in a word, to the clash of civilizations (Huntington 1996). While it is true that historically, and right up until the present day, individuals, institutions, and collective movements that have identified themselves with a given religion have often been actively involved in such conflicts and clashes, it is equally true that it proves very difficult in nearly all such cases to generically call to mind a face-to-face clash between two or more religions in abstract terms, as if they *in themselves* were war machines. Historically, wars of religion have really been about something else, or a number of things combined together. Political and economic motives have often been mixed with the religious and ideological motives that a society's powerful members or movements from below have voiced, in the past as in the present day.

Seeing how a religion sees itself thus means escaping the temptation to view it as a universe of beliefs entirely unrelated to the universe of beliefs of another religion, because every single religion came into being and lives in an environment populated with beliefs, gods, other religions. This is what we call the socio-religious environment. So a religious belief system cannot be studied without its own socio-religious environment. That is not to say that the system is more important than the environment, or vice versa; methodologically speaking, systems theory leads us to assume the system-environment relationship as the fundamental element on which to base our analysis of the religious phenomenon from a sociological approach.

Having said as much, this work is arranged along the following lines:

a. A definition is given of religion as a belief system that interacts, right from its birth, with an environment.
b. This obliges observers (the social scientists) to consider the relationship between the original impulse to form a new religious belief and the process of building a belief system as a fundamental object of their analysis, and
c. to monitor this relationship in order to arrive at a dynamic understanding of whether and how a system is able to develop according to a principle of relative internal autonomy, to assert its own identity and mark its differences with respect to other systems of belief.
d. For this purpose, we focus on the centrality of the concept of communication, as defined in systems theory, to analyze religion as power of communication;
e. we measure its explanatory validity in several directions (though not all, for obvious reasons of space and the writer's limited competence), concerning the relationship between *word* and *scripture*, the performative strength of ritual and liturgy, the elaboration of a *concrete* doctrine, that *takes shape* in daily life, and finally the oscillation between ethnic identification and claim to universality, which seems to characterize religions in their evolutionary process in relation to the different social environments in which they become established as dominant cultural regulators.

In particular, Chapter 1 focuses on the crucial passage from *living word* to *holy scripture*, as a fundamental device in the construction of a system of religious belief. In this setting, we shall introduce a first conceptual distinction between system and environment, applied to the religious phenomenon. On the basis of this distinction, I can arrive in Chapter 2 at a global definition of religious belief system, showing how a religion generally tends to reduce the complexity of the social environment, producing meanings that are capable of sustaining the challenges of every situation—otherwise it would be liable to an irreversible crisis. The approach I have chosen does not draw entirely from systems theory because—as we shall see in Chapter 3—religions cannot be conceived from a sociological viewpoint (nor, more in general, by the social sciences of the religious phenomenon) as a functional apparatus without a subject. They draw their energy from the capacity for improvisation that is sometimes expressed by a charismatic personality, sometimes the end result of the sum of a multiplicity of ecstatic and visionary experiences of groups of individuals.

This leads to another crucial issue that I am interested in studying (and I do so in Chapter 3), that is, the transition from what we have called the capacity for improvisation to the process of building a genuine belief system, from the original creative force of the founder of a religion to the definition of the symbolic boundaries of a completed system. The hypothesis that I intend to present is that the virtuoso of religious improvisation operates in a place where there are already various layers of previous beliefs that he or she reinterprets, sometimes changing their global meanings and presenting them as if they formed a new horizon of sense. That is why the great belief systems often appear, while they are under construction, rather like a *cliff*, a complex layering of symbols nourished via different *channels* that flow from other religious systems, that have been partially incorporated, partially overcome, but never entirely cancelled. Sometimes they may even have crumbled, only to become consolidated again elsewhere, in the new system gaining ground in a given environment. So every religion, as any historian of religion will tell us, is affected by syncretism: from the particular viewpoint of the sociologist, this is the structural and functional principle that enables a system to enter into relations with the environment, seeking to dominate the complexity that continuously overrides the attempts constantly being made by belief systems to create, or recreate *order.*

The topic of order will be further developed in Chapter 4, considering the constant tension that we can see in the great systems of religious belief between the principle that brings together the multiple and the variable characteristic of the movement of history and human societies on the one hand, and the force of the spirit on the other (meaning by spirit what Simmel called "religiosity"). The search for sense is not satisfied with what organized religions say on the strength of an encoded tradition; whether they are movements of reawakening, spontaneous groups of seekers of the divine, wandering pilgrims, or normal individuals dissatisfied with their respective churches, they all explore *beyond* the confines of sense established by an institution, an authority or a religious tradition.

Applying systems theory to the study of religious phenomena with a critical spirit enables us to evade the quagmire in which the sociology of religion has sometimes become bogged down, divided between strenuous support for the theory of secularization on the one hand, and the hypothesis of a return of the sacred on the other. If we seek instead to understand how religious belief systems *think* in relation to the various environments they encounter in their historical and evolutionary process, we shall see that their characteristic power of communication can vary in intensity and force, depending on whether they are more or less able to face the challenges of social complexity in a given time and place, reorganizing their internal means of communication, learning how to communicate with changing environments. Religions are therefore constantly on the move because their systems will always retain a core that stays vital and continues to circulate in human societies.

Chapter 1
Religion as Communication

The Mystery of the Text, or Telling the Story of God

Religions have produced repertoires of stories and narratives about their deities and the latter's relationship with the cosmos and with human beings: stories that have been handed down by word of mouth, or spoken revelations subsequently put into writing. In religions that derive from the figure of a prophet, the passage from living word to *scripture* can be seen as an act of communication that aims to reduce the ambiguities of comprehension and recall. The authenticity of the message is thus fixed in a text, then the authentic becomes true. The originally spoken message gains a supplementary statute of truthfulness. In some religions, this happens not just because a prophet who founded a new faith has died, it is done by one of the prophet's successors in an effort to avoid the community of believers coming up against the recurring problem of how to choose a legitimate successor to guide the community after their leader's death. This is what happened, for instance, in the Sikh religion. In 1708, the tenth and last guru, Govind Singh (1675–1708), decided to end the chain of transmission of power that had hitherto involved a series of nine heirs of the founder, Guru Nanak (1469–1539), and to transfer this authority to the Sikhs' sacred book, the *Granth* (or *Adi Granth*, the Original Book, also—significantly—called the *Sri Guru Granth Sahib*, the Venerable Book of the Guru), a document compiled at the time of the fifth guru, Arjan (1581–1606). The book was thereby sanctified and it takes pride of place in all Sikh temples, as on object of veneration and a constant source of inspiration. This is a good example of how fixing the word in a scripture has the advantage—within and with all the limits inherent in any scripture—of eliminating the risk of conflict over the succession and reducing any memory-related controversies (McLeod 1968; Piano 1996). Producing a written text reduces the abundance of the spoken communication between prophets and their first intimate disciples, which will already have suffered from errors of interpretation on the part of the latter even while the prophet was still alive. In transmitting the message to others, these privileged witnesses, who have been lucky enough to know the prophet and benefit directly from his teachings, come up against genuine conflicts of memory. As an example, we might mention the passage of the Gospel according to St. Mark (8:27–30), which reads:

> And Jesus went out, and his disciples, into the towns of Caesarea Philippi: and by the way he asked his disciples, saying unto them, *Whom do men say that I am?* And they answered, *John the Baptist; but some say, Elias; and others, One*

of the prophets. And he saith unto them, *But whom say ye that I am?* And Peter answereth and saith unto him, *Thou art the Christ*. And he charged them that they should tell no man of him.

I do not doubt Mark's story, so I assume that it provides useful information: the evangelical words reflect the words spoken by Jesus himself. This story also shows us the effort made to define the symbolic boundaries that were beginning to be marked around the figure of Jesus immediately after his death. The evangelical texts have two fundamental sources: an ancient account of the life of Jesus on which Mark worked in particular, and the so-called *logia*, a collection of Jesus' sayings used effectively by both Matthew and Luke. Both of these sources can be seen as the outcome of a self-analysis by the first community of Jerusalem. The translation of the original draft in Greek posed a far from negligible intellectual and spiritual challenge, since it had to transfer the original message from one language to another (from Aramaic to Greek, two languages that have far from marginal structural differences). The community of Jerusalem preserved a living memory of the Master, because it included some of the disciples who had known him personally. Their memories did not always coincide perfectly with what was being remembered by other communities, however. The early followers of Jesus' message were all Jews (Lupieri 1997: 90), but there were communities of *Hellenists* (that is, Hellenized Jews), and other groups of Jews who continued to observe the precepts of the Torah. The latter can be considered as genuine *in-between* believers, who were fascinated by Jesus' message, but they did not wish to definitively break away from the religious tradition of their birth, that is, Judaism (Blasi, Turcotte, and Duhaime 2002; Destro and Pesce 2004; Ehrman 2003). In these communities, Jesus the miracle worker, Master and Messiah, was more important than Jesus resurrected. Other communities, like those developing in the Hellenist environment, focused instead on the redemptive force contained in the message of the Resurrection. The very word *messiah* is dear to Jewish tradition and it was taken up again in the Christian environment in its eschatological sense, synonymous with the notion of Supreme Judge at the end of Time (Matthew 25: 31–46), as well as in its salvific sense (Flusser 1997, p. 145 et seq.). The boundary that was progressively established between the new religion of Jesus and Judaism came to pass right over the living *body* of Christ who, when put to death, was believed to have returned from the dead. For some, therefore, the Messiah had already arrived, while the Jews are still waiting for him. Hence the controversy concerning the question of "Who do you say that I am?" and "Who do men say that I am?".

These two questions emblematically contain the sociological problem of the relationship between the *founding act* of a belief and the process of *building* a belief system. I could use a formula to say that I am interested in studying *religion before there were religions*, that is, what came before the creation of a complex system of belief that tends to function according to its own internal logic, coming to terms with the multiplicity of social environments in which it takes root (or attempts to do so), and with a variety of historical situations through which it passes more or less successfully. The above example is of interest because, in the evangelical account, it is as if the authors (that is, Matthew, Mark and Luke, to whom the so-called Synoptic Gospels are attributed; the Gospel of St. John is another matter, since it follows a mystical or Gnostic line of interpretation) were describing the scene of a conversation in which two speakers are trying to understand each other, to find a shared interpretation of a leader's behavior and, as a consequence, of that of the leader's followers. They represent a communicative interaction. Communication has to do with at least two dimensions: of believing as individuals and of believing as a group. The object of the belief lies at the heart of the group's acknowledgment, it aims to become the shared language of the group, while at the same time it is seen as the faithful copy of the leader's *words*. The bond of solidarity that links the leader to the group develops gradually through a continuous interaction, of which the evangelical story gives an effective account. If we compare the narrative structure of the Synoptic Gospels with the scriptures of other religions, we find that they often describe scenes involving conversations between deities and human beings, or between masters, or prophets and their reference groups, the "early disciples."

In the religion of the Hindus, for instance, the scriptures consist of texts that have been revealed and others that hand down the content of the faith as it has been revealed through time. Now, the original nucleus—of the revelation—is really scattered in a vast and articulated sequence of texts; the whole set goes by the name of the *Veda* (Wisdom), prepared over the course of time, approximately between 1500 and 500 BC. In the beginning, in these documents too, there was the *spoken word* heard by seers, who only subsequently put what they had *heard* into writing, or handed on to others what had been revealed to them and, in the end, the latter transferred what they had been told into a body of hymns and prayer repertoires. For many centuries, there existed nothing more than a chain of faithful agents, very like the oral sources in Islam, or in other religions. When the work of transcription began, it was completed under the rigid control of a priestly caste (the *Brahmin*).

Among the many texts worth mentioning, one in particular is of interest for our present discussion. This is the *Bhagavad-gita*, literally *The Song of the Blessed Lord*. This is a document probably prepared in the second century BC, that was subsequently absorbed in another important religious document, the *Mahabharata*, which tells of an ongoing dialogue between Krishna, the principal incarnation (*avatar*) of the God Vishnu, and Prince Arjuna, a mythical hero of the Hindu sagas. The object of their discussion is war, or rather whether it is justified to resort to violence to deal with conflicts. The Prince is strongly opposed to violence, but he is obliged to command an army in order to combat the enemies of his kingdom. Krishna seeks to explain his doctrine by saying, "To action alone hast thou a right and never at all to its fruits." Man must learn to take action, but offer the fruits of his actions to God. By doing so, even violence can have a sense, it can be transformed into a sacrifice to the deity. It is only in this way that Arjuna can prevent the actions that he abhors (violence and war) from becoming a cause of attachment to the *world*, rather than just the backdrop of a representation in which everything that happens is really mere appearance. In other words, the book in question represents a psychological drama and an ethical dilemma, in which the reference to the deity is used to draw considerations on the sense attributable to human actions (be they individual or social). This sense is the fruit of a communicative interaction between two subjects, one belonging to the divine world, the other to the human world, and more in particular to that part of the human world that has to do with the wielding of power.

This dilemma regarding war and the justification of resorting to violence is also contained in the second phase of Mohammed's prophetic experience which the Koran describes with a certain dramatic emphasis in numerous places. It is well known that Mohammed went through at least four distinct phases in his prophetic experience: the original mystical phase, when he had his first revelations and his first ecstatic experiences in the desert; then came another immediately afterwards when he became aware of his new moral status as the announcer of a religious message to the peoples and tribes that inhabited the Mecca and surrounding areas in 610. Later, the prophet became fully aware of his mission and also conscious of the growing difficulty that it was to encounter (even among the members of his own clan); and finally came the phase that developed after the migration (*hijra*) from the Mecca to Yathrib—subsequently renamed Medina—in 622, when he was governor of a city. It is in this last phase, when he combined in his person the figure of the religious reformer and that of the political leader, that Mohammed finds himself having to organize an army and motivate his followers to become good fighters too, in order to defend the monotheistic faith that he had proclaimed, and that the enemy tribes of the Mecca violently opposed (Cook 2005; Pace 2004b).

What it worth highlighting is the communicative model that religion adopts to effectively implement the passage from thought to action, from imagining something to getting it done.

Religion as Communication: The Approach of Systems Theory

The model can be simplified as follows: between God and human beings there is an intermediary, who acts as interpreter for the former and can speak to the latter. This intermediary is basically a means of communication, initially pure word—in the sense that he serves as an echo of a superior, divine word, and as the human instrument for transmitting a *novel idea*, a new view of the world, a word that human ears would otherwise be unable to hear. So when the word becomes scripture, it is configured as a story of the communicative exchange that took place between God and a prophet, and between the prophet and a community of followers that formed around him or her. Hence the communication of the communication: a medium (the scriptures) working on another medium (that of the pure word received and reiterated by a prophet or spiritual master who founds a new religious faith). The interpretation of what has been written in the scriptures thus constitutes a third important step: this third-level communication challenges the growing complexity that progressively develops when a religious message is successful, becomes spatially widespread and prolonged in time, coming into contact with all the different human societies that have succeeded one another in the lengthy course of history.

In short, religion as a *communication medium* therefore means at least three things:

a. It suggests the idea of a God who speaks, always choosing privileged interpreters to whom He transmits a symbolic code.

b. It gives the latter the power to establish social links that can no longer be conceived in purely ethnic, territorial, tribal and parental terms— worlds that tend to wrap individuals up in details (ethnic group, tribe, family, territory); these links must be traced back to a higher code that *separates from these particulars* and makes individuals feel and act *as if* they belonged to a universal community. The symbolic boundaries of this community are defined by a communication code, the key to which cannot be duplicated indefinitely, because it is guarded by those who programmed the code and only made accessible (as a sign of their goodwill) to someone they trust. Religions basically ask human beings to place their trust in the person that God has entrusted to open and close the communication code. Faith is thus primarily *trust in somebody* (be it a prophet, a spiritual master, a guide, or a shaman).

c. The community of faith that is created relies on a constant process of ritualized communication, by means of which its members renew their pact of loyalty to the code transmitted to them, learning to discriminate true signs from false, confirming the socio-linguistic evidence that enables the community to consider itself as such. Its unity is essentially the product of a communicative investment, of a communication that publicly ensures a formal understanding of the evidence, of the fact that everything is continuing true to memory; the rites and liturgies of religions can be seen as great public communication systems that serve specifically to reiterate (so as to acknowledge and have acknowledged) the content and confines of the communicative pact that the community of "faithful" has signed in order to come into being.

I can use another example here to clarify these considerations. According to the story in the Hebrew Bible, God sent Moses the Tables of the Law, or Ten Commandments (though it would be more accurate to call them the ten *words*)— to Moses and to him alone. Only Moses climbed Mount Sinai and stood before the burning bush … rather like Odysseus, when he had himself tied to the mast of his ship so that he could hear the sirens' songs while his men rowed on with wax in their ears. The power that Moses and Odysseus gained in so doing was enormous.

In particular, Moses was then able to communicate to the sundry tribes of Israel that their new destiny was to be no longer just tribes, but a people called upon by God to go to the Promised Land—a land that is not just a territory to colonize, but *the* place where they can become a "people," where they can become established as a community beyond the ties of blood typical of a society based on the family. The Promised Land is the place where they fulfill their mission to transform the sense of their actions as individuals by charging them with a new liberating force that they did not feel before, or that they only sensed confusedly. Their religion (Judaism in the case in point) became a communication medium that enabled them to see unity where beforehand there had been division and differentiation (into tribal and ethnic segments). This power of communication of their religion has proved so strong that it has enabled the Jews to survive the appalling tragedies of their history (Walzer 1985).

When the operation to overcome the symbolic frontiers is complete and tends to become consolidated, one of the most reliable indicators for identifying the passage from movement to institution, to put it in Alberoni's words (1977), or from the founding phase to the building of a religious belief system, lies in the development of rites and liturgical practices. Very often what we read in the scriptures reflects the need to establish order in the rituals used by a community of believers to celebrate their symbols, to *speak* collectively about *their* God, and the way in which individuals must interact with their God.

To Communicate to Believe

Religion as power of communication operates in relation to belief. In many ways, believing goes back to the idea of a relationship with an individual—a relationship that, in order to have the features of *religiosity*, must appear to another individual as an *event*, something new and repeatable at the same time, equally changeable and stable, that illuminates the mind and awakens the senses. The notion of spirit, often used in different religious traditions, frequently alludes to this idea of an event that was sought after and dreamed of, but that ultimately takes place as if the individual had not really been expecting it. Among other things, this guarantees its endless reproducibility. Despite attempts made by this or that religious organization to control its power, the spirit blows where it will. In other words, it can function as a communication code and the key is not in the exclusive possession of any established religious organization.

The reason for this, in sociological terms, can be explained by the fact that religions can also function *without a subject*, but in the long term they meet with difficulties created by the *spirit that blows where it will*. To function without a subject, a religion tends to establish itself as a self-sufficient belief system capable of self-regulation, without necessarily always having to depend on people in flesh and blood. But taking this approach means that it runs a constant risk not of losing consent, but of losing control that is, the keys, or the symbolic monopoly over and of the innovative force of the *spirit*, over and above the communication that opens the mind and warms the heart, that moves the symbolic boundaries of the religious belief and reduces the complexity of the social environment, which is changeable in time and space.

It becomes important to clarify the difference between *communication as dominion* and *communication as power* in the religious arena. Dominion is that of a religion organized as a system that claims to permanently control its own symbolic boundaries, defending and protecting them for all time. Power, on the other hand, alludes to the capacity to shift these boundaries, to combine and recombine experience and sense of the relationship between believers and the *event* of believing, between what is, by definition, the environment for a belief system on the one hand, and the original, symbolic nucleus that constitutes the success or prestige of a historical religion on the other. In fact, religious symbols also go through a phase in which they build up their original symbolic capital, the combined fruits of experience and sense. For some religions, we know a good deal about this phase: the experience of the first community of a prophet's followers is *narrated* by the people concerned and, from their accounts (that is, their communication of the prophet's original communication), we can grasp the sense of the actions of the early protagonists—even though (as the historians will tell us) not everything is comprehensible.

It is interesting to compare the pioneering season of a religious belief with its subsequent evolution into what are sometimes complex forms of religious organization, because it shows how difficult it is for an organization to contain— to retain within limited and stable boundaries—the original force of the founding experience, because this is seen as a novelty in the (religious) communication, something capable of shifting the boundaries of people's imagination, their feelings, thoughts, and actions. Once religions became organized into systems with any claim to stability (what we might call the religions of *deposition*), many of them attempted to fix their symbolic boundaries once and for all, but this often gave rise to very strong internal and external tensions, capable of destroying the system as a result of lacerating conflicts that sometimes irreparably disrupted its internal unity and cohesion. Religions of *deposition* generally develop sufficient capacity for self-reflection to be able to transform their legitimate claim to *possess the truth* into pure will for power, to be superior to other religions, to have clearly distinct coordinates for marking out their differences vis-à-vis other belief and power systems and, finally, to draw from their symbolic nucleus—re-elaborated and fixed in the *depositum fidei*—a complete and integrated view of the world, a social recipe for all seasons ... or, in a word, an orthodoxy, but in the sense in which this category was used by the French social psychologist Deconchy (1971). This means a complex device that can be studied by observing the functioning of three variables:

a. the discrepancy between religious propositions and rationality,

b. the organic nature of religious propositions (the fact that each of them is perceived as belonging to an established and coherent body of propositions), and

c. the membership regulating function of religious propositions.

Deconchy sees the beliefs that a religion proposes to its followers as a number of *doxemes*, small units of information that make up a universe of sense that is perceived as being coherent, unchangeable, and irrefutable. A set of *doxemes* of this type is exactly what is defined as orthodoxy.

An example of a fundamental and at the same time elementary *doxeme* is that of "God incarnate" (in Christianity), or "There is no god other than Allah" (Islam), or again "He who is my *bhakta* (or devotee) is dear to Me" (in the Hindu *Bhagavad-gita*), or finally, "If there were no unborn, not-become, not-made, non-compounded, there would be no escape" (in Buddhism). Each of these propositions has an informative value that, by definition, is not immediately comprehensible to the human mind. The discrepancy between the proposition and its rational comprehension measures the degree of orthodoxy. If the discrepancy is nearly nil (or, in other words, if there is no question of the rational reliability of the propositions), then we can say that we are dealing with an orthodox system and believer. In this case, it is as if we were dealing with "a certain type of mathematical operand that, on the strength of current usage, does not need to be submitted to any particular axiomatics" (Deconchy 1971: 373). In the same way, if a believer is able to correlate a given proposition, or *doxeme*, with others and thereby grasp the contiguity and consistency of the body of proposed beliefs (that is, their centrality in relation to other secondary claims), then we can say that the discrepancy in perception between individual and system tends towards zero. Finally, all this consequently enables us to measure whether, and to what degree, a belief system is able to regulate the sense of membership of its faithful: the stronger the convinced adherence to the *doxemes* perceived as a coherent system that can neither be separated into parts nor partially revoked or doubted, the greater the transformation of the doxeme into current opinion (as Rokeach put it [1960]), or a mental *habitus* that induces every devotee to assume that the body of doctrine reflects the truth, the only truth possible on the matter of belief. What counts in this case is the apparently rational correlation between different *doxemes* that, taken one by one, might even seem *irrational*, incomprehensible in terms of the true/false logic on which a belief system ultimately relies. This is not so much a matter of whether single propositions are true or false, it is *the set*, that counts as a construct for interpreting a certain symbolic message, which exhibits its own internal rationality, its own internal cross-referencing and logical linkage between different propositions, or *doxemes*. If God became incarnate, then Jesus was God and human at one and the same time. If there can be no god other than God, then those who associate several gods are polytheistic and are consequently entirely in the wrong. Those who do not practice their devotion to Krishna do not understand the sense of human action. If you do not believe in the possibility of reaching Nirvana, you can never understand and eliminate the source of pain and suffering. Many great religions have also developed a powerful and vigorous capacity for analysis and self-analysis, which has often adopted the analytical and reasoning procedures typical of analytical logic. If we were to try and combine the notion of *doxeme* (as it is conceived by social psychology, which can essentially be translated into a quantity of information provided by a religious authority and accepted more or less trustingly by a believer) with the notion of *hermeneutic variability,* then we could probably retrieve a dimension that escapes the psycho-social approach.

In fact, information always contains a communicative factor. A belief system consequently functions not only on the strength of the logic of dominion, but also thanks to the power of communication—a power that the system does not necessarily always succeed in controlling completely. This power may also be wielded by *those without authority*, and even by the simple believer who, in certain circumstances, may express what we might call the *capacity for improvisation*. To take an excellent example, St. Francis of Assisi exerted this power and, in doing so, he profoundly innovated the Catholicism of his time, reacting to a church (in the sense of an organized belief system) that he saw as being immovable and lacking in fervor and radical evangelical passion. In other words, even when we are dealing with a *doxeme*, for example, with a statement that is unquestionable according to an established religious authority, it can be interpreted by single believers according to a theoretically very broad range of meanings, in principle at least, on an ideal scale of appreciation that can go from a maximum to a minimum of convinced adherence. There may be multiple spaces between these two extremes. Those who control the definitions for a set of *doxemes* can never be sure that their power of transmission can always count on an effective medium (or power) of communication—unless they resort to coercion. As a matter of fact, to be sure of being effective, they sometimes feel the need to modernize their communication tools, to create new places and spaces in which to channel their communication, to combine traditional liturgy with unconventional forms of mutuality, and so on. That is why we think that an orthodoxy cannot really be seen as a closed belief system, but rather as the precarious result of an effort to strike a balance between possible interpretations of the same piece of information (be it as small as you will) that, combined with others, contributes to the composition of a theo-logical fabric that is complex and (in the case of a religion that has become a system) coherent.

The Relationship Between System and Environment with a Religious Matrix

Let us call this fabric *a belief system organized on religious grounds* and establish that this system evolves only in relation to a social environment that is, by definition, more complex and changeable than the system. For a belief system, the socio-religious environment is, by definition, vaster, more pluralist, more dialectic, in a word, multiple and changeable. It is up to the system of religious belief to produce sense in an environment that, for its own part, produces a continuous surplus of sense.

An example may help to clarify what we are trying to say. In the long march that sees Christianity become detached from its Jewish roots, up to the moment when it completely and definitively abandons them in the second century AD, many Christian intellectuals of the time (Filoramo 1997: 145; Stroumsa 1999, 2005) sought to justify the unavoidable need to abandon their Jewish background by focusing on the fact that, in the light of the Hebrew texts (the Torah), they could demonstrate that Jesus had brought about the ancient prophecies concerning the coming of the Messiah. He was the Messiah announced by the prophets of Israel, so Christians were the new Israel. This interpretation complied with the rules governing the exegesis of the scriptures at the time, rules that were obviously also shared by the learned rabbis. It suffices to read a classical text on the anti-Jewish debate of the time, Justin Martyr's *Dialogue with Trypho*. Justin was a Christian who demonstrated his knowledge of the techniques of exegetic debate in vogue in his time when he imagined that he was conversing face to face with Trypho the Jew. The essence of Justin's reasoning was that Christ had now recapitulated the whole story of salvation in that, being the Son of God, He was the one and only Israel. As Filoramo reminds us (1997: 149), Justin was speaking to an audience of Christians who were still particularly sensitive to the attraction of their Jewish heritage and, in doing so, he relied on a logical armamentarium that was to be used surprisingly often in the course of subsequent centuries. The Jews were in error because they were essentially "*murderers of the righteous*" and Christ was the quintessence of righteousness. The Jews had not realized that Jesus represented the New Alliance that God signed with the whole of humanity.

This example can be interpreted not only in the light of historical facts, but also as a good pretext for emphasizing our sociological point of view. In fact, Justin, like many other intellectuals of the early Christian Church (which is why they are remembered as the Church Fathers), represents an attempt to build a belief system with precise and stable boundaries, capable of clearly distinguishing what went before from what came after, the identical from the different, those within the boundaries from those outside them, those who are for from those who are against. In the socio-religious context in which Justin moves, however, the information that he processes and proposes cannot be taken for granted, that is, that Christ is the only true Israel, so Judaism is obsolete or—worse still—it has been tainted by the terrible crime of having put the Savior, the Messiah, the Son of God, to death. In Justin's environment, there is a surplus of sense in circulation that covers a whole kaleidoscope of attitudes and beliefs, from the Jewish person convinced that Jesus is not the Messiah to the one who has decided to follow Jesus without abandoning his Jewish roots, from the Christian who still feels Jewish and does not see why he should abandon the practice of circumcision, to the Christian who moves ever further away from the law of Moses, to those pagans who are converted to Christianity and for whom any reference to Judaism consequently makes little sense.

A system of belief is thus built by means of a complex process of definition of its own boundaries in a continuous, dialectic relationship with an environment. If the belief was founded originally on a communication, on the vital relationship between the living word of a leader (prophet, reformer, spiritual master, seer, and so on) and an early community of followers, then there can be no belief system without a corresponding social and religious environment. This is, in essence, Weber's great lesson on the matter of charisma.

When we speak about religion, we are alluding from now on to the distinction between system (of beliefs) and environment (of reference). This means that we are not interested in discussing the essence of religion: this is a conceptual challenge already attempted by philosophy, theology, and the social sciences, with uncertain and often dubious results. Much less are we attempting to say that the object of sociological investigation must necessarily confine itself *exclusively* to describing empirically observable behavior. Our starting point lies elsewhere. It may be complementary, and not necessarily antagonistic to other approaches. What I intend to do is to ascertain the feasibility of a comparative religious belief systems theory that substantially does two things:

a. It acknowledges the fact that, over and above the diversity distinguishing the various religions of which we have a historical record, the fundamental tension between the act of foundation and the construction of a system constitutes, in religions, is a good starting point for understanding how a religion functions, even before it becomes a religion (or belief system, with higher or lower levels of internal complexity and differentiation), as power of communication, making us imagine new symbolic boundaries of believing that chart new courses in the search for sense.

b. Depending on the original force of this power, we can *socio-logically* understand (using the categories typical of sociology) how the fluidity of the initial experience of the power of communication leads up to the creation of a belief system, that can reproduce itself in time and spread to different places from where the announcement of a religious message originated, if we study the *relationship* between belief system and different, changeable socio-religious environments in which the former seeks to become established, gain favor, withstand time, and compete with other belief systems or other forms of social power (from the economic to the political).

To summarize in an image, religions are like formidable compasses with their tips fixed in a precise point in time and space; as they open wider, they trace increasingly ample circles, designing new spaces. Leaving aside the metaphor, they become rooted in other social environments, often far away from their original roots from the cultural and linguistic standpoint.

Toward a Religious Belief Systems Theory

Let us assume, therefore, that religion is something that can be observed inasmuch as it is a relationship between system and environment, because it is based on another relationship: on the one hand, there is an innovator who traces the new symbolic boundaries of the belief and there are people who identify with them; on the other, there is an environment that, from the socio-religious standpoint, is by no means a *tabula rasa*. Quite the reverse: it is scored with consolidated beliefs and with a plurality of beliefs coexisting or competing with one another. Our approach consequently cannot do without the typical stance of the historian. Max Weber attempted a comparative historical sociology of belief systems in his monumental *Sociology of Religion* (1993). More modestly, what we propose to do is to see whether a theory such as systems theory can usefully be applied to the field of sociology of religion to solve certain problems that scholars of the religious sciences face (Davie 2001; Filoramo 2004; Trigano 2001). We might list some of these. The first concerns how to overcome the dilemma between secularization and a return of the religious without necessarily having to take a stand for one or the other point of view; how to analyze religious phenomena from a sociological standpoint without losing sight of their historical profundity; whether and how to compare belief systems without falling into the methodological error of canceling, as Durkheim said (1912), the differences that can characterize different societies.

This means that we must consider the relationship between system and environment in the religious field as a form of communication, which can be configured (even though it varies depending on the environment) according to an operating principle that tends to be repeatable and universal. We can thus assume that a belief system goes through history and experiences alternating cycles of adjustment and maladjustment to the various environments to which it belongs, and with which it must cope. So not everything will necessarily always go well: there will be times when the system has a marked capacity to shape an environment in its own image (possibly facilitated and supported by outside forces, such as a politician's decision to elect a belief system as the state religion or the official ideology of an empire), times when the environment becomes diversified to such a degree that a variety of interpretations of the beliefs prevails, and times when there may be a tendency to individualize the belief and to restore religions to the public stage at one and the same time (Casanova 1994; Garelli 2006). In relation to an environment, a belief system lives in time and the idea of cycles alludes to the fact that there is no linearity in such historical processes, just as there are no deterministic cause-effect relationships, such as: where there is modernization, religion is bound to suffer and there may even be an eclipse of all things holy. That is why a comparative sociology of religions can only evade the trap of theoretical schematism by taking into account the view of other disciplines, and of history of religions in particular. A sociology of this type certainly does not tread in the methodological steps of the historical sciences, so what we have written here is not intended to be a small-scale comparative historical treatise. The approach that we take is different: it is basically an attempt to go back to the inimitable work done by Max Weber, coherently adopting the comprehending method on which the German sociologist founded his conceptual edifice. In other words, we are interested in focusing on an aspect that we consider heuristically central, and that is *the relationship between the act of foundation of a religious belief on the one hand, and the process of construction of a belief system that takes shape with time, evolving and adapting to different social environments.* To study this relationship, a comparative sociology of religion cannot avoid relying on the secondary analysis conducted by the specialists in the various religions known to us, using their findings as a source of information to generate data that can be interpreted using sociological categories, which necessarily differ from those used by a historian. Drawing from systems theory, we are interested in delineating an ideal type (in the sense used by Weber) of the relationship between the original constitution and the subsequent construction of a religious belief system. Reference to the various religions and to single aspects that others have already studied is therefore functional to our purpose. Far from wishing to compare different religions, we intend instead to take an abstract approach to the great flux of religions in history. Having selected one aspect—the above-mentioned relationship—we can concentrate on what might be functional to our sociological reasoning: there is no thirst for omnipotence in our usage of details borrowed from the specialists of the history of religions as if they were mere *laboratory* samples or reproductions of documents, revisited—in a sense—under another microscope: that of the sociologist.

So the time has come to explain that the theoretical reference framework in which we place these samples: this refers to systems theory, and particularly to the attempt made by Niklas Luhmann to apply this theory to the study of religion (Pace 1986).

According to Luhmann's systems theory (1977, 1984, 1995, 1986, 2000), observation always implies a dual procedure: identifying something and then establishing what distinguishes it from the environment. By proceeding in this way, I identify and differentiate. This analytical procedure does not necessarily correspond to what we conventionally call reality, if we assume that reality involves identifications, distinctions, and differences that fail to follow lines that are clear-cut once and for all. The approach of systems theory seems to our mind to be very useful for developing a theory of religion without falling into the traps either of essentialism (having to define the essence of religion, with the corollary of fixing its perennial features in the universal anthropological structure that religion would express, or making it coincide with an aspect of our genetic code and thereby satisfying its claim to universality and timelessness), or of functionalism (religion as dependent on the structural conditions of a society or psyche, that is, reflecting the same logic as the rational choice that makes every human being calculate the costs and benefits of their actions), nor even of naive enlightenment (religion as a phenomenon with a social weight that will progressively decline as scientific understanding and technological modernization help to provide rational answers to the questions of sense that have traditionally been the sphere of religions).

Taking a systemic stance, what we see is a dynamic relationship between a system and its environment. In other words, we need to consider the continuous changes taking place both in a system and in its environment, and how they influence each other. In abstract terms, what does not change is our observation point, as we identify, distinguish, and differentiate something in relation to the surrounding environment. That is why it is impossible, in our case, to arrive at a definition of religion that is good "for all seasons," for all times, and for all places. This is because we are talking about the *relationship* between a system and an environment, in our case between a belief system and a socio-religious environment. We focus less on what defines the system's stability and more on the continuous "border wars" conducted by the system to set itself apart from the environment and, by so doing, to find a principle of self-definition and self-regulation that is not necessarily due to or dependent on other systems, or at the mercy of changing conditions occurring in the environment outside. What comes to mind in this setting is a concept dear to the sociology of religion of Ernst Troeltsch (1990), recalled several times by Jean Séguy (1972; 1980), of the relative autonomy of religion, of religion as a belief system that is. If we juggle with the terminology and talk about belief rather than religion, we can identify a specific social type of belief that enables feasible comparisons to be drawn between different symbolic and religious worlds.

This concept has been better explained in systems theory using a concept drawn from modern biology, that of *autopoiesis*, that is, the minimum premise, be it as small as you will, that a system must logically possess in order to present itself as such and be identifiable as a network of relationships obeying certain rules that make it distinguishable from other systems and differentiable from the surrounding environment. In other words, the link between the different elements or component parts of a system is established and governed by a principle within the system itself, on the strength of which it traces the boundary between inside and outside, between what is relevant to the system and what is not. The fundamental issue for a system is the strength of the boundary that enables it to distinguish the external (environmental) differences that pose no problems from those needing to be taken into consideration and made the object of transformation from external to internal difference in order to better withstand the interchange with the outside environment. Here lies the relative autonomy of a system of religious belief.

The problem for an observer lies in grasping first where the boundary passes that distinguishes a system from the environment, and then how the *border wars* take place between different systems. This means that we must study the conditions and modes of constitution of a system, and follow up its evolution as if we were dealing with an organized structure capable of functioning as a closed system (an indispensable condition for it to be open to the environment). According to Luhmann's theory, in fact, a system can only be open inasmuch as it is closed, meaning closure and openness in the sense of the system's capacity for self-generation in time through an exchange of energy with the environment, deciding case by case how much of the environment's external complexity can be converted into the system's internal differentiation. We are in a circle of thoughts that reflects a well-known definition of system proposed by the Chilean biologists Maturana and Varela:

> ... the structure of a society as a particular social system is determined both by the structure of its autopoietic components and by the actual relationships taking place among them while they integrate it. Therefore, the domain of social phenomena ... results from the autopoietic operation of the components of the society while realizing it ... . (Maturana and Varela 1980: xxvi)

The macrosystems that we know (the living, psychic, and social systems) are therefore *autopoietic*, because they rely on their own, specific operating principle: for living systems, this means cellular reproduction; for psychic systems, it is the thought process, and for social systems, it is communication. There can be no thought without the awareness that generates it, and there can likewise be no cell generation without a living organism made up of cells. A social system is a system because it produces *communication*, and communication takes place within a social system. The mind (the psychic system) is not just a set of brain cells, but a sophisticated way of linking thoughts, information, and messages in a constant thought-generating process. Everything belonging to the mind is in the shape of a thought or a link between thoughts; and everything that does not have this shape lies outside, as far as the mind is concerned; it is the environment in which a mind operates. When something is thought or imagined, it becomes an element that enters the circuit containing the network of thoughts and links, so it is no longer *only* something outside, separate and different from the mind. When I think something, it enters the familiar space of my mind. Observing the operations that a cell or a mind, or a social system, implement to chart their boundaries involves distinguishing between the explanation that an observer gives of what he or she sees on the one hand, and the operations that we assume cannot be brought within the observer's perspective on the other. These are data, or facts, that we are inclined to *take for granted*, that we believe exist irrespective of whether or not somebody claims to observe them. This is very similar to the concept of the *life-world* (that, as we said, is taken for granted) developed in Schütz's sociological phenomenology (1967).

From the methodological standpoint, the systemic approach introduces a shift, as Esposito rightly pointed out (1992: 21), from the question "What does x see?" to another question, "How does x see?" If we restrict ourselves to considering the implications of this change of sign in the question, insofar as concerns social systems, then we can say that the way in which we observe something (rather than the *something* being observed) helps us to understand the further methodological advantages of systems theory. In fact, studying a social system has less to do with defining the contours of something, confining it to the Procrustean bed of empirical analysis, and more with retaining the conviction that, in order to study it, we need to understand how it relates to one or more other systems. This is what

Luhmann defines as *double contingency*: every *autopoietic* system is closed in relation to another, but it is still influenced by the functioning of other systems, and vice versa. This double contingency characteristic of social systems means that a system continually draws experience from the instability of the meanings attributed to information and situations experienced in the environment where it operates. Every system seeks to shape the experience of a meaning that is open to other potential meanings. Every external or internal item of information is systematized, converted into a relationship that has meaning for the system (be it psychic or social) and referred to a series of relationships that the system can control in a serial sequence. It certainly acquires a current meaning as soon as it is taken into consideration, or taken into care, by a system, but it recalls other possible meanings and other possible interpretations at the same time. It is as if, every time the information were analyzed and classified according to the internal parameters of a social or psychic system, thereby lending it a meaning, it were also revealed as potentially ready to generate other meanings, in a continuous surplus deriving from the environment that, by definition, offers a greater abundance of possibilities and alternatives, up to a point where the previously attributed meaning might even be denied.

As Luhmann sees it, drawing also from Husserl's philosophy, sense is the fundamental modality that enables reality to be experienced, enabling the orderly arrangement of people's impressions of what is presented to them as actual and potential. The moment we experience something as real, sense makes us consider potential other meanings to attribute to what we have experienced. Communicating (that is, social systems) and thinking (that is, the mind, or psychic systems) are operations of sense: they actualize the sense, while remaining constantly open to other possibilities. We communicate and we think something, but on a horizon of meanings open to other possible communications and thoughts. One communication enters into a relationship with another, just as one thought enters into a relationship with another in a sequence of communications and thoughts that is not closed, but open to a surplus of communications and thoughts. Seen from this point of view, a psychic or social system is founded on sense in a continuously- enacted game of actual and potential. So, everything makes sense to the system, whether it relates to the themes it covers or to what remains as background or latent potential for other meanings.

Theoretically, this infinite number of possible references is what we call the *world*, that we could define more simply as what constitutes, for a system, a boundary beyond which there extends a space that cannot be embraced in its "gaze," let alone controlled completely once and for all. From this point of view, sense grasps the theoretically endless complexity of the world; by actualizing, it selects what can be *understood* by the system as apart that engage with other parts of it, while at the same time it refers to other possibilities. So every system is induced by its very nature to build its boundaries of sense. Hence its dynamic nature: it can never shut itself in or withdraw within itself once and for all, as if it were satisfied with *staying put*, because every choice (of sense) is open to and refers to other possibilities (Luhmann 1995: 172). Sense, for Luhmann, is a product of the evolution of psychic and social systems, or rather of their parallel evolution, since they are both influenced by each other. He basically defines this as the availability of a redundancy of possibilities for the experience or action that actually take place (ibid.: 172). He also said that all experiences of sense that seek to determine the reality always incorporate, like a fundamental constant, a *sentiment of disquiet*. Sense *obliges itself to change.* (ibid.: 173).

Sense is therefore a way of processing the experience of events that are read and interpreted on the basis of the states of a system, selecting some rather than others so as to be able to cope with the event that questions the system. Luhmann gives all this the name of *information*, which constitutes the elementary unit of the relational processes between system and environment. Being an event, it is also configured as an experience of something that is, by definition, unrepeatable. As Luhmann said, if the sense of such information is repeated, then it is no longer information (ibid.: 67).

For complex systems (that is, psychic and social systems, which therefore have a capacity for self-analysis), this information is not so much the experience of something that happened beyond the boundaries (the environment) of a system, but rather the experience of a change of state that the information induces within a system. This influx from outside increases the system's self-analysis and self-determination. This can be translated, with a positive effect on the system, into an increase in complexity compatible with its internal balance, or else the information may have a negative, conflictual, and contradictory dimension that the system has difficulty in assimilating, because the information introduces a possibility previously not entertained in the system's hitherto "calm and clear" horizon of sense.

Luhmann gives an example that is particularly helpful for the purposes of our present discussion of religious belief systems (that we have already mentioned and that we shall return to again more extensively later on) when he refers to the case of the Protestant pastors, who were once all men, but now there are increasing numbers of female pastors. Should they be called *pastoress*? Should we kiss their hand? (ibid.: 68). We might find ourselves asking the same questions at some time in the future should the Catholic Church decide to allow women into its priesthood, which has traditionally been reserved for men. The same applied when this tradition was abandoned by the Anglican Church, arousing some doubts among its followers, and even outright criticism in some cases. The psychic system of the believers processed the information either as an event that extended the boundaries of sense, or as a threat to the reassuring framework of meanings attributed to the function of the priesthood in the life of *their church.* For individual believers, their church is the environment in which they act because they believe; just as believers, each in their own way, constitute the environment for the church system. So, if some believers disagree with decisions made by the ecclesiastical authorities, the resulting situation is a *double contingency*: it means that the latter have been unable to communicate effectively to the former what sense they should attribute to the decision to ordain women priests; and, for their part, the dissident believers create an external differentiation that is hard to transfer inside the system.

How Religions Communicate

This terminology should not come as a surprise because, in all the historical religions of which we have a knowledge, there is a functional principle at work that we can define as *communitas* (or *ecclesia*, literally the ideal assembly of people who identify themselves with a shared belief in something or someone, and who also generally share several fundamental modalities of belief), that does not necessarily focus on any explicit clerical hierarchy or an organized structure with a unique, acknowledged, and visible authority. As Durkheim has already explained, for us the word "church" is really a synonym of *system of sense*, experience of an event that is transformed into a complex network of symbolic elements, nourished by specialists in religious matters and by ritual forms that are intended as procedures that select allowable symbols, a specific way of communicating that enables the repetition of an otherwise unrepeatable event, *as if* it were always topical and up to date. The fact that a ritual must be identically repeatable in order for it to be considered valid by the system of (religious) sense is no accident: it incorporates information that preserves the sense of the experience of an extraordinary event, without adding other information. Rituals are forms that have already processed the information and already selected what can and cannot be done in the liturgical space that they design. They are configured in this way because, as a rule, they are part of the internal language of a belief system, an internal system of signs that *preserve* the original information (as in the case, which exists in many religions, for instance, of victims being sacrificed), without necessarily producing new information.

Every time a liturgical action is enacted, it is as if the audience, under the guidance of an officiating authority, were to open an imaginary archive of symbols deposited in their religious belief system, the inalienable heritage of their religion, and thereby bring it alive. This reiterates where the boundary passes between what it is allowable to believe and what has been judged *impossible* and *unspeakable* to believe (subject to external changes that alter the system's internal state). This heritage that can always be used for the purposes of communication, as a stock of topics and conceptual collections that can circulate every time system and environment engage in communication. The reasoning that the Catholic ecclesiastical authorities have often used, for instance, to say no to women in the priesthood, and to explain this to a wider audience of its followers, draws from a heritage of reasoning and interpretations considered selectively by the church as binding and handed down from one generation to the next.

In relations between religious belief systems (and within a system that begins to experience increasing levels and degrees of internal differentiation), no question can be considered of little moment, because even the smallest of issues may conceal large questions. As Luhmann explained (1995: 163), this is because in all experiences of sense there is a *difference*: the difference between what is *actually given* and something else that is possible, starting from what is given. In religions, in the beginning there is the difference, and it is only through difference that it can establish its identity.

Moving away from the monotheistic religions, Buddhism, for instance, is a belief system was sparked by the capacity for improvisation of a person, Gautama, of the royal house of the Sakya, who had been the lords of a small feudal state territorially located between India and Nepal for generations. He came to be called the "Enlightened one," or Buddha, and he probably lived between the fifth and fourth centuries BC. Buddha tested the sense attributable to pain, and to the origin of pain, and how to avoid it in life, through difference with respect to the belief system dominant at the time, which was Hinduism. When he delivered the message to his disciples, we see that the first community, *sangha*, or assembly (that Piantelli [1996] also translates as *ecclesia*) of wandering beggar ascetics (*bhiksu* or *bhikku*) very soon became divided on the issue of how to interpret Gautama's teachings. In other words, what took place was a process that, having been generated by difference, then produced further differences: between what Gautama put into practice with his experience and his doctrine deriving from a dialectic differentiation from Hinduism, and the possibilities of sense that originated from his spiritual message. Like other religions, Buddhism has generated approximately thirty different schools, born from schisms and bitter ideological controversies. Around 130 years after Gautama's death, the first of these schisms led, together with others that took place afterwards, to the formation of different schools, which also multiplied as a result of the expansion of Buddhism not only to most of India, but also to Central and South-east Asia.

In particular, Buddhism met with considerable success thanks to an enlightened prince belonging to the Maurya dynasty, called Ashoka, who became converted to the Buddha's doctrine and adopted the Buddhist ethics as a system of public and civil norms for his whole kingdom, including the principles of nonviolence (*ahimsa*) and respect for animal life. But it was under his government, between 268 and 233 BC, that the first two trends (which had already existed in Buddhism in the early days) became consolidated. On the one hand, there was the *sarvastivada* school of thought (literally, the theory according to which all exists), which was declared heretical by the Council of Pataliputra (the capital during the reign of King Ashoka, now Patna in Bihar), but it subsequently spread throughout the Kashmir region; on the other hand, there was the *vaibhajyavada* school (literally, the doctrine of distinctions). This latter trend, promoted by Ashoka himself, would appear to have caught on thanks to an intensive missionary activity in what was then Ceylon (now Sri Lanka). In the first two centuries AD, this first division was to lead to creation of another important separation within Buddhism, in which one branch referred to the school of the *greater vehicle* or *mahayana* and the other, by contrast, was called that of the *lesser vehicle* or *hinayana*. The distinction between these two schools also crosses geographical boundaries: the former is more widespread in northern India, China, Japan, Korea, Nepal, and Tibet, the latter in southern India and particularly in the southern Asia (Burma, Cambodia, Sri Lanka, and Thailand). The school of the lesser vehicle refers to a body of scriptures in the Pali language and emphasizes the core, exemplary function of monastic life, submitting to a rigid moral discipline, isolated from the rest of the world in the monastery (*sangha*). The school consequently believes that it jealously preserves the purest spiritual tradition inaugurated by the Buddha. This school can be further divided into various groupings that it is unnecessary to mention here.

The school of the greater vehicle, on the other hand, focuses on the figure of the *bodhisattva*, a person who embarks on the arduous course charted by the Buddha, striving to draw near that culminating point where he or she can go beyond the threshold of pain and reach an understanding of their origin—that is, enlightenment; but the *bodhisattva* tarries a while to serve as an example for all other human beings, common mortals and laypersons, who cannot opt to dedicate themselves entirely to a monastic life. This branch has also developed many shoots, particularly in the process of adapting Buddhism to the Chinese and Japanese cultures and mentalities, as in the case of *zen* (or meditation) Buddhism, which reflects particular features of the Japanese and Chinese mentality.

The third Buddhist school of thought is conventionally called tantric (or *vajrayana*, the diamond vehicle), which developed a set of esoteric doctrines that a spiritual master teaches to his disciples as a mystical, secret path, reserved for a chosen few. This line of thought became widespread in Himalayan Tibet starting from the sixth and seventh centuries AD, and also in Nepal, Bhutan, Manchuria, Mongolia, northern China and Sikkim (now a small state in the heart of the Himalayas, with its capital in Gangtok and approximately 6 million inhabitants).

The example of Buddhism is interesting for many reasons in the economy of our present discussion. It did not originate as a religion, although this somewhat inept and imprecise notion could be applied to it. It was really more the spiritual experience of a person who gathered around him a first community of followers, who recognized his personal charisma and who, after his death, took it upon themselves to define the fundamental principles of his teachings, what was subsequently to become his doctrine, even if it is configured (as we have seen) as a heritage that is contended by different schools. Now, changing linguistic register, if we look at the whole historical and social parabola of Buddhism, we can extrapolate from the course of events and conflicts that have characterized its alternating fortunes in the world up until the present day (not only and no longer *oriental*, since a well-tempered Buddhism exists in Western culture too) a series of elements that can be interpreted in the light of systems theory. These can be listed as follows:

a. The figure of the virtuoso who creates (improvises) an original spiritual model gives rise to a process of construction of a system of religious belief.

b. This system (and this was already implicit in the new course charted by the founder) becomes established by differentiation with the environment, and particularly with a stratified and complex socio-religious environment, if for no other reason than the fact that it had been dominated for centuries by a cultural regulator in the form of Hinduism and co-inhabited by other spiritual options, some dating from the same time as the Buddha (for example, the spiritual way of Jina or Jainism). This differentiation is translated into a precise symbolic boundary that partially separates Buddhism from Hinduism (for example, by preaching the elimination of the caste system as encoded by the hegemonic wisdom of the Brahmins, the noble priests of the highest Hindu caste) and partially places it in continuity and competition with other belief systems.

c. The passage from the living word or living experience of the founder to the belief system can be seen as an effort to define the symbolic boundaries of the system made by those who took it upon themselves to solve the question of succession to the founder's charisma, and to ensure continuity, substance, and force to his original message in the conviction, with the *best intentions* (but is this not an act of faith too, enabling men to ensure that the power of communication of a leader who has died is not lost?) to preserve its authenticity generation after generation.

d. It is in relation to this very definition of the boundaries that controversies of sense subsequently develop within the community; they give rise to different schools, or in other words, to attempts either to limit the excess of sense or to allow it to give a glimpse of a broader horizon of possible meanings. The boundary marking the distinction between the schools of the greater and lesser vehicles, for instance, basically expresses the intention to narrow down or broaden the field of the possibilities of sense, between what is actually given (only the monk who withdraws inside the *sangha* can arrive at enlightenment) and what *may be given*, starting from what is already given: that others, who are not monks, can also come close to enlightenment.

e. On the basis of the differences of sense, different traditions become consolidated. In other words, people live, communicate, take action one way or another, closing or opening the horizon of possibilities that enables a system to *read* the complexity of the environment (or prevents it from doing so) by transforming the possible into the practicable, producing new, non-dissonant information if it has chosen to open the casket of the *unspeakable* and to make it *speakable*.

What I need to remember from the example that I have given is that, irrespective of the individuals who actually occupied the stage, right from the beginning of the history of Buddhism—Gautama (the tip of the compass, to go back to an image that we used earlier on), with his uncertain biography, and all the great masters or princes who developed and contributed to establishing his teachings as a belief system, however differentiated and open to other, different environments from the original one—sense (when it comes to religion) has a social dimension. It cannot be experienced by a single individual, because what the charismatic figure does and says is really a door opening onto a multitude of meanings. The improvisation of the charismatic leader or reformer needs an audience, it is nourished by a social relationship that enables the leader to put his charisma to the test, as Weber explained. In other words, the sense that he experienced becomes an object of communication. In addition, those who continue the work begun by the leader inevitably come up against the problem of subsequent interpretations of the founder's message, which continuously give rise to controversies of sense. They find themselves having to produce communications about the original communication. Their job is to *communicate the communication.*

From this point of view, religions (we could even say every religion) are potentially a horizon of possibilities of sense, some actualized, others not, in a continuously open and mobile reference to other meanings. The efforts made by the historical religions to establish the criterion or standard consequently appear like a Sisyphean task because they are destined to be continuously threatened by the eruption of other belief modalities, starting with what has already been actualized.

Socio-religious Differentiation

In the Christian religious scenario, differentiation can be interpreted in different ways. Taking a historical perspective, we can analyze the theological and political (and economic) reasons that have produced schisms and lacerations which have remained impossible to repair. Looking at the present, we can speak of an increasingly plural market of faiths and of a religious mobility typical of modern man (Hervieu-Léger 1999) within what is conventionally called Christianity. Just how many churches professing to be Christian are there today in a near-continent such as Brazil? It is hard to say. In some cases, the sense experienced by a church or a community is open to a number of possibilities that other communities and churches classify as superstition, syncretism, or expressions of the devil, the *other* in a negative sense. I can explain the competition for the definition of sense in the same terms as market competition, as the theorists of *rational choice* do; but taking this approach of political economics to religion paradoxically emphasizes the social dimension of (religious) sense. For there to be competition, there must be subjects who compete with one another, acknowledging that there is an impassable horizon of sense, that is, what establishes that it is right to compete, leaving other possibilities in the background. The competition is between individuals in flesh and blood, but they obey an abstract social law that transcends the will of the single individuals, or rather the single individuals refer to it as an impassable horizon of sense. What a group or community experiences of the sense attributed to Christ is dialectically related to what another group elaborates on the matter.

If it is right to take into account the experience of these individuals (the believers), it is likewise legitimate, for systems theory, to consider the production and reproduction of the (religious) sense as a social process in which every identity also acts as a difference. So every experience, when it takes place in the context of a system of sense (be it a part of the organized forms of churches, or of sects, movements, cults, or the like), it is no longer just that, but also an element that produces *con-sent* or *dis-sent* vis-à-vis what the system has elaborated to decide on the "right sense" to attribute to the things people believe in, not so much as individuals, but as a community, or *ecclesia*.

Every belief system that has somehow given voice to a sense to attribute to a religious or spiritual message (elaborated by a prophet or a charismatic figure) consequently has as its environment not only the many, sometimes undefined subjective experiences of single believers, but also (and above all) other systems of belief that may converge towards the same or other objects of belief. The much-discussed religious pluralism, that was once identified as a marker of changes underway in the modern socio-religious landscape, really exists already in the beginning, it lies at the very foundations of the original process of construction and constitution of a belief system. A new way of believing seeks to occupy a space in an environment "crowded with deities," it must cope with the existing pluralism and distinguish itself from the other systems in order to become established. Pluralism here essentially means that observers (the sociologists of religion) are mistaken, methodologically speaking, if they think they can study a religion without extending their gaze to the setting in which the religion is placed and considering the relationships existing between system and environment in the religious field they are studying.

Faced with the flow of meanings that have been attributed in the history of Christianity, at various times, to the message of Jesus of Nazareth, at first glance we could say that the interpretation of the experience of the Christ-event has always been multiple (not unequivocal) and, more importantly, changeable—not so much in relation to the single churches that have attempted in the course of time to decide on the sense of the message transmitted by Jesus and his disciples once and for all, saving it from a series of hermeneutic disputes (for example, the Christological controversies), but rather in relation to the continuous flourishing of new movements and religious groups that refer to Jesus' message, often interpreting it differently from the historical churches. For instance, Moon's Unification Church in South Korea and the Universal Church of the Kingdom of God in Brazil both refer to Christ, but they see him very differently from how the Lutheran or Catholic churches see Jesus. Nor could we expect it to be otherwise. Their establishment as self-proclaimed new systems of sense relies on these very differences with respect to other existing systems.

In any case, sense becomes a resource with two primary functions: it enables us on the one hand to mark a clear boundary between actual and possible, and on the other, to put a stop to the flow of experiences of sense (that could theoretically be limitless, or at least multipliable at will), which is translated into a sign of recognition of its identity as a system. People and their experiences certainly count in religions, but so do the institutions that are created to assure continuity to a religious message. What we call the flow of experiences of sense therefore concerns not single believers, but all of them together; it includes them and transcends them, *ecclesia* as a system that can function in time even though the individuals identifying with it change—even when an *ecclesia* does not take the form of a complex organization guided by a unique, recognizable leader. Now, when the sense is fixed in a network of meanings that enable the complexity and variety of the experiences occurring in a socio-religious environment to be contained, then in systems theory we speak of *symbolic generalizations*.

A system cannot absorb all the external complexity, otherwise it will crumble: a church as a system cannot contain all the sects that might develop from the sense given to the religious message of its foundation, otherwise it will break down into a number of micro-systems. A system of sense uses symbolic generalizations to succeed in referring to itself and coping with the external complexity of the environment. A symbolic generalization reduces and defines: it reduces the potential plurality of meanings attributable to an object of social and human experience, and it defines the system's identity. This is the only way for people to indicate their *religious ID*: they can call themselves Muslim, Sikh, Orthodox, Mormon, and so on, maintaining and declaring their distances and distinctions from other possible interpretations and other identities.

To give an example of the above considerations, I can consider the first conflict that split the young Muslim community approximately 30 years after the death of the Prophet Muhammad. The great upheaval (*al-fitna al kubra*), as it was remembered in the historiography of Islam, saw the party of 'Ali (*shiat'Ali*, whose name gave rise to the term Shi'ite) at war with the upholders of the Sunna (from which the word Sunnite derives, which literally means the followers of the tradition of the Prophet) between 640 and 680 AD, and not only for political reasons (a battle over the legitimate succession between different clans), but also for theological reasons. Muhammad had taught his followers that divine revelation was manifested through different prophetic figures (from Moses to Jesus, just to mention the two main figures with which Muhammad drew comparisons to illustrate the differences between his own religious message and those of the Judaism or Christianity), and this had come about in Islam in the person of Muhammad himself (with the seal of the prophecy), so that, after his death, it was impossible to imagine another prophet. Who could legitimately guide the community of believers (*umma*) that had gathered around the word revealed by God through his Messenger? The solution chosen by the majority was the institution of the caliphate. Weber would call it an institutional succession to the charisma: in fact, a caliph (in Arabic *khalifa* means vicar or deputy) is a person who has the function but not the charisma, who acts in lieu of Muhammad without having the status of prophet. The dissent voiced by a minority who rejected this solution focused on the figure of the Prophet's son-in-law, 'Ali, who had married Muhammad's best-loved daughter, Fatima. The point of rupture that developed between 'Ali's party and the Sunnites concerned the idea that the Prophet's legitimate successor had to be chosen from among the members of his family, of his own *house* (*beit'Allah*: Muhammad's house or family, which was especially blessed by God, because God had chosen Muhammad as his messenger). The issue led to a genuine schism, with the Shi'ites becoming established as a minority sect, that has always succeeded in withstanding the persecutions and repression at the hands of the Sunni dynasties thanks in part to a particular theological doctrine (that of the hidden Imam), that has nurtured the hopes of redemption for the injustices it has suffered.

I am not interested in telling the whole story here, but can restrict ourselves to drawing from the example a few considerations that are functional to our discussion on sense and symbolic generalization. After Muhammad's death, the Muslims had to come to terms with the practical problem of his succession and their search for an adequate solution had to take into account the religious as well as the political aspects of the problem. What did all this mean? It meant wondering about the sense to attribute to Muhammad's message ("I am the seal of the prophecy") and it very soon became clear that they disagreed on how to experience the sense attributable to his words. It was in the crossfire of conflict that the Sunnis managed to set a limit on the flow of experiences of sense that had been emerging since the Prophet's death, of which the Shi'ites represented a rising peak. The Sunnis wanted to impose a symbolic code that, from their point of view, would fix the sense to attribute to Muhammad's message once and for all. It is no accident that the solution they adopted is theoretically (in terms of political and religious theory) a form of de-personalized government of the community—neither a theocracy nor a purely personal government by a wise prince. The institution of the caliphate—which should have existed regardless of the figures of the caliphs themselves (though history shows that it subsequently became hostage to at least two great dynasties, the Ommayyadi first and the Abbasidi later on)—means and defines in abstract terms a function, and an official appointed to said function, not a person boasting an extraordinary power in his own right. At a certain point in their history, marked by defeat and persecution, the Shi'ites were likewise having to decide on the sense to give to their experience. The doctrine of the hidden Imam (the last spiritual leader of the sect, who disappeared in the second half of the ninth century and who will become visible again at the end of time, bringing justice and restoring truth) is a symbolic code that fixes the flow of experiences of sense that in the Shi'ite world, in the early times of their diaspora, developed as a form of self-analysis on the reasons for their defeat, even though their leaders and martyrs of the faith, 'Ali and his son Huseyn, had been in the right. In both cases, symbolic generalizations progressively enabled two belief systems, the Sunnis and the Shi'ites, to define their identity within a given framework of belief (Islam), each differing from the other, each the environment of the other.

Symbolic generalizations also make sense of the contradictions and paradoxes in religions. This is the great mystery of religions. In fact, for religions mystery is really a semantic field where what would be logically unthinkable becomes thinkable and can be experienced as if it were all real by means of the specific social activity of religions—rite, or liturgy. This is the only way for religions, established as systems of sense, to succeed in closing themselves in and claiming their self-sufficiency. In conclusion, liturgy enables us to observe one of the structural traits of systems of religious belief, and that is the power of communication.

In fact, "sense can be part of a sequence that is based on physical sensations of life and thus appears as *consciousness*, but it can also be part of a sequence that demands another's comprehension and thus appears as *communication*" (Luhmann 1995: 175). A sociology of religious belief systems is more interested in the latter aspect, although it does not disregard the former—and anyway, the one without the other would have no ... sense. So, it is a case of choosing which access point enables us to gain a better understanding of how religions function as (organized) systems of belief in which people in flesh and blood take action and experience the sense of the holy. So it is time to see how systems theory considers communication and how, moving from the general theoretical paradigm, we can obtain useful indications for a religious belief systems theory.

Chapter 2
Religion and Sense

Sense and Communication

Simone Weil claimed that human language can never succeed in speaking about God, not even when it attempts to use images and mystical suggestions. When we think that we can do so, that we can define the essence, then it has already escaped us. At best, we have described an idol. The contradiction, or *coincidentia oppositurum*, belongs to the action of thinking in images, which is typical of religions. They shed light on the sense, but only incompletely. With her typical acuteness, Weil basically tells us that any effort made by human beings to pronounce a word about the supernatural is destined to be thwarted every time it aims to provide a definitive, closed, and normalized answer on the topic (Weil 1951). What we believe in—in religious terms—can be perceived as a set already defined in every aspect, or as a set of actualities and potentialities, that can consequently still be unraveled, spoken and made the object of living experience.

It is common knowledge, for instance, that there are different ways to approach a reading of the various religions' holy scriptures. We can read them as texts that have incorporated an unchangeable sense, or as pages that are open to interpretation by the hearts and minds of men and women living in different historical periods. In point of fact, the first approach is never adopted, whatever those who defend their absolute value say. The text is always interpreted somehow the minute it is read and an orientation of its sense is specified (a given verse must be read this way and no other way). But other ways are always there, between the lines, because there will always be somebody who sees another meaning there.

In the Talmudic schools, or *yeshivot*, the texts include the various commentaries on the Torah that the rabbis have made with time. These comments often reflect discordant points of view and opinions. In fact, the Talmud is a set of documents that have been produced at different and not always easy times and conditions for the Jewish communities. It is difficult to date them, especially when it comes to identifying the different schools of thought that these texts have contributed to forming. The disputes that are reported in the texts and that are the object of debate even today (and used as a training method) in the *yeshivot* have to do with different, past, and present ways of reading the sense attributed to a given precept, or a certain verse in the Bible, or a passage in the commentary of one rabbi or another. In rabbinical Judaism, what is written in the Talmud has traditionally been considered as divinely inspired (*Ruach haKodesh*), and the orthodox and ultra-orthodox Jews of today loudly claim that the Talmud is entirely inspired and consequently an unquestionable source of norms and certainties of their faith.

The reformist commentators and even the traditionalists tend to believe, however, that the Talmud is really the result of a complex stratification of texts produced at different times that reflect different socio-cultural conditions, so they see it as a plexus of interpretations open to an infinite number of possible comprehensions (Libson 2003). We could therefore say, in this case, that the sense is polysemic.

Much the same could be said about the prevalent approach to the reading the sacred text in Shi'ite Muslim tradition. As explained by Corbin (1971), one of the greatest experts on Shi'ite theology and exegesis, from the doctrine of the hidden Imam onwards, we can see why the Shi'ite scholars and theologians see the text as having two meanings, one manifest and the other hidden, one readily accessible to the simple believer, the other reserved for those trained to understand the mysterious and esoteric signs of the divine that shed light on the path to follow, that will enable them to perceive when the time is ripe for the Imam's return. The people capable of interpreting God's signs are called *ayatollah* (from *ayat*, meaning a sign, but also a verse in the Koran, and *Allah*, or God). The Sunnis take a different approach that allows no space for such a dual interpretation. In the orthodox Sunni way of thinking, the prevailing idea, if any, is that the Koran cannot be interpreted from a historical-critical stance because it is as if it had been handed down from the sky exactly as it is (Abu Zayd 2002, 2004).

In short, a communication problem is generated by the sense and its excess of polysemic possibilities in the religious field. When we deal with this topic, we need to bear in mind that, for systems of religious belief, we have to distinguish the subjective actions of the faithful from the functioning of the system as such, which may (to the eyes of an outside observer) have little to do with the people concerned. Religious belief systems are a variant of social systems, one of the more or less complex of society's possible systems. The social dimension of systems, including those based on religious grounds, exists in the sense that action takes place within a system through communication. If Weber had conceived of social action as a type of action oriented towards calculation or value (the intentional or subjective domain of action capable of producing "sociability") and Parsons, dissatisfied with the point reached by Weber's theory, went so far as to claim that action *is* the system, in the sense that social action is only possible within socially pre-defined norms (the role, for instance, and the hierarchy of compensation in terms of status), Luhmann said that the fundamental element of a system lies less in the action of social subjects and more in communication.

In fact, communication is a process for reducing the complexity that needs action for it to succeed, or rather it needs to be separated and reconstructed in actions (Luhmann 1995: 204). So it is not that actions that construct social systems; vice versa, it is the latter that need to be separated into actions in order to function. When we speak of communication, we mean not just the transfer of information from a source to a recipient, but rather a *selective process of sense*. Communicating means drawing a meaning from among the possible meanings, processing it and making it the object of a potential symbolic transaction with another party, who does not merely receive it, but also performs a similar operation in selecting its possible sense.

Communication relies on the fragile balance of the double contingency: what seems an unequivocal and clear selection for *ego* may not be so for *alter,* who makes his own selection. Given a certain repertoire of possibilities (of sense), we can choose something that is then circulated as discourse. The communication is therefore not conceived as action, discourse, the act of announcing and then awaiting a response, it appears instead as a unit simultaneously comprising the information and also the acts of its communication and comprehension (or the expectation of its acceptance, which may obviously be granted or denied). When, as Luhmann says (ibid.: 147), "One reads, for example, that tobacco, alcohol, butter, and frozen meat are bad for one's health, and—whether one believes it or not—one is changed (into someone who should know …)." Once we have received the information, we may or may not believe it, but the communication changes our state of mind and obliges us to decide whether or not to believe what we have been told. This new state that we are in did not exist before and it *did not exist without the communication.* Accepting or rejecting (believing or disbelieving) are consequent actions that are not part of the structure of the communication, which already allowed for the selection of possible meanings (and the rejection of others). Communication creates the framework social conditions in which actions (of acceptance or rejection) may or may not take place.

As a result of this selectivity, communication must cope with the coordination of the reciprocal selections being made in a social system as a whole. Politics, the economy, science, law, and other component parts of a social system all process their own internal communication strategies: the problem that each of them faces is how to coordinate their own selection with selections structurally made by other systems, each with their own communicative competence.

On this issue, it is interesting to study not only how this or that politician or entrepreneur acts in relation to the financial system, or a given scientist in relation to a government that decides whether or not to approve a law on artificial insemination, for instance, but also to see whether there is what systems theory defines as a *symbolically generalized communication medium.* This is one of those media that "use generalizations to symbolize the nexus existing between selection and motivation and to represent them as units" (ibid.: 161), who meant by motivation the level of acceptance that a given selective proposal manages to gain. In the list of such media that the author draws up, we find truth, love, property/money, power/law, art, and religion. These are media that enable us to reduce the space of the excess of sense: when we speak about politics, economics, religion, science, and so on, we take it for granted that we understand what we are talking about. We generally distinguish between a politician and politics, just as we distinguish a priest or a church from religion. The difference lies in the relationship between action and communication: a politician takes action or a pastor takes care of his flock within a more general horizon of sense that we abstractly call politics and religion, respectively. This what makes communicative selection possible, as something that takes place between individuals, but it refers to a higher social command than the individuals involved. Generalized communication media are one of the possible ways to control communicative processes; the other two most important ways are language and the means of their diffusion (including modern mass communication media).

If I apply the above considerations to religions, I can say that a belief system functions through communication since agreement or disagreement concerning the content of truth (the sense to attribute to a given set of propositions of faith) depends not only on the will of single individuals, but also and more importantly on the system's capacity in a given situation to select "signs of identity," that is, beliefs that can be shared by the largest possible number of people (allowing for the fact that some people will not share them), beliefs capable of being represented socially as *ecclesia*. In our daily language, we conventionally speak of Muslims, Catholics, Buddhists, and so on. But we know from empirical investigations that societies with a Catholic majority include many different ways of being Catholic, just as in Islam there are different ways of practicing the Muslim faith, and so on. Such a behavioral pluralism (in actions) is reduced by a symbolic generalization— Catholicism "nevertheless," or Islam "nevertheless"—that communicates something different from what single believers may communicate in their actions and practical experiences.

A religion that functions as a generalized communication medium has symbolically reached a high level of self-awareness and self-referencing capacity. It can claim to be universal not because it has extended its influence to different parts of the planet, but because it has become a belief system that disregards whether its "official" beliefs—selected and communicated as such—are more or less well received. The growing expectation that many will be accepted is a consequence of the communicative action that a system uses continuously in its generation and regeneration (its *autopoietic capacity*).

For a Definition of Religious Belief System

Having come thus far, I suggest a definition of religious belief system. So far, we have clarified what we mean by system, identifying the three aspects characterizing it according to systems theory, that is, a) difference vis-à-vis the environment, b) the elaboration of sense, and c) communication. To apply these three concepts to religion, we need to clarify another aspect: we are talking about a religious belief system, and the term *belief* is broader, although it is commonly used to mean religion. In point of fact, there are other forms of belief resembling or differing from religion. The authors who coined the terms *secular religions* (Piette 1993) or *civil religion* (Bellah 1967) alluded to all those symbolic universes with which we can identify collectively without necessarily referring to a religious confession or to a church. In many ways, Communism was a utopia in which great masses of people believed, a sort of paradise on earth that was to abolish all forms of social injustice and rid humanity of the alienation produced by paid labor. The fact that people in the United States of America, leaving aside the religious diversities of different churches, sects, and movements of all kinds, speak of a shared feeling that would induce the majority of its citizens to identify with a poorly defined God and that this would serve as a constituent element of their national identity, could make us speak of civil religion in the sense of a quasi-religious unwritten pact of solidarity that overrides their clearly evident differences. They are Protestants, Catholics, Muslims, Jews, Hindus, and so on, but they are Americans, and they feel part of a national community with a moral mission assigned to them by a supreme being.

Even today, political rhetoric expresses the idea that civil religion and sense of national unity coincide thanks to a shared religious belief, which goes beyond the confines of the different faiths. The American presidents use a symbolic generalization medium to reduce the complexity of the social and religious environment and transform its pluralism and differences into a resource of political consent to shared national values. Their civil religion gives the impression that Americans are united, despite all their many (not only religious) differences.

We could say that both secular religions and civil religion are ways of representing a collective consciousness, enabling a plurality of individuals (sometimes whole populations) to identify with a community of election or destiny, to nurture sentiments of attachment to their homeland (for example, the fatherland) and to fight to defend it in the name of ideals of justice, as in the political utopias that give strength and passion to the desire to eliminate social injustice and inequality. In any case, there is a social dimension in action that has to do with believing (de Certeau 1987). It is worth mentioning again what Durkheim (1912) said on the matter of collective consciousness: we create it, but then we end up seeing it as something that overrules individual human will. In fact, Durkheim tended to imagine collective consciousness as a secular god that human beings adore and celebrate since they live together in a society, renewing the pact of solidarity that makes them feel united. For Durkheim, the sacred is really a collective experience that makes us discover the binding nature of belonging to a society, enabling us to stipulate an unwritten ethical pact. Without this basic belief, society would not exist. If we did not see it as something transcending our own individual will, to which we must submit like it or not, in order to avoid losing the sense of our actions, we would be unable to believe in anything. The alternative to collective consciousness is significantly called *anomia*, that is, the absence of norms, a condition that makes individuals feel homeless, with no acknowledged and widespread power to impose the social norms on an individual's behavior. So, according to Durkheim's sociology, the act of believing provides the very foundations for social order (Rosati 2009).

Studying religious phenomena led Durkheim to see the cogent force of the sacred as the source of social norms and of the normative principle without which society does not exist and individuals no longer see the sense of their actions. Religions consequently have absolutely no autonomy; they can be completely broken down into specific forms of a more ample genus: believing. Believing in society *as if* society were a deity means that religions are administrative variants (influenced by history) of the sacred nature of society per se. For Durkheim, the gradual drive towards individual autonomy on the one hand, and towards a fragmentation of social work division on the other, would have endangered the very normative principle that makes a cohesive society possible and capable of seeing itself as such. So it is hardly surprising that he should have been a promoter of religious education in the early years of junior school to educate the younger generations to adopt a moral sentiment capable of compensating for the entirely individual propensity to seek one's own benefit and profit, which tends to loosen the bonds of social solidarity.

Taking our systemic approach, however, and contrary to Durkheim's convictions, religions gain some degree of autonomy because they are, by definition, considered as belief systems capable of organizing themselves—if for no other reason than because they are capable of representing the *place* occupied by individuals, in society and in the world, according to a general framework that makes *sense* of what individuals do in society (their actions) and imagine being able to do beyond the horizon of possible sense established by the world, in competition with, or through differentiation with respect to other sub-systems operating in a society (the economy, politics, science, and so on).

Religions *think and make people think* along the lines of a superhuman principle (transcendent or immanent as the case may be) that governs society and the cosmos, developing complex symbolic models in order to be able to *speak and act* as a consequence. For a religion, believing intercepts three domains: thinking, speaking, and acting. In other words, it deals with the domains of the possible representations of sense, communication, and action, respectively. The operating principle of a religion organizes the belief on these three levels corresponding, in sociological terms, to different degrees of internal differentiation. Thinking refers to the preparation of a class of specialists or professionals appointed to defend the symbolic boundaries of its representations of the superhuman; then there are the liturgical officiants needed to organize the routine reproduction of the ritual, intended as a specific language for communicating the symbolic content of a religious message. Finally, there are the individuals who act, orienting their actions in the symbolic arc thus designed and confirmed in rites functional to the production of social norms, or through self-discipline, or respect for an institutional authority.

When Max Weber focused on the elective affinities between the Protestant ethic and the spirit of capitalism, he proceeded in reverse order: from modern forms of rational organization for the capitalist enterprise to the lifestyle of the entrepreneur, and then to the ethical and social norms he adopted, ending with a reconstruction of his symbolic-religious universe. It is as if Weber were monitoring two domains—the economic and the religious. His chosen observation point enabled him to comprehend the symbolic code lying behind the capitalist entrepreneur's rational action, that is, to decipher how the Calvinist *perceives* the superhuman and how this perception has important consequences both on the ethical plane (how this superhuman is spoken about, and what sense is derived from it in the action) and on the socio-economic plane (the action itself). We can hardly fail to see that Weber's debating method *actually* (though it was obviously not the author's intention) assumes that (Calvinist) religion as a belief system distinguishable from another system of social action, such as the economy, enters into a relationship with the latter, adapting to the specific meanings attributed by the social agents acting on the strength of the *spirit of capitalism*. In this case, the sense is not deduced from the action of individuals (who generally constitute the environment for the belief system), but a selection of possible meanings that the doctrine of Calvinist predestination provides to explain the individual's place in society and in the world. By doing so, however, it becomes ingrained in the way of thinking and lifestyle typical of the capitalist entrepreneur (Poggi 1984). By closing the symbolic boundaries of sense, Calvinism as a religious belief system proved capable (more and better than others, according to Max Weber) of dominating the social differentiation that capitalistic modernity produced, according to which every entrepreneur must pursue his or her company's profit, therefore operating according to a scheme of things that makes profit-seeking the object of human action. Because of its elective affinity for the capitalist economic ethic, according to Weber, Calvinism was able to produce a sense (of the action) that transcends the purely profit-seeking dimension, *perceiving and making people perceive* the entrepreneur's social action in meta-utilitarian terms.

Religion as a belief system is therefore founded on the system-environment nexus, which is a constitutive link of religion. It is only by holding strongly onto this assumption that we can understand why religions (as we know them historically) cannot be studied by the social sciences as if they were units unrelated to one another. This does not mean that the difference establishing the relationship between system and environment in the religious field can be translated into a sort of implicit hierarchy between one and the other—as if to say the system is more important than the environment, for instance, because the environment is synonymous with multiplicity and the system with unity, and unity is essentially more important than multiplicity. Nor does it mean underestimating the already often-mentioned weight of subjectivity in religious belief system-building processes. The important thing to bear constantly in mind is that the premises for the development and the articulation of a religious belief system lie not only in the individuals in flesh and blood, but also in the socio-religious environment where the system becomes established as such through differentiation. This ultimately means that the system-environment distinction applied to religion implies no division into two separate parts, like two halves of an apple, but simply the *adoption of an observational stance* that social scientists of religion can choose, from among the number of approaches that might legitimately be adopted, in order to arrive at a broad-spectrum theory of the phenomenon they wish to study.

A point of equilibrium that our observation should maintain is based on what we could call the *principle of respect* in our study of a religion. Our interest in observing it as a belief system must first lead us to identify its symbolic boundaries, which have enabled it to distinguish itself from the environment. Secondly, it must induce us to consider how a religion sees itself or, in other words, how it guards the symbolic boundaries that it has charted. Finally, it must prompt us to develop analytical models suited to the specific object we are studying, respecting its autonomy (or capacity for self-generation as a system). A religious belief system usually distinguishes what it is believable—within it—from what it considers *unbelievable* outside it.

When I compare different belief systems, I can also establish how much the field of possibilities concerning belief proposed by one or other belief system is wide or narrow, tolerant and flexible, or rigid and impenetrable. This is because I can assume that *the environment is always more complex than the system* (Luhmann 1995). However complex a religion may be, it can never produce a communication on all the things that it sees as "the rest" of the religious field, or the rest of the world, where other "faiths" exist and elaborate different interpretations of the world. That is why it has to compensate strategically for this structural weakness in its communication, using a tool that enables it to adapt its own code to the different cultural registers that it encounters in the environment. For instance, studying how a belief system such as Buddhism (though to what degree it is wholly religious is a debatable point), that originated in India, can adapt to the mentality and culture of the Chinese and Japanese helps us to understand the degree of internal differentiation that it has succeeded in developing during its evolution in order to cope with the complexity of new, different environments where it has come to operate for historical reasons. The same considerations would apply to explaining the relative success of this belief system in the West.

Much the same considerations would also be pertinent for all the religions that, with time, have become great world religions, whose environments have become so vast and complex as to coincide with the boundaries of the world. The fact that the feedback from this complexity affects a system's functioning is another aspect upon which sociological (and other) observation can shed light, providing it constantly takes into account the dynamic relationship between system and environment.

Belief Systems and *Autopoiesis*

When we analyze how an environment has a feedback effect on the system, an important hint comes from the liturgical rituality that a religious belief system usually generates. It can be seen as a generalized symbolic communication medium, a formal scheme capable of reiterating the sense the system has chosen to attribute to what it believes in, and keeping "outside the door" (of the holy precinct or liturgical area) any alternative and potentially deviant, misleading or irreverent behavior—in a word, any excess of sense that the system cannot cope with. If, in order to adapt to a new environment presenting hitherto unknown levels of complexity, a system proves willing to absorb unusual symbols and rituals, and unconventional types of behavior with respect to the formal schematics of its liturgical apparatus that it had originally standardized once and for all, then we can measure how the system copes with symbolic elements that do not belong to its own code. It is as if we were studying how a belief system deals with the insecurity generated by information that does not belong to its own internal scheme of things. This information may be treated either as a sort of threat that must be cast out, or as a resource for producing a new and more widespread consent. Either way, the system is always obliged to take stock of itself, to see itself as being capable of incorporating an external difference by transforming it into an internal difference.

This is what we mean by *autopoiesis* in religious belief systems, that is, the capacity for reproduction through an increasingly articulated internal differentiation. The study of religions as living organisms can provide some important empirical contributions to help us construct indicators to measure their internal complexity, such as the division of labor, or the specialization into the spheres of influence, with the related training of one or more professional classes, or the management of financial and human resources, the organization of corporations (based on age, social category, gender, and so on). The differentiation processes observable in religious belief systems can be fundamentally brought down to the following antonymic pairs: *center/periphery, conformity/deviation, formal/informal, superior/inferior,* and *functional/segmental.*

Historical sources permitting, I can pinpoint the central nucleus of a religious message in a given religious belief system and its offshoots, often in a declining order of importance of their meaning. This is the relationship between what is *fixed* and what is *mobile* in the lengthy course of a religious belief system's evolution, between what represents the original, unchangeable core and what is presented instead as the system's open-mindedness in relation to the environment. Taking the first pair, for instance—center/periphery, the different colors used to distinguish individuals belonging to different castes in the Hindu system of belief are certainly important, but they do not form the central nucleus of their symbolic universe. It is likewise quite easy to find examples of the conformity/deviance dichotomy: inasmuch as they are systems that become organized as a center of knowledge and power founded on their claim to possess the truth (which may be seen as having been revealed directly by the deity or handed down in scriptures), religions must constantly defend the symbolic boundaries that they have raised in order to distinguish themselves from the environment, and they must consequently classify everything coming outside their boundaries or threatening their solidity, under the heading or in the category of deviance.

The formal/informal pair can be reworded in terms of a liturgical/para-liturgical polarity, because it has to do with the set of rites that a religion develops. A rite follows an official code and involves precise procedures; it is implemented under the control of the specialists in holy matters. But alongside or in parallel with these classified practices, the devout and faithful may introduce more or less well-tolerated variations. They may invent complementary practices that are celebrated outside the official sacred precinct, maybe up against its walls. To use a spatial image, it is as if we were right outside the walls of the temple. In some Catholic sanctuaries, for example, the boundary between official liturgy and para-liturgical practices is clearly visible, marking a space that is tolerated by the Catholic authorities, but there can be no overlap with the canonical space. To give an example, during the annual celebration of the Madonna at the Polsi sanctuary in Aspromonte (Calabria), the ritual cutting of the lambs' throats in the stream running alongside the church is a form of popular para-liturgical devotion that stops right on the threshold of the sanctuary, clearly marking the distance between formal space and informal space in the celebration of the sacred.

Finally, the superior/inferior polarity recalls both the structure of the religious power and knowledge that a belief system claims to possess and several of the previously examined conceptual pairs. A peripheral belief may be considered inferior, and any informal behavior may be seen by the religious powers that be as marginal or almost intolerable. The best-known case is that of the Hindu caste system (Dumont 1966; Piano 1996; Bayly 1999; Shah 2001).

Since the word "caste" (*varna* or *jati* in Sanskrit) means a pure race, it was coined by the Portuguese settlers when they arrived in India and discovered how Indian society functioned on the strength of a particular form of social stratification. A caste is a closed social group to which every individual belongs by birth. The word *varna* means color and every caste has a color for its clothing to distinguish it from the others. The caste is indicative of a precise religious or social status: first came the superior caste of the *Brahmin*, or priests (the only people entitled to officiate at sacrificial rites, whose distinctive color is white); then came the warriors, or *ksatriya* (princes and noble warriors, identified by the color red), and then there was the population of traders, or *vaysya* (whose color was yellow). Later on, those who held the religious power and knowledge added a fourth to the first three castes (distinguished by the color black), called the *śudra*, that is, the laborers, on the lowest level of the social scale, who had to serve those belonging to the higher castes. Anybody not belonging to one of the above-mentioned four castes "had no color": these were the so-called outcasts, defined as Untouchables because they were believed to be impure by definition. People are born into a caste and that is where they remain, each generation handing down the set of ritual duties assigned to its own caste. With their caste, people inherit a whole set of ritual rules that, in theory, every member of the caste must follow. The caste system thus establishes a hierarchy of ritual purity: those who belong to the higher castes can perform ritual actions considered of high symbolic rank, while such actions are forbidden to those of the lower castes. This rigid hierarchy subsequently gave rise to a stratification of occupations and professions, and a strict regulation of any social mobility from one class to another. The Brahmin were considered the purest, and consequently the closest to the core truth of the *dharma*, the heart of the Hindu religious message, so they had to remain isolated from people of the less pure, lower castes. In Hindu cosmology, moreover, the social order designated and designed by the caste system coincides with the cosmic order and consequently reflects a law that is seen as being unchangeable. It is as if the social system were a replica of a complex cosmogony.

The caste system thus relied on a model of belief that imagines society as having always been divided into a number of segments with precise boundaries marking the ritual distance between the people who belong to one or another segment. Such a segmentation of society is naturally functional to the maintenance of social order as a reflection of the cosmic order. This system had already been weakened when the condition of outcast was abolished by law and it is now proving unable to stand the test of modern-day social differentiation, which facilitates the formation of new classes, amplifying economic opportunities and expanding people's occupational options.

Determinate and Indeterminate

Believing, when it is referred to a religious system, means *believing in the feasibility* of connecting the determinate with the indeterminate. An individual's social position in ancient Indian society was clearly defined, even if it was not readily comprehensible to all concerned: the caste system enabled society to see itself as a factual and symbolic unit at one and the same time. It led people to accept an otherwise unthinkable order. It made people behave as if they acknowledged this order, and somehow saw the sense of it and how it selectively guided their actions. This was not a matter of any mystification of reality, in the sense suggested by the Marxist approach to religion. A socially unjust order may appear justified in religious terms—and that is why believing is always an act of alienation according to the classic Marxist view, because it focuses the repressed desire for justice elsewhere, into the world beyond the grave, that many religions have described in great detail to lend more sense to that desire. In point of fact, believing has to do with the *desire to communicate* with the superhuman, with more or less help from an intermediary.

Seen from this point of view, the sacrifice is a communication medium *par excellence*. It is very difficult to find a religion that does not contain some sacrificial ritual. As Hubert and Mauss demonstrated (1929), sacrifice is a term that contains the idea of differentiation: an animal becomes a sacrificial victim when it is separated from its natural environment and elevated to a *different* sphere of meanings. The animal crosses an ideal boundary and is thereby transformed, it acquires a new status and consequently goes to a special death, that is sacred because it involves an equally special figure, the sacerdotal officiant (from the Latin *sacerdōs*, priest) performing the sacrifice. In this setting, believing means separating in order to recompose, uniting through difference, distinguishing in order to communicate, departing from the determinate in order to arrive at the indeterminate.

The ambivalent structure of believing in the religious sense has been much discussed by historians, anthropologists, and sociologists of religion, so it is not worth spending too much time on the topic here. Religions—like mythology—

represent a free and creative source of symbols that enable humans to construct causal relationships that make sense. To draw from the ideas of a contemporary ethologist, who reflected on the psycho-biological grounds of religion (Hinde 1999), there is empirical proof of the fact that states of ecstasy or contemplation induced by religious practices (prayer, meditation, yoga techniques, and so on) can give people an intense sensation of interior well-being that spreads to their consciousness as a feeling that they are able to control exterior situations or face the difficulties of daily life, and even withstand physical pain and psychological suffering. Without wishing to fully embrace the strictly socio-biological approach that others have coherently tried to take (Acquaviva 1990), Hinde's idea can be interpreted in the light of systems theory as follows: believing—referred to what is conventionally called religion—always means believing in the existence of a possible link between "all things," that ultimately allows us to see as thinkable and possible what is ordinarily not so. Ordinary experience is filled with an extra-ordinary power, and the sense experienced in such cases contains a very wide range of possibilities. It is as if a door were opening onto a limitless panorama of possible meanings—an excess of meanings that other systems cannot cope with and contain. Every religion, on the other hand, is capable of developing a set of symbols and rites, sometimes with very wide degrees of freedom and with a creative spirit that closely resembles that of mythology, of poetry and music, if for no other reason than because it involves the experience of many, many individuals, who expand on the meanings that their belief system attributes to a given dogma or a certain liturgical gesture, offered as a simplified formulary of beliefs (as catechisms generally are).

It is also true that, to distinguish itself from the environment and from other religions, every belief system tends to restrict itself—in the sense that it develops a number of variations on a central, core theme that are configured as a way to emphasize how it is different. But such variations on the theme must have a stop at some point to enable a system to retain its differences vis-à-vis other systems with which it competes in a given social and religious environment. The theme of a deity's death and resurrection, for instance, recurs in many religions. In Christianity, it lies at the very core of the belief system. There may be variations on this theme, but only up to a point, if a given system is to preserve the identity of that central core of the original message from which the system originated; otherwise, it encroaches on the area occupied by other belief systems and the claimed specificity of Christianity (to give an example) risks vanishing or becoming relative. If significant numbers of people say they believe in reincarnation after professing generically to being Catholic, then either the symbolic boundary between resurrection and reincarnation is no longer clear, or it has been trampled down, dilating the sense attributable to the word "resurrection" until it coincides (albeit often only vaguely) with the meaning of reincarnation as used by the New Age religions of Far Eastern inspiration (Cesareo 1995; Garelli, Guizzardi, Pace 2003).

The difference in religious belief is thus reduced to causal relationships that can be influenced, not rationally but on the deeper plane of the emotions. As Benveniste wrote (1969: 442), the Greek word *spendo*, which is translated as "to make an offering" (in honor of a deity) refers to the idea of an *offer of security*. Before a hazardous journey or a military expedition, offerings were made to the gods to implore them to ensure their happy outcome, like a sort of life insurance. More or less every religious belief system seeks to reduce the risks to which every individual is intrinsically exposed in life. But the offering also recalls another dimension: when an agreement is made, it has always been customary to drink a toast, especially if the agreement takes the form of an oath of fidelity. In some religions, the pact between God and human is fundamental. For instance, the idea of the Alliance between God and Moses is central to Judaism, and an alliance, an agreement, a pact, an oath are all words that indicate a relationship.

In fact, believing always has to do with thinking in terms of a *relationship in a situation at risk* in an environment that is variegated, changeable, and uncertain, especially when it comes to seeking the sense of our actions. The relationship reduces the risk. Belief systems tend to suggest that the key to this relationship is not in the sole hands of human beings and, by doing so, they lead people to believe that they can reduce only the risks *within certain limits*, because their reduction relies on a superhuman force. The autonomy, or *autopoiesis*, of religious belief systems lies not only in the sense that they seek to elaborate to interpret this structural relationship (between determinate and indeterminate), but also in their extraordinary capacity to produce *narratives* that arrange the communication between the system and its environment on several, differentiated and, at the same time, complementary levels. That is why the power of communication that a religious belief system claims to possess, that enables it to function as an autonomous organization of sense, must necessarily translate the *narratives into actions*. The link between narrating and acting in religion is decisive: when it is weak, individuals acquire secularized lifestyles, tending to tailor their religion to suit themselves; when it is strong, people behave *as if* a divine will were taking effect and involved in their actions (Turina 2006).

It is generally agreed and has often been said that the particular, autonomous terrain of religions is rituality. Rites are communication in action, narratives transformed into gestures indicating a meaning, a sense. They enable religious belief systems to patrol their symbolic boundaries, seeking to channel the flow of communication between believers (each with their own psychic system), and to set a limit between what is and what is not consistent with the great narratives generated by the system (which are *brought to life*, or *relived* in the liturgical action), adapting the narrative in the process to different environmental situations, which never remain the same. Rites are basically opportunities provided by a belief system so that its faithful can experience the sense attributed to what constitutes *the core of the message for the system*. This clearly does not prevent individual believers from taking another course, from the mystical path to an initiation guided by a spiritual master. In all such cases (including the mystical experience), special spiritual methods must be used to ensure reproducibility—in other words, people must always fall into line and follow a master (Maccarinelli 2001; Filoramo 2002).

Let us take yoga, for example. The etymology of the term is interesting for a start: it derives from a Sanskrit word, *yuj-i*, which means *conjunction* and *control* (in the causative sense), but also to *focus the mind*. In current usage, the word has come to be synonymous with a meditation method. In one of the classic Hindu texts, it is also defined as *concentration*, alluding to the act of combining, finding agreement, making harmonious, and also to the capacity to fix one's gaze. If we reduce the complexity of the definition of yoga found in the scriptures and adopted by various masters in the course of time, in a nutshell we might say that a person is guided, step by step, by a master along a path that should ultimately make the person self-sufficient. The goal is to rid oneself of the conditioning influence of the ego's attachment to material things and thus (as a supreme moral and spiritual condition in order to become free) to escape the cycle of deaths and rebirths on which the Hindu message is based. At the end of this journey, the mind should experience a state of indifference to nature, material things, and the individual's conscious ego, thereby achieving the *mokśa*, emerging from the round of continuous deaths and rebirths, and attaining to the supreme ideal of salvation in Hinduism.

In many ways, something similar to what we have said about yoga can also be found in the Christian world. In the Orthodox Church, for instance, as of the twelfth century (and with an extension that echoed the same spirit and method right up to the sixteenth century), there was a meditation and spiritual technique called *hesychasm* in circulation. The word literally means "solitude and interior calm," and the purpose of the set of techniques involved was *naturaliter*, and intimate and mystical communion with God in the here and now. Emerging from a monastic environment (in the elite community of the Greek monasteries of Mount Athos, to be precise), where it was already customary to follow a daily cycle of liturgical prayers, fasting, and times of silence, *hesychasm* was seen as a method that took effect simultaneously on body and spirit. It involved continuously repeating the name of Jesus (the so-called "prayer of the heart," or "Jesus prayer") accompanied by regular, rhythmic breathing patterns to help the mind concentrate on that mystical point the person strives to achieve: of communion with God himself.

The repetition of a holy name, or of the holy names of God, is a practice found in other religions too. In Islam, for instance, many Muslim believers repeat the 99 names of Allah (*al-asma' al-husnā*) several times a day with the aid of a necklace consisting of 33 beads (the hundredth name is symbolically the key to the mystery of the ineffable essence of God).

What we mean to say here is that rituality in religious belief systems lies on at least two levels: one is public, as it were, the other private; one concerns and celebrates the community, the other has do with individual asceticism. Both these levels may be strictly structured, according to standards that leave no space for inventiveness or deviance. There is one public moment and another that could be defined as "diffuse," that could be illustrated graphically as a scatter plot of discrete points, each of which represents an individual managing their interior rituality on their own. They may also be arranged, however, so that—while the "public" ritual continues to reiterate the same, clearly distinct, hierarchies and gestures— individuals in their private lives have a greater degree of freedom, providing their behavior does not interfere with the orderly sequence of the collective, public rites.

All this generally divides religious belief systems into systems that are more or less *deaf* to the environment in which, and in relation to which they establish themselves, and systems that are *noisy*, that is, that tend instead to exchange information with the surrounding environment more intensively and more frequently. On this issue, Luhmann reminds us that the construction of social systems follows Heinz von Foerster's "*order from noise principle*" (Luhmann 1995: 207). Foerster was born in Vienna in 1911 and had the opportunity to come into contact with the intellectual environment of the Vienna Circle. He later moved to the US, where he set up a biological computer laboratory in 1957, that attracted such personalities as Norbert Wiener, William Ross Ashby, Margaret Mead, and Gregory Bateson. Foerster developed a theory very similar to Constructivism, that is, the world does not exist before my experience, it is my experience that is the primary cause and the world is a consequence of it (Foerster 1996: 34). The objects (of reality) are constructed through our action in the world, and the characteristics and properties that we attribute to things are ultimately properties of the person observing them. The observer is therefore the person who arranges and organizes a world constructed from his or her experience, establishing an order of meanings among the many possible available meanings. In the same way, a social system establishes an order "of things" on the strength of the "noises" it picks up from individuals who are seeking to *communicate to each other* what meaning each of them attributes to the world around them. In plain words, a social system selects the sense of social action and communicates it to the psychic systems, taking what the latter have elaborated into account (Foerster 1960, 1987; Foerster and Porksen 2001).

Rituality as an Intersection Between Systems and Individuals

The existence of the two levels of rituality thus helps us to understand the specificity of religious belief systems, that few other systems can boast, because the two ritualities effectively interpret the concept of *interpenetration* discussed in social systems theory. This concept is used to allude not only to the intersection at elemental level, but also to the mutual contribution to the selective constitution of the elements that results in such an overlap (Luhmann 1995: 210 et seq.). The principal, "natural" environment of a belief system consists of its believers, that is, as many psychic systems as there are individuals who refer to a given system of belief. The two levels of rituality reflect this mutual contribution, what the psychic systems give to the belief system as a whole, and vice versa. This is the only way for the double contingency determined by the sense experienced and communicated by one system to another, as one of the possible meanings among the many available, to be reduced and made tolerable for both the system and the "believers" (intended as psychic systems). An empirical analysis of the objective correspondences between the two levels of rituality could shed some interesting light and help us to measure whether and to what degree the sense officially intended and established by an institution that organizes public liturgies coincides with the sense experienced by the individuals taking part in them, or in all those other rituals classifiable as private or domestic, that are often performed outside the places designated by a religious institution.

By being open to outside meanings, a belief system can paradoxically also seek to reinforce its claim to having *closed* symbolic boundaries. The Latin Mass belongs essentially to Catholic tradition, and it is the asserted object of a sort of *symbolic copyright*. So, systems promote openings in order to better control their own boundaries, but if this strategy fails because their being open makes them no longer able to control the rules of the communication game that apply to the liturgical space, then any evolution or change can pave the way to a symbolic *invasion* of elements belonging to another religious or social system.

Speaking of evolution does not mean that we can imagine a linear adaptation to the environment, however. Every opening implies an increased internal complexity and therefore a symbolic boosting of a given religious belief. Even such technologically rudimental societies as that of the Mbuti Pygmies (who survive in the forests of sub-Saharan Africa), for instance, have a complex belief system and sophisticated rituals, the outcome of a gradual adaptation to an unfriendly, difficult, and hazardous environment. The evolution of which we speak when we refer to belief systems is always circular, that is, it is characterized by an interpenetration between systems that *remain* open to one another. Saying that they remain open is not tantamount to saying that they influence one another. Psychic systems effectively *co-penetrate* with one another within a belief system whenever they adopt another sense proposed by the system. Being open to another system means that a given system (for example, the psychic system) adopts the *alter's* difference "on probation," because it sees the sense of the *alter*'s action as an element *worthy of faith*, that the individual may accept with such conviction that they makes it a part of their own horizon of sense. Any *alter* may not necessarily do the same, or in the same measure; they may accept the alternative sense that another psychic system proposes, but still feel free to combine it with their own strategies of sense.

When the alternative sense becomes communication and action at one and the same time, we are faced with what is conventionally called conflict, a deafening noise that the system cannot avoid hearing, but that it is unable to translate using its own approaches to sense selection. A metaphor that might make it easier to represent what we are trying to say with a graphic image is not that of two circles touching one another, and less still of two concentric circles (a larger one containing the macro-system and a smaller one containing scattered psychic systems that seek to communicate with one another through a medium called religion or, to be more precise, rituality, when it comes to religiously oriented actions). The idea suggested by systems theory is that, in order to survive, every system can go beyond the boundaries that distinguish it from the environment and enter into relationships with other systems, functioning as an environment in relation to the latter. Its previous, stable, and dependable boundaries thus become movable. If, after an exchange between two systems, they both ultimately succeed in preserving their own specificity, then the outcome can be considered positive for the *autopoiesis*, self-generation and, at the same time, self-preservation of the systems. This process enables every system to stabilize its instability, guaranteeing its constant reproduction by means of hitherto unexpressed potentialities.

Chapter 3

From the Capacity for
Improvisation to Belief System

The Virtuoso and His Feats

Having clarified in what sense we mean to speak of religious belief systems, we need to deal with the problem of the relationship existing between the system's constitution and construction process and its genesis. This is not a case of chicken or egg paradox, or of which comes first, the founder of a religion or a religion that, given the impulse of a charismatic personality, becomes organized and established in time. Our hypothesis is basically that the founder of a religion creates nothing new in absolute terms, that is, nothing that does not already exist in some form in the environment where the founder acts. He or she draws inspiration from symbolic material already in circulation, possibly reinterpreting it in an original way, and communicates it effectively, finally transforming it (and this is the fundamental, relevant aspect) into living experience. In abstract terms, the sequence of actions can be summarized in three words: information, communication, and action. The thought, the thinkable, and the unthinkable.

We can consequently define as capacity for improvisation that extraordinary talent (or charisma) exerted by a mobile personality—someone capable, in other words, of transforming symbolic material existing and pre-existing in a given socio-religious environment (rituals, beliefs, messianic expectations, forms of religious organization) into a new system of meanings, a new scenario set against an existing backdrop, lending a new sense to a universe of sense that no longer succeeded in dominating the contingency of a given socio-religious environment. The personality of the founder of a religion is described as being *mobile*, meaning that they are capable of going beyond the symbolic boundaries of a consolidated, existing belief system and of charting new boundaries, partly by rearranging the relationships between the constitutive elements of the previous system, that is, inventing new symbolic boundaries from the existing substrate. The term "mobile" also alludes to the power of communication that the founder exerts over his early followers, the purpose of which is to *make them have* a first experience of mobility of the symbolic boundaries.

Suffice it to recall the well-known sentence attributed to Jesus in the Gospel of St. Mark (2: 27–8): "The sabbath was made for man, not man for the sabbath. Therefore the son of man is also Lord of the sabbath." This sentence does not mean that Jesus intended to go against the Jewish precept of the *shabat*, that is, the abstention from all activity in the Lord's honor from dusk on Friday and all day Saturday. He complied with the Law of Moses, but criticized the excessive formalism preached by some of the influential groups of Jews of his time. In the story of one of his miracles being performed on a sabbath day (judging from the account in the Synoptic Gospels, at least), the man from Nazareth healed the unfortunate by means of the word, which was permitted by Hebrew law. As we see from the passage in Luke 6: 6–11:

> And it came to pass also on another sabbath, that he entered into the synagogue and taught: and there was a man whose right hand was withered. And the scribes and Pharisees watched him, whether he would heal on the sabbath day; that they might find an accusation against him. But he knew their thoughts, and said to the man which had the withered hand, Rise up, and stand forth in the midst. And he arose and stood forth. Then said Jesus unto them, I will ask you one thing; Is it lawful on the sabbath days to do good, or to do evil? to save life, or to destroy it? And looking round about upon them all, he said unto the man, Stretch forth thy hand. And he did so: and his hand was restored whole as the other. And they were filled with madness; and communed one with another what they might do to Jesus.

The episode is rather eloquent: on the one hand, Jesus attributes a sense to the sabbath, suggesting somehow that the formal barriers that a certain type of Jewish tradition had erected around the precept of the Lord's day could be overcome; on the other, the group of Pharisees was clearly worried about Jesus' personality, because he was a *living* indication of a new meaning attributable to an action taken during the *shabat*. The episode is a good example of how the capacity for improvisation is exercised mainly on the plane of communication: not only because words are exchanged, or because it gives a measure of the conflict existing between the demand for novelty and the prospects of preserving or defending the established symbolic power, but also and above all because it gives us an idea of the stuff of communication in religious belief systems, both in their genesis and in the social and historical process that leads them to become established. In fact, Jesus chooses one of the many possible meanings to attribute to his healing action—a meaning that for the Pharisees had faded into the background; it had been lost along the way while they were scrupulously and obsessively abiding by the law. Why should I be considered a deviant if I do a good deed on the *shabat*? This is the very simple, but effective reasoning of the man from Nazareth. The comment that Luke adds to round off the episode is significant: it is as if the Pharisees realized that Jesus had not actually gone against the law and yet, for them, the sense Jesus attributed to the meaning that for the Pharisees *shabat* fell outside the symbolic boundaries that they had constructed in relation to the dominant belief system.

It is worth bearing in mind that the Pharisees were important in the Judaism of Jesus' times, but they were certainly not the only authoritative interpreters of the Jewish religion. There were publications speaking against the Pharisees, written by other Jewish groups, and there are also traces of a violent controversy against the Pharisees in the texts of the Essene sect. Unlike the latter, who strongly opposed the dominant group of Pharisees in Jerusalem, Jesus often repeats what is reported very clearly in Matthew 23: 2–3: "The scribes and the Pharisees sit in Moses' seat. All therefore whatsoever they bid you observe, that observe and do; but do not ye after their works: for they say, and do not." This is an invitation to go beyond the symbolic boundaries, but without abandoning the ethical and religious core that Judaism had handed down over the centuries. The formula that Jesus uses to express all this, and that we find several times in the Gospels, goes along the lines of "It is written, but I tell you … ."

Figuratively speaking, the written word is like a sort of impassable frontier in the conceptual maps of Jesus' listeners. He tries to make them imagine the possibility of going beyond. The belief system of a practicing Jew is based on the idea of the revelation of God, whose Word is preserved in the holy Book. Hence the widespread practice of consulting the holy Scriptures and therefore also the formula (only partially precise) of Judaism as a religion of the Book (Stefani 1997: 23; Flusser 1997).

The example that I have drawn, in referring to the charisma of Jesus of Nazareth being put to the test, really provides an indication—from a methodological standpoint—of how I mean to proceed in my analysis of the capacity for improvisation. Because this capacity usually belongs to an individual who is recognized by a group of individuals (that subsequently becomes a community of followers or faithful) and because the relationship takes the form of a charismatic, affective and secure bond established between the former and the latter, we need to adopt a comprehending method, as Max Weber put it, assuming the personal dimension as the interpretative key, inasmuch as concerns religions that refer to a figure who has given the *incipit* for a new way of believing, at least.

Basically, what we aim to do is to concentrate our attention on a particular way of *producing faith*, that is, the *personal* genesis of a belief system. Here lies the real miracle of the great religions: the personal experience of a prophet or spiritual master gives rise to the construction of complex and imposing religious belief system that is able to withstand time. All this entails remaining faithful to Weber's comprehending method for analyzing social phenomena, but integrating it with the genealogical perspective, along the lines of the studies conducted by Talal Asad (1993). By combining these two methodological approaches, we can proceed more effectively with a comparative study of religions in the context of the social sciences.

Drawing comparisons, for instance, between the various figures of prophets or masters who founded belief systems is no easy matter, especially for the sociology of religions, a discipline that is not very familiar with the history of religions. In fact, comparing means observing the religious phenomenon while bearing in mind that the empirical materials on which we work are drawn from a non-sociological laboratory, that is, the laboratory of history, *equipped* (from the documents to their interpretation) by those specializing in the history of religions. Comparing is not so much a matter of being determined to find the universal and general within the particular, the fundamental structure over and above the differences between the various stories or experiences of the prophets, but rather of grasping whether and how the capacity for improvisation affects the religious belief system-building process, starting from the premise that we must expect major differences between different systems, and from the assumption that, despite these differences, the capacity for improvisation is expressed in action, as a chance to *move* beyond the boundaries of sense established by previous belief systems.

This enables me to clarify the viewpoint that I intend to adopt as observers of belief systems. It can be summarized in two words: genealogy and constructivism. A system of religious belief is not something that is defined once and for all, but the outcome of a *process* that originates at a precise moment in history, possibly around an epicenter that triggers an earthquake in the ancient dwellings of the spirit, and something new is then built on the rubble—so, right from its origins, the mobility of the boundaries of sense is intrinsic in the *process*.

I therefore expect this mobility to be preserved somehow, occasionally continuing to jolt the walls built around the original message and progressively consolidated. Systems that tend and pretend to restrain that original mobility from which they were born for ever after are often destined to crumble and disappear. In fact, a great ideal line can be traced, from this point of view, between the *dead* and the *living* religions.

The living and the dead refer not to the account book that we could write, recording an inventory in the cemetery of history of how many and which religions have failed to survive. It would be a difficult task, anyway, because the layers of very ancient belief systems, that we considered dead and buried, even today can reveal an unexpected vitality. I only need to consider the shamanic layer that is resurfacing and that, in actual fact, had never really stopped launching signals from backstage in the history of this or that religion (Buddhism, Shinto, Hinduism, and so on). The living and the dead allude specifically to the ability of belief systems to reproduce the original capacity for improvisation in the course of time, even though the figure of the prophet or master who developed a new conception of the world, and of the relationship between human and superhuman, is usually no longer available in flesh and blood. I can define a belief system as *dead* if it fails to preserve the principle of mobility and the capacity to convert this originally acquired resource into an *autopoietic* functioning principle, proceeding through differentiation with respect to the environment (or the many environments with which a system must deal) and striving to convert external differentiation into internal differentiation. Vice versa, a *living* belief system succeeds in performing these two fundamental operations.

There is a sort of link between what I have written above and the hypothesis advanced by those who support the concept of *rational choice* applied to religion (Stark and Bainbridge 1987; Stark and Finke 2000). They claim that a religion operating in a state of monopoly tends to lose *faithful customers*, whereas in a situation of pluralism (an open market of religious faith), the competition prompts the different faiths to compete with one another and consequently to offer a religious product that can consolidate and maybe even increase its share of *audience*.

Seen from the *supply side*, a religion is all the more alive the more it adapts to the market logic and strives to increase its share of faithful customers, offering them something that fulfills their expectations, their hopes, their ideological view of the world, their liturgical preferences, and so on. It risks dying when it turns inwards and does nothing to cope with the challenges coming from outside. This theory clearly relies on a basic assumption: that it is the market which governs the level of vitality of a religious organization. Even leaving aside the strictly economic terminology adopted by the supporters of *rational choice*, we would find ourselves faced with the issue of religious pluralism and the meanings attributed to it, moving from the observation point of the sociology of religions.

If we limit ourselves to considering the religions that the historians have studied and brought to light even from the faraway past, we realize that no religion can boast an illustrious birth, as if nothing had gone before it. In sociological terms, this is tantamount to saying that the so-called religious pluralism is not a specific trait of modern society. Religions are like cliffs: if we study their characteristic features from close up, we discover just how many layers they are composed of, incorporating reflections and scraps of prior religions, transferred inside from outside, metabolized and reinterpreted, but therefore never actually cancelled.

In our opinion, the capacity of a religion, or of a complex universe of religious beliefs, to contain different layers of beliefs provides a good indication of how the belief system was built and became established, and to what degree the complexity it has interiorized can be seen as a resource of sense that enables the system to reproduce and regenerate itself (in the *autopoietic* sense) in the course of time and in relation to socio-cultural environments differing from that of its origins.

Above all, I need to take the temporal dimension into due account in order to study the evolution of systems—and of religious belief systems—and, from this perspective, the historical and political conditions that influenced or interfered with their evolution. Then, to the temporal domain we are observing, we must also add the spatial or territorial domain: the diffusion of a religion—the territories that it inhabits in practical terms—helps us to analyze how it has been acculturated when it has been successful in a different socio-cultural environment from where it originated.

It is useful at this point, when I take the spatial dimension into account, to keep control of a conceptual pairing that is crucial to understanding the relationship between system and environment inasmuch as concerns religions. A system of belief, especially if it starts with a virtuoso of improvisation, tends to be presented and represented as bearing a universal message, a salvific formula intended for all human beings, with no exceptions, and for the whole cosmos. Historians of religion have shown, however, that at some point in their evolutionary process, religions may become the belief of a particular population instead, gradually becoming transformed into a religion on an ethnic basis. The promise of doing good for the whole of humankind (that, for the sake of simplicity, we call the universal ethic) changes to become the certainty of a given population's purity or ethnic superiority. Ethnicity is an essentially social construction, as the best anthropology (Gallissot, Kilani, and Rivera 1998; Tullio-Altan 1995; Kilani 1994) and the best social psychology have often repeated (Mantovani 2004); when ethnicity interpenetrates with a religion, it raises its followers to the kingdom of the elite, thereby subtracting from its claim to universality.

One example will suffice: let me take a look at Hinduism. When I speak of this religion what do I refer to? Based on the findings of Hindu studies, I can say that it is a label with which we conventionally describe a beliefs stratification process that took place approximately between 1500 BC and 1500 AD. That means three thousand years of history, during which there has been a very rich story written by different peoples, from tiny kingdoms to great empires, amidst invasions and wars. Following the lucid reconstruction provided by one of the greatest Italian experts (Piantelli 1996: 7), if we were to schematically design the *cliff* of the Hindu religion, we could produce the graphic representation illustrated in Table 3.1.

This complex stratification is interwoven with an even more intricate internal differentiation within the belief system, if we observe it from the point of view of *the gods* that populate the Hindu pantheon.

Apart from the absolute impersonal principle (*Brahman*), the Hindus worship a variety of deities. Starting from each of these, we can trace the symbolic boundaries of a like number of belief sub-systems within the whole conventionally going by the name of Hinduism (Madan 1991; 2004; Copley 2000; Dirks 2001; Patel 1992). This is further proof of the concept that we have mentioned several times of *internal differentiation*. The important point to emphasize is that a system is generated from an original matrix and it then develops various sub-systems within it, each of which has the other sub-systems as its environment, and each of which gives an effective indication of the system's capacity to evolve through differentiation. The overall picture is illustrated in Table 3.2.

Table 3.2 deliberately provides a very concise summary of the broad spectrum of beliefs that come under the umbrella term of Hinduism. Moreover, those who have had an opportunity to visit any Hindu temples will be well aware that their iconography effectively reflects the sophisticated framework of this belief system.

I have deliberately chosen to draw attention to the particular features of Hinduism so as to demonstrate how the ethnicization process that this religion underwent during its evolution certainly did not prevent the system of belief from *learning* to deal with the external differences in the environment and partially transferring them within—thereby succeeding in withstanding the challenges of centuries. By including and excluding at the same time, even though it remained geographically confined to the subcontinent of India, Hinduism was able to function as an environment for the formation of other belief systems, such as Buddhism, Jainism and—as we shall see later on—the Sikh path. It also succeeded in guaranteeing a fair degree of internal unity by means of a set of relatively homogeneous religious practices, shared by the various sub-systems of belief.

I could say that, over and above the different meaning attributed by the various sub-systems of belief to the divine principle, the communication deriving from them takes practical shape in the liturgical actions that have somehow followed a

Table 3.1   The differentiation of the Hindu religious system

Layer of belief	Period	Sources and contents
Vedism Founded on the ancient holy scriptures (the Vedas)	1500–1250 BC Expression of the Ārya peoples, who settled first between Iran, Pakistan, and Afghanistan, and subsequently in the Indus Valley	Traditions transmitted orally and later transcribed in the form of hymns and prayers used in sacrificial rituals referring to an impersonal divine force
Brahmanism The elaboration of a conceptual system produced by the caste of *brahmin* (priests) who, for centuries, right up until the eighteenth century, controlled its interpretation	700–600 BC A classification progressively developed by the *brahmin* as the kingdoms or city states of the Ārya populations became more and more settled and firmly in control in the north of India.	The Upanishad (literally the secret doctrine), in particular, contains a cosmological account that refers to an absolute and impersonal Being governing all things through a personal Demiurge, who is entrusted to guarantee cosmic order
Hinduism The ethno-belief of the Hindu people, founded on the two previous layers, and consolidated by the principle of ethnic identification	The definition of Hindu dates from the time of the Muslim invasions of the tenth and eleventh centuries, to distinguish the non-Muslims, who were treated as protected communities; under Muslim rule, these people—like Jews and Christians—could continue to profess their own faith and follow their own judicial systems	The writings that reinforced this process of ethnicization are the so-called books of tradition (*smrti*), containing information on astronomy, grammar, etymology, ritual rules, and social norms
Neo-Hinduism Tendencies that developed under colonial rule, and that still survive today; they are presented as a reform of the spiritual message contained in the holy texts, or alternatively as a return to the pure Hindu origins	From the eighteenth century to the present day	First example of a reform movement is represented by Brāhma Samaj (born in 1828), while an instance of ethno-religious reawakening was created in the past by the Ārya Samaj (1875) and, by the Hindu People's Party.

shared design. Similarly, despite the traditional division into castes, which led to a diversification of the rituals, the symbolic axis around which the rituality rotates is substantially common to everyone, whether they belong to a higher caste or to a lower one. It is primarily a matter of faithfully adhering to the fundamental

Table 3.2   Brahman—the perennial impersonal principle

Shaivist sub-system	Vaishnavist sub-system	Shakti sub-system
The worship of Shiva, further divided into at least six schools of thought	The worship of Vishnu, divided into two branches, depending on which of the two manifestations of the god (Krishna or Rama) is worshipped	The worship of the great goddess Shakti, divided into various branches, the most important being the one that gave rise to Tantrism (from *tantra*: esoteric books)

rites that accompany the four phases of a human being's life—the naming of the newborn, the initiation into adult life, marriage, and death. Each of these steps involves (or involved … some of the ritual practices—with the possible exception of marriage, which continues to take place according to the traditional rhythms and rules—have lost their social plausibility in modern times) the performance of elaborate rites generally adopted by everyone, albeit to variable degrees depending on the caste to which people belong.

In conclusion, Hinduism may seem to be a religion *without a subject*, without an explicit founder, but in point of fact, as in other cases, it is very difficult to determine who possessed the capacity for improvisation at the beginning of this belief system, mobilizing pre-existing raw materials and shaping them anew. The fact remains, however, that—if we look at the effects produced by this macrosystem over the course of its thousands of years of history—we can see that it has undergone an *evolution*. This is what we have briefly attempted to describe in the tables above: an evolution that obviously follows a law of stratification rather than that of exclusion. That is how the universe of Hindu beliefs has succeeded in keeping alive its relationship with the environment (that is, its difference), establishing itself as an *autopoietic* system, that has certainly developed in history, but according to its own internal evolutionary line of expansion, and not only of expulsion.

The Virtue of Expansion

I can speak here of syncretism through expansion in opposition to a syncretism through cancellation or crushing: in the former, new layers of belief are added without causing traumas or contradictions with the horizon of sense shared before the arrival of the new religious faiths; in the latter, a new religion seeks to annihilate its predecessor, crushing it under the weight of its (purportedly) superior truth.

A good example of the former case is Shinto, the Japanese symbolic universe of beliefs onto which another system of belief—Buddhism—subsequently became grafted without any particular friction. The reason for this fortunate coexistence can be found in the fact that the success or appreciation of Buddhism decreed by the Japanese has not meant any denial of the Shinto religion. Buddhism has been seen as a more effective communication medium for dominating the topic of death, that Shinto traditionally associated with the idea of defeat, the corruption of the body and the triumph of the shadows. It is as if there had been a mutual exchange of elements between the two belief systems that have increased their respective internal differentiation. One has made the environment of the other operative, and vice versa. Even today, Japanese people are said to be born and marry, and to celebrate the most important festivities according to Shinto rituality, but that they turn to Buddhism when they are nearing death and for their funeral rites.

Shinto is a belief system populated with spirits (*kami*) that become vitally manifest everywhere, but especially in nature. Hence the extreme care taken of the trees, water courses, flowers, and so on in Japanese places of worship, and the election of certain evocative places (mountains, volcanoes, bays) as divine epiphanies. The fact that nobody knows the founder of Shinto might help to clarify its apparent ductility in absorbing other systems of belief. Because it has no father or mother, an orphaned religion can accept other fathers and mothers. This is not really the case, however. Anyone with an understanding of the Japanese world knows that Shinto is like the air we breathe: everything is Shinto, including the theater (*kagura*), and *sumo* wrestling. In other words, when scholars speak of Shinto as the "original religion of the Japanese," they allude to a set of beliefs and rites deposited in the long-term memory of the people who have inhabited the island of Japan. While it is true that it is not easy to identify its genesis, there are some traces of it available. Thanks to recent studies (Raveri 1984, 1993, 1998), we can say that Shinto is really a label covering a whole array of symbolic elements drawn from different ancient mythological and religious universes.

In ancient Japan, there were probably societies divided into tribes and every tribe or clan had its own micro-system of belief, with its own deities, cults, and rules of conduct. To be more precise, each clan worshipped a single spirit (*kami*) identified as the mythical father of the clan. When one clan expanded and took over another, the defeated clan's *kami* was not destroyed, but incorporated in the belief system of the victor. A belief system substantially founded on believing in the spirits meant that all the spirits could be considered as essentially good, unless they proved otherwise.

Besides, the word "Shinto" seems to have preserved this original pluralist concept: it literally means the "path of the gods" and it was still meant in this sense much later on, thanks to the use made of it by modern Japanese scholars. Someone has traced this path back to a popular ancient Japanese version of Chinese Taoism. Others have sought to organize the evolution of the Shinto belief system into four periods (the ancient times, the period of the clans, and those of the Yamato Kingdom, and of the Kojichi), starting from the oldest sources that date back to the third century BC.

Leaving aside the various specialists' opinions, what appears interesting to note is the reference that even the ancient, traditional religions of the Japanese people made to shamanism. The word "shaman" derives from a usage of the people of

eastern Siberia (the Evenkes), who used the term to designate a person with special
powers that enabled him to act as intermediary between the human world and that
of the divine, or of the spirits; the shaman is a figure that incorporated the features
of the prophet, the miracle-worker, the magician, and the fortune-teller. Siberian
shamanism thus served as a mould for classifying other, similar types that can be
found amongst the Inuit people (the Eskimos), the Mongolians, Turks and Koreans,
and the Japanese, among others. In Korea, for instance, the shamanic substrate has
more or less influenced all the religions that subsequently arrived from outside, that
is, Confucianism, Buddhism, and Christianity to some degree, and ultimately, in the
present day, even the new churches and sects that have multiplied in the last thirty
years, for example, Reverend Moon's Unification Church.

It is particularly important to remember at this point how Buddhism has
absorbed several shamanic deities and made use of forms of dance and song that
are typical of the shamanic tradition in order to better spread the belief among
the people of the rural villages. Korean shamanism is believed (though the issue
is somewhat controversial) to derive from the Siberian version. Some have
claimed, however, that the figure of the *mudang*—the female shaman in Korea—
reflects autochthonous traits that we also find in other enclaves of South-east Asia
(including ancient Japan). Actually, if I take a look at the features of this figure, I
find that it has sacred elements similar to those we might encounter in Africa or
Latin America. The *mudang* is a person who has the gift of going into a trance and,
after reaching a state of ecstasy, of entering into contact with the spirits, capturing
their strength or their grace; they serve as *informers* about a person's destiny, to
heal, or to cast out the evil powers that threaten an individual's life. The fact that
the early sovereigns of the Korean kingdoms were also shaman and it was only
afterwards that there was a separation of the religious workload (in the same way
as in the Native American Indian tribes) is significant. The male or female shaman
basically had a clearly distinct function that we could call the processing of
information in the form of communications and performances, making sense of a
world that was otherwise overloaded with multiple and indecipherable meanings.
The shaman was able to select a possible sense and, through ritual action,
succeeded in lowering the threshold of risk and uncertainty in the environment in
which human beings live, and with which they must come to terms.

Shamanism is therefore a belief system that puts in order a world populated
by spirits, appointing someone to mediate with this world. This is consistent with
the well-known definition Mircea Eliade (1951) gave to shamanism, that is, it is
simply the ritualization of the raw religious experience, made accessible by means
of ecstatic techniques or trances. In a way, the world of the spirits with which
the shaman enters into contact is the multiple and changeable environment that,
through differentiation, establishes a relationship with a person who has a gift
considered and acknowledged as extraordinary. This person is seen as the holder
of the power of communication, in its dual role in reducing the external complexity
and selecting a sense from among the many possible and making it the object
of further communication within the society. As we have seen, it matters little

whether it is ancient or modern, since shamanism has not only not disappeared with the advent of modern and urbanized society, it has been restored—even in the United States of America. First, the Native American movements retraced it along with what remains of the heritage of the Native American Indians confined to the reserves, then it was relaunched and circulated by such an intellectual as Carlos Castaneda (1968; 1999), whose books have introduced topics and features typical of shamanism into the New Age circuits.

Turning back to Japanese Shinto, I can conclude that the cult of the spirits (*kami*) that, up until the third and fourth centuries AD had been controlled by the single clans (and particularly by some of the leaders of these micro-social units, which were founded on the ties of expanded families), was transformed into the cult of the mythical ancestors, with special reference to the most powerful clans that had progressively emerged as the new political and military forces, capable of unifying increasingly vast territories, reducing the other clans to liegemen of the new imperial sovereigns. The epic of the mythical ancestors of the first emperors (of the dynasty of the so-called Yamato, literally the State of the Great Kings), who chose Naiwa for their capital, in the Osaka region, which was then one of the most fertile areas for rice farming, is told in a text called the *Kojiki*, that appears to have been commissioned by one of the first Yamato emperors. The *Kojiki* tells the story of the divine origin of the first sovereign, direct descendant of a *kami* called Ninigi, who belonged to the family of the great Goddess of the Sun, Amaterasu Omikami. Amaterasu was the daughter of the original divine couple of the Japanese cosmogony, Izanagi and Izanami (rather like the metaphysical couple that we find in many cultures in South-east Asia, and in the Chinese culture in particular).

It is worth briefly outlining the story in the *Kojiki*, because it enables me to draw a few final considerations on Shinto, and not only on Shinto. The story is told that, after the birth of the island of Japan, which was the fruit of a union between Izanagi (the male principle) and Izanami (the female principle), the couple continued to generate various other *kami* (spirits or vital forces of nature). But, in giving life to the *kami* of fire, the irreparable happened and Izanami was burnt and died. In his anger over the incident, the male god killed the *kami* of fire and divided it into many tiny pieces, which all turned into other, less important *kami*. After meting out justice upon the fire spirit, Izanagi went to the afterworld, to the reign of the dead, to retrieve his much-loved wife-goddess. She could not return from the world of the dead, however, without permission from the *kami* who superintended the afterworld. While waiting for her freedom to be granted, the impatient Izanagi dared to look upon his wife, which was something he had been forbidden to do. Only then did he discover what a pitiful condition she was in and the disgusted Izanagi attempted to flee, with the infernal deities in hot pursuit. When he succeeded in making his escape, he realized that his contact with the world of the dead had made him impure, so he stopped to wash in order to cleanse himself. This act of purification prompted a final prodigious event: while he was washing, the great Sun goddess (Amaterasu) and her brother, Susanoo, were born, and Izanagi entrusted them with the government of the world. But the story does not end here, because Susanoo very soon revealed his willful character: he began to sow the seeds of discord in the world and his deplorable behavior made the Great Goddess decide to hide in a cave and leave Susanoo on his own. So the light of the sun disappeared from the world (this suggests the fairly obvious interpretation that there was an eclipse of the sun at the origin of the myth). Without the sun, life on Earth began to perish, so along came all the *kami*, the good spirits of nature, who formed an alliance and tried to persuade the goddess to come out of her cave. The negotiations were ultimately successful when one of the *kami* (a female spirit) launched herself into a lively and amusing dance that drew the goddess out of her hiding place. As soon as she set foot outside, Amaterasu was surrounded and held firm by all the other *kami* and the sunlight—as in all stories with a happy ending— shone on the world once more. At this point, the goddess sent all her offspring to reign over the islands of the Japanese archipelago. This mission was ultimately completed by the *kami* Ninigi, who was to become the head of the divine family of all the Japanese emperors. Ninigi then handed over the three symbols of the Empire—a mirror, a sword, and a jewel—to the first king of the Japanese dynasty.

The last part of this complex and contorted story enables us to grasp an important passage from the religion of the spirits to Confucian wisdom. For Confucius, in fact, the world is divided into three levels: the sky, mankind, and the earth. The emperor is the element linking sky and earth, since he was appointed by the heavens to govern the world. This is the notion of *tenno*, the Celestial Emperor, that we also find in Japanese tradition. Confucianism thus provides a political-religious frame for the central figure of the emperor: all this is apparent in the Japanese constitution of 604 AD, in the 17 articles of which Prince Shotku Taishi (573–621) strives to establish the Confucian ethic as the unifying foundations of the new Japanese society (Hérail 1986; Gira 1997).

The story that I have briefly outlined above is an imaginative, complicated fresco, rich in symbols and an excess of meanings, that seeks to represent the one–multiple relationship, projecting it in a world that is transcendent and immanent at one and the same time. It describes how the one is always given in relation to the multiple, and how the one can exist when it succeeds in interiorizing some of the force of the multiple. The story is functional to the belief, not only to the explicit belief that legitimizes the absolute power of the sovereign, but also the more pervasive belief that enables people to imagine a multiplicity of spirits existing in nature, with which they can enter into communication if they accept the sense attributed to them by the belief system.

Finally, when Buddhism arrives in Japan in the middle of the sixth century AD, after many initial difficulties and thanks to the mediation of an influential imperial family, it contributes to structuring the belief system typical of the Japanese people into an even more complex picture.

The belief system thus ultimately consists of various layers. The ancient and deep-seated substrate of shamanism provides the basis for the construction of the original Japanese religion, Shinto, upon which first Confucianism (originating in China) and then Buddhism (also from China) subsequently are deposited, without canceling the former religion. Se we have a plexus of at least four segments of a symbolic universe that, seen as a whole, already in the sixth century of our era presented a remarkable level of complexity and differentiation. Schematically, we can illustrate this stratification as follows:

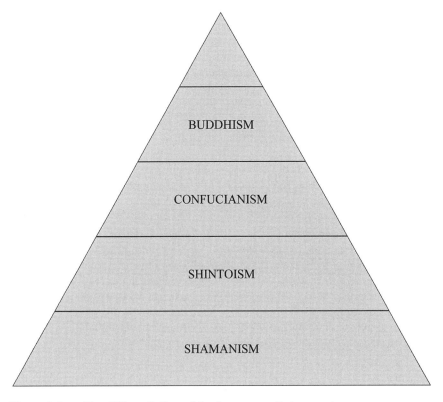

Figure 3.1   The differentiation of the Japanese religious system

The diagram is very rudimental, a hyper-simplification of the internal differentiation that occurs within a belief system, that is gradually restored to a certain unity when the force needed to make the four levels coexist is wielded by a political power, that is, the first imperial dynasties reigning in Japan from the sixth century onwards.

Each level represents an internal articulation that progressively developed in the relationship between system (in its original state) and environment; by environment I mean that multiplicity of views of the world, some of them autochthonous and remote, typical of the mentality, and historical and religious heritage, of the early inhabitants of the Japanese islands, as well as others from outside, like Confucianism and Buddhism, and foreign to the cultural categories of the Japanese peoples.

I could consequently say that this was neither a case of syncretism, nor of a more ancient layer of beliefs being defeated by the newer ones coming from nearby China. Instead, this is an interesting example of persistence through change, of mutual adaptation between system and environment. The symbolic boundaries of Shinto expanded and became articulated on several planes, just as the symbolic boundaries of the Confucian and Buddhist systems became integrated with those of Shinto, without canceling the former's profundity and value. Buddhism ultimately proves stronger than the others, however, when it can give a more convincing explanation of the meaning of death during the Nora period (when the Japanese emperors chose their new capital there between 720 and 794 AD). The choice of the sense that Buddhism succeeds in suggesting to Shinto was not really antithetical, but rather an enlightening interpretation of the theme of death—an interpretation that, to return to the language of systems theory, favors an interpenetration between the two belief systems.

In addition, the complexity of Buddhist doctrine, which included a number of different schools, offers a choice of aspects and concepts that can subsequently become ingrained in other religious conceptions of the world. Its initial success in Japan was partly due to the fact that it became the religious language best suited to a clearly distinct segment of the population, that is, those who were better educated and were involved with the emperor's court. Shinto has continued to survive as the backdrop of Japanese sensitivity, a sort of background music, firmly rooted but mainly among the lower social classes. So there has been a social division of the religious workload and this has proved functional to the internal differentiation of the belief system.

What has been said so far on the matter of the Japanese belief system could also apply to another great nation, China, judging from the fundamental research conducted by John Lagerwey (1987, 1991, 2007). Here again, a simple diagram can give an idea of the complexity of the Chinese belief system and help us to see how, despite the heavy censorship that it suffered for many years at the hands of the communist regime established by Mao and his successors (a censorship that now seems to be disappearing), their religion also appears to be articulated and differentiated on several levels as follows:

The first and most ancient layer, as in the Japanese case, is represented by the nucleus of shamanic beliefs. This probably dates back to 1500 BC, and it existed up until around the second or third century AD, at least, in the form of the cult of the ancestors (often the heads of the reigning families). It was expressed in divining techniques and sacrifices. In the substrate of the cosmological story that it told, it was based on belief in the existence of the *unique man*, the sovereign, the mediator between sky and earth, capable of governing the forces of good and defending his subjects from the forces of evil—in other words, a sort of man-god, around whom a genuine cult developed, administered by a sacred figure such as the shaman. Scholars have sought to demonstrate that the first shaman was in fact the first king of the Shang dynasty (1550–1220 BC). Later on, the direct power of the king was replaced by that of the heavens, and the emperor was seen as his delegate, order being assured by the State as a reflection of celestial harmony. This idea gave rise to a complex astrological conception and a calendar that marked time

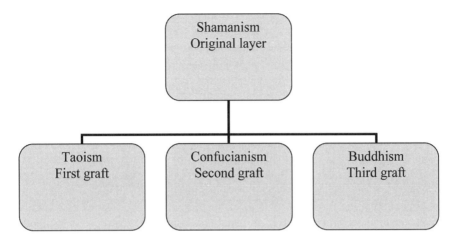

Figure 3.2   The matrix and differentiation in the Chinese religious system

on earth according to the rhythm of the seasons. It was in this period, under the Zhou dynasty (1100–249 BC) that a distinct class of professionals in holy matters was to emerge, who continued to exercise the ancient powers of the shaman.

The second important layer was occupied by Taoism. This dates back to the time of the Han dynasty and particularly to the reign of Wen and his son Jing (179–141 BC). Under their reign, the philosophy in the book of Lao-Tzu (a name attributed both to its author and to the text itself, which means *Venerable Master*) was promoted to the role of imperial ideology. Central to Lao-Tzu's thinking was the need to educate the governing classes about virtue and spiritual elevation: his book is the object of veneration, almost a holy scripture and the object of meditation and daily recital. The initial tendency to make Taoism the state religion was brought to completion only later on, at the time of the Northern Zhou dynasty (between 557 and 580 AD). The fundamental doctrine always rotates around the simultaneously transcendent and immanent principle called *tao*, literally the *way*, *path*, or *principle* tending towards infinity, that exists in all things in various and multiple forms, a principle that came even before creation. It is a universal rule that governs the whole universe, an internal order to which all human beings must adapt if they are to aspire to overcome the death of their frail physical body and release their aura so that, after death, it can fly up into the sky where it can finally celebrate its own immortality. Becoming light enough to emerge from the mortal body involves complying with a number of behavioral rules in life that relate to breathing and physical exercise, diet (for example, foods containing cereals are forbidden) and sexual behavior.

The third layer consists of Confucianism, a philosophy and a spiritual wisdom all in one, developed by a master, Confucius (Kong Qiu) (551–479 BC), who had a decisive influence on the formation of the imperial governing classes and the functionalist and hierarchical conception of society: "The king is king and the minister is minister ... the father is father and the son is son." Single individuals have value only as a function of society and their actions must consequently always be oriented to achieve the good of the community.

Finally, the fourth layer is represented by Buddhism, which gradually penetrated into China as of the first century AD, but its definitive expansion dates from the time of the Han dynasty (second century AD), arriving from India along the silk trading routes and other maritime trading routes. The result was that the Chinese learned and adopted many different versions of Buddhism, from the *theravada* to the *mahayana*, and even the *tantra*. Faced with such a complexity, the Chinese Buddhist monks sought to elaborate a more unified view, producing their own original Buddhism as a result, which was called *chan* (or *zen* in Japanese). The important element to remember is that Buddhism managed to be successful in an environment shaped for more than 15 centuries by a highly sophisticated civilization that was steeped in philosophy and had its own religious conceptions, based on Confucianism and Taoism. These were cultural universes that, in principle, "contrasted with the fundamental concepts of Buddhism" (Zürcher 1996: 372), particularly as concerns the relationship between the role of the monastery and the monks (the *sangha*) and the political power. The *sangha* was seen in Buddhism and by the pro-Buddhist kings as independent, not subject to the sovereign's orders, but this concept of the monks' role was in contrast with the Confucian idea according to which the emperor was the sole representative of Heaven and consequently unwilling to tolerate the existence of an independent center of religious power, such as that of the Buddhist monastery. Then there was the fact that, according to the Confucian view, every human being had to engage in an activity that was advantageous to society, so the Buddhist monks, who had chosen not to work and who relied on charity or the work of others, appeared entirely incompatible with the organic Confucian view. The key to understanding how Buddhism succeeded in evading the cultural obstacles it encountered in the (new) environment of ancient China lies in the complex relationship—sometimes even conflictual but still a relationship—that developed between the Buddhist religion and Taoism. In other words, Buddhism became Chinese by incorporating several elements of Taoism within its system of belief and, vice versa, the door to the Chinese mentality was opened when Taoism in turn incorporated ideas and practices of Buddhist inspiration. This is another case of interpenetration between two belief systems. Finally, we might add that the Buddhist belief system's success was also facilitated at a certain point by the fact that the Buddhist *sangha* (monastery) came to be seen as a powerful and beneficial institution that could have a protective effect on the environment in which it stood (Zürcher 1996: 374). Thus adapted to the Chinese, Buddhism could not only take root (especially in its *mahayana* version, which focuses on the ethic of good deeds for the benefits of all living beings), it was subsequently able to expand beyond the boundaries of the vast Chinese empire into Korea, Japan, and what is now Vietnam, while exporting Chinese mentality, culture, and arts to these countries at the same time.

I could go on providing other enlightening examples like the case of Japanese Shinto or of the Chinese belief system. For these, as in other, similar cases, we can adopt a practical formula: we are dealing with *religions of accretion*, as distinguishable from the *religions of annihilation*. By the former, we allude to a type of belief system that, in differentiating itself from the environment, succeeds in incorporating a part of the external complexity; elements belonging to different symbolic universes are correlated with one another so that their original autonomy is not cancelled, but remains recognizable. In such cases, the internal differentiation is very high because it is founded on a principle of "multiply and grow" or, in other words, on a device that we could call a systemic integration of something in the environment that might appear impossible to integrate, an integration that makes one belief system much more flexible than others claiming instead to possess a unique common denominator of sense. Moreover, when a belief system carries with it the stamp of its original capacity for improvisation, the tendency for accretion or annihilation depends on the *compass* that the religious or holy authority uses to trace that perimeter of sense that a system strives to define and contain, distinguishing itself from possible polysemics and misunderstandings occurring in the environment.

In what we have called the religious belief systems of *annihilation*, the difference in relation to the environment functions operatively as a continuous reduction of the complexity, in the sense that the *alter* (the other belief systems constituting its environment) is obliged to accept the choice of sense proposed by the *ego*. The *alter's* structures of sense are ultimately cancelled by the hegemonic belief system. In actual fact, all this does not coincide with any definitive disappearance of the subdued religions. It functions rather like the mechanism involved in Hegel's dark night, when all the cows are black: the cows are still there, but the system does not see them … though one day we shall see them float to the surface again from the seabed of history. The differences of the other systems of belief are erased; they do not become the object of the system's capacity for self-reflection. Hence the frequent difficulty these systems based on the logic of annihilation have in penetrating well-structured but still flexible socio-religious environments … and the alternate and uncertain fortunes of Christianity, for instance, particularly in China or Japan, seem to provide an eloquent empirical instance of this (Yang and Tamney 2006).

The capacity for improvisation, that may be part of the original DNA of belief systems, can be seen as an energy that a system may retain or lose. If it retains this energy, we can expect the system being built and evolving to grow. If it loses this energy, it is more likely to end up losing strength and the capacity for self-generation and social reproduction. In other words, annihilation refers to the internal functioning of a system incapable of converting external difference into internal difference, and consequently destined in theory to become aphasic in its communication with an ever more complex environment. The external complexity takes effect in this case as an entropic factor for a system, that can no longer cope with the mass of information coming from outside because it is no longer able to evolve, as a religious organization of sense, in a differentiated manner. We need to bear in mind that a belief system like Catholicism (if it is still correct to speak in the singular these days because, being a world religion, it has become acculturated in every continent, albeit with varying degrees of success) really reveals a very high degree of internal differentiation.

Over time, in fact, Catholicism has functioned like a scale of beliefs, from the official or canonical to the barely tolerated or para-liturgical. By means of the latter, it has often absorbed the multiplicity of popular cults and devotions existing in the environment (and certainly not deriving from the Catholic doctrine) in *self-persuasive* articulations of the sense that the system as a whole has selected. There is no doubting, however, that by doing so the Catholic belief system (specifically organized as a hierarchical church with a recognized and visible authority) has defused the difference expressed by the local cults or the autochthonous religions.

For instance, when historians compare the question of the relationship between paganism and Christianity in the process of building the Christian identity from the second century onwards (Filoramo 1997: 204 et seq.), they show us that, by tracing a clearly distinct symbolic boundary vis-à-vis what Justin would have called heresies (no longer synonymous with different schools of thought, as in the Greek tradition, but intolerable deviations from the true doctrine), Christianity came to see itself as a self-sufficient system for producing sense, even reducing all the differentiations that had grown up all around it in the meantime.

Improvising and Transmitting

The distinction introduced earlier between religions of accretion and religions of annihilation takes us back to the problem of the genealogy of a belief system. While it is true to say that a system can function without a subject, it is equally true that no religious belief system can exist without one or more subjects that bring the system into existence by exerting the capacity for improvisation—just as a system can reproduce only if it has a real "following" of people in flesh and blood as its environment.

A comparative sociology of religious belief systems cannot allow itself the luxury of disregarding the ideal type of the prophet that Max Weber sketched, along with other specialists in the sacred, such as the magician, the shaman, or the priest. Although the charisma of the last of these figures is due to the function assigned to him in the context of the professional order to which he belongs, in certain circumstances he may behave as if he were a prophet or had his own, personal charisma—and the history of religions provides numerous examples of such cases. The magician or shaman may likewise exercise a personal power that "bursts from the heart," to borrow an evocative expression used by the historian of religions Culianu (1991), releasing the spirit it contains and opening the mind to new meanings and horizons of sense.

Let us now sketch the features of the virtuoso of improvisation. In order of importance, these are:

a. The existence of symbolic materials in the socio-religious environment that a personality with a *charisma* acknowledged from below (by a spontaneously constituted community), or legitimized from above (that is, through its recognition by a political authority, or because it is tolerated by an institution of salvation) uses to create a new religious symbolic universe.

b. The method used to create this new symbolic system relies on a *power of communication*, that allows people to imagine other possible worlds and different boundaries from the dominant conceptual maps adopted in a given society and in a given historical context.

c. The communication is configured as a genuine *communicative action*, as the actual experienced (initially by the virtuoso) of the new sense to attribute to the existing religious symbolic material, which is reinterpreted and differently oriented; and, from this action, he draws the *force of the word*, a new grammar for expressing the religious discourse—a word that does not stop at preaching, but that *gets things done*, a *performing* word.

d. In fact, the virtuoso makes people imagine that it is possible to go beyond established *symbolic boundaries* and mark new boundaries responding to culturally latent expectations in a given society; they makes people think the unthinkable, and their personality can therefore be defined as *mobile*, in the sense that it sets new energies in motion, transforming them into resources for perceiving a new sense of believing. The virtuoso lets people see how they can shift the boundaries and see the feasibility of another way of believing, that sometimes looks like a whole *other world.*

e. The mobile personality is characterized by his or her ability to *generate belief*, starting from materials already existing in the social environment, through differentiation with that environment and the adoption of a sense that is new, but was somehow expected.

The virtuoso of improvisation certainly has charisma, but he also has something else, and that is a power of communication that triggers a dismantling and rebuilding of the symbolic boundaries of believing. Already during his time on earth, he shows his first followers how to *gain experience* from this process, how to experience the new sense of believing. The gap between the virtuoso's charismatic phase and what comes afterwards, that Weber discusses when he analyzes the problem of succession and of the routinization of the prophet's charisma, is not just a matter of the problem of who is to be the charismatic leader's legitimate successor, but rather—and more importantly—of how to deal with the collective task of constructing the belief system, which becomes necessary after the leader has died.

So the crucial point concerns not only the legitimization of the authority who becomes the leader of the community after the charismatic leader has died, but also and particularly the stability of the boundaries, the definition of reliable frontiers of the belief that enable his followers to avoid having conflicting memories and recurrent interpretation issues concerning the message left by their leader. From the original improvisation, therefore, we must move on to a period of systematization of the boundaries.

This is a social construction process that swings constantly between the need to remain faithful to the *given word* of a prophet or spiritual master (the virtuoso) and the need to enclose the content of his message within stable boundaries. As a system of belief progressively takes shape, in order to remain faithful, it tends to preserve something of its founder's capacity for improvisation. If this were not so, the system of belief would end up by betraying that given word. From this point of view, faithfulness and faith are one and the same thing. Keeping the boundaries secure means giving proof of both faithfulness and faith. The moment the given word is betrayed, the system is destined to self-destruction. So faithfulness constitutes an inexhaustible resource of sense, occasionally capable of producing changes or adaptations to the environment, that is by definition excessively changeable and unreliable.

But there is more to it than that. In fact, faithfulness is also an important organizational resource for belief systems and that is why a system is exposed to the recurrent risk of its boundaries being questioned every so often, and seen as "movable partitions" rather than the rocky foundations "on which to build a church." The principle of conservation of the energy set in motion by a virtuoso seems to function like a regulating mechanism for a belief system's evolution, the condition that enables a system to distinguish itself from the environment as it advances along the path of history, passing through a sequence of events and arriving in the various different places where a religion subsequently takes root. It becomes stabilized on the one hand, while on the other we can say "and yet it moves." Having said as much, we feel that we have moved beyond the stale, old debate of whether religion is a factor of conservation or innovation, beyond the binary logic of tradition/modernity.

A Typology of the Virtuoso of Improvisation

The aim of the analysis that we propose to conduct on several figures of virtuosity is therefore to show how certain types of virtuoso may differ from the abstract type outlined above, thereby measuring not only the distances (conceptually speaking, between different types), but also the structural features of the different religious belief systems depending on whether they stem from one type of virtuoso or another.

We shall use a few examples to introduce our typology. The first concerns the figure of the founder of the Sikh path, Guru Nanak (1469–1559). This new religion was born in a particular place, the Punjab of northern India, and in a particular historical and political setting, under the domination of the Muslim Mogul emperors. A first, over-hasty interpretation of the Sikh path by the colonial scholars defined it as a form of syncretism: a combination of motives drawn from Islam and Hinduism. Subsequent research soon demonstrated the originality of the Sikh system of belief, however, and its independence vis-à-vis the above-mentioned two great religions. Its really original trait lies, in fact, in the exaltation of a motive that already existed in the Indian socio-religious environment: the doctrine of the *sant*, or spiritual master, who indicates an entirely interior path to salvation and belittles anything that might be configured as an organized institution, dogmatic thought, exterior rituality, and so on. A *sant* creates a network of relationships, mainly because he attracts disciples or people wishing to follow his example—a path, or *panth* in the Punjabi language, that leads them to experience a mystical fusion with the deity.

In northern India, at the beginning of the sixteenth century, three spiritual masters—Kabir, Nanak, and Dadu—stood out amidst numerous other minor figures. But it was Nanak who succeeded in lending continuity and historical breadth to the high route of the spirit that he had explored and subsequently indicated to his early disciples. Nanak is basically a figure very like many others that we have seen in religions: he is a prophet, originally influenced by a mystical, ecstatic experience (a revelation, when the Lord was to tell him "You are the Guru, the Supreme Guru of God,", and present Nanak with a goblet of ambrosia—*amrita*), that convinces him to reflect on an enlightening truth contained in a simple sentence, as is often the case in the more or less hagiographical stories relating the early steps of a prophet or virtuoso, that is, "There is no Hindu, there is no Muslim, so which path shall I follow? I shall follow the path of God. God is neither Hindu nor Muslim, and the path that I follow is the way of God" (Cole and Sambhi 1978: 9). Nanak preached this apparently simple truth in the style of his time, as a pilgrim wandering over a vast territory, singing the glory of God and creating a first network of followers and disciples. His journey lasted twenty years, at the end of which he returned to the Pañjab and established a stable, resident community in a new village that he was significantly to call Kartarpur (the city of the Creator). In this first community of disciples (*sikh* in Sanskrit), Nanak appoints his successor before he dies. It is significant that, after his death, he was to be remembered as "guru of the Hindus and a guide and master among Muslims", giving the impression that his devotees had yet to fully understand the innovative core of his message, but they had begun to move along the boundaries of the two great religions, and had begun to learn the art of encroachment. Nanak was followed by another nine gurus; however, the tenth guru, Govind Singh (1675–1708), put a stop to the chain of succession by no longer appointing a person, but naming the holy book, the *Adi Granth* (or *Guru Granth Sahib*, as it subsequently came to be called), as the sole source of authority and guidance for the community. Meanwhile, Govind had taken steps towards reform, creating an elite of soldier-ascetics (the *khalsa*, or community of the pures), ready to defend the community against increasingly frequent attacks and persecutions at the hands of the Hindus or Muslims.

For the sake of space, it is best not to attempt here to reconstruct the whole complex story of the Sikhs, who are now present all over Europe. It is more important to focus attention on the genealogy of this religion. What interests me is not so much the biographical profile of the master, Nanak, but his position in relation to the socio-religious environment of his time. He was faced with an environment divided and distinguished between two dominant belief systems, one of long-standing tradition (Hinduism), the other of more recent acquisition (Islam). Both had clearly defined symbolic boundaries, either because they had become ossified in the shape of the caste system (in the case of Hinduism), or because they were guaranteed by a political authority (that of the Moguls in the case of Islam). What Nanak had in mind was to overcome these rigid boundaries, to reshuffle the cards, as it were, and to rewrite (metaphorically speaking) the conceptual maps that oriented how millions of people felt and believed.

The experiment that he conducted involved borrowing a part of the symbolic material contained in the environment of the two belief systems to invent a new spiritual path. As a system of belief, Islam was the environment for Hinduism, just as the latter was the environment for Islam, and it is as if Nanak had stepped over their boundaries, running along a narrow frontier that he saw no longer as an impassable barrier, but rather as a communication medium or, metaphorically speaking, a bridge joining the two banks of a river. His capacity for improvisation was expressed as the power to give a new sense, differing from the shared sense that confined the beliefs within pre-set borders, dominated by (at least) two major belief systems. The idea of one God, like the idea of the centrality of the master-disciple relationship, dear both to a part of the Hindu spirituality and to the Sufi Muslim tradition (of the *pir*, who introduced disciples to the mystical path), and like the opportunity to arrive at the mystical experience of being united with God and the sentiment of brotherhood that gave rise to the conviction of the need to do away with the caste system, make the Sikh path a good example of the *boundary crossing* that can take place thanks to the performance of such a virtuoso of religious improvisation as Nanak.

Much the same can be said of Zoroaster (who probably lived between the seventh and sixth centuries BC) and the religion that he founded, Mazdaism (from the name of the supreme deity, Ahura Mazda, the Wise Lord). The holy book of the Zoroastrians, called the *Avesta* (or Eulogy), especially in its oldest parts (attributed—albeit with a great deal of caution on the part of the specialists—to Zoroaster himself), describes a laborious process whereby earlier polytheistic conceptions are abandoned and a metaphysical dualism is developed. It proclaims the existence of a Power of Evil, as opposed to the divine Power of Good, the latter being impersonated by Mazda, creator of the cosmos, while the former is outside the world created by God and is responsible for the pain and death, misery and injustice, that looms over human beings, who are responsible for themselves and free to choose between good and evil.

In the light of the limited sources available, the figure of Zoroaster can be defined as that of a virtuoso who abandons the priestly robes to wear those of the ethical-religious reformer, which explains why he was opposed by his ex-brothers in the priesthood who officiated for the cults relating to the many deities in the ancient Iranian pantheon. In a nutshell, we are dealing with a mobile personality who tried to *explore beyond* the safety of his own territory, abandoning his institutional role and, like all prophets, accepting the risk of meeting with failure.

To better support our considerations, another useful example can be drawn from comparing the figure of Jesus of Nazareth with that of Muhammad, starting from the premise that we are dealing with a mobile personality in both cases, and bearing in mind that this comparison concerns two religious families that, for various historical reasons, are related to one another. It is worth emphasizing that we are not interested in comparing two prophets from the classic perspective suggested by Max Weber, but rather in shedding light on the *relationship* between the mobility of the personality and the belief system that came after them. To use a seismic image, it is a case of observing how the shock waves of an earthquake irradiate outwards from its epicenter in a given time and space, then the situation stabilizes; this movement is condensed in the power of communication exercised by the virtuoso of improvisation on an existing set of beliefs and practices that he reinvents and then others, that follow him, take it upon themselves to systematize.

For a start, why was it that, according to a well-established tradition and general consensus, neither of the prophets, Jesus or Mohammed, ever wrote anything down? A possible, simple answer lies in their mobile personalities. Their ability to go beyond the boundaries—or mobility—could be communicated more effectively by the spoken word than in writing. The society of their time made more use of the spoken than of the written word and this facilitated the emergence of charismatic figures whose strength lay in their words.

There is also the fact that the written word, especially on sacred matters, carries a charge of symbolic force that the spoken word tends to reduce: writing basically *strives*, by means of a sort of coercion, to constrain the living word in a given sense once and for all, that is, to establish the legitimate boundaries of the system of meanings of the founder's original message. Spoken words fly, as the saying goes, written words remain. The words of the prophet stretch the horizons, while the written words seek to confine them. It is important, however, to analyze how a mobile personality—despite all the work of sacralization (to define the legitimate boundaries of sense) done by those who spread the original message—somehow infects the system of beliefs that it generates. We must expect the symbolic boundaries of a system of belief to be (possibly in different stages of its evolution) infected by the *mobility factor* of the personality of its founder.

The characteristic ability of a person with (religious) charisma to *make a society move*, changing the minds and hearts of its members, is expressed in the invention of new media for communicating symbols that are already known, but they acquire a new meaning under his inventive influence. In other words, a mobile personality is characterized by an aleatory impulse: he basically faces a risk (which brings us very close to Weber's notion of putting the charisma to the test) when he offers an interpretation of the world that tramples over the shared boundaries of sense adopted by a people or a social group to represent itself socially; in a word, he says things that are *extra-ordinary*. In a way, a charismatic leader has already allowed for the risk of his preaching being rejected, given that his words question a universe of beliefs that enables a people or a social group to see itself as united. In this case, speaking of religion means evoking sentiments of collective identity, universes of shared values. The prophet's charisma changes all this, so there is a very high risk of his hypotheses being rejected and prompting hostility or, at best, being misunderstood.

The above considerations seem to be confirmed by the early story of Muhammad, when he was still active in Mecca, between 610 and 622, and even more so by the story of Jesus, during the time he was preaching in public, when the established religious and political authorities began to take his words, and the following that he had attracted, more seriously. Both Muhammad and Jesus had dared to go beyond symbolic boundaries that looked like the load-bearing walls of a stable, secure home for whole groups of human beings. But the ability that they revealed, to place "minds and hearts" in movement, paving the way to new horizons of sense, was not extinguished with their earthly demise.

So, going back to the question that I've asked myself, what are the cascading effects of the mobile personality on the evolution of a belief system that begins with *his living word*? I hypothesize that, during the course of its evolution, the system develops a *mobile tradition*, despite all the attempts it makes to become immobile and immutable. This inherent mobility belongs to the organizational strategies rather than to the symbolic capital that a belief system accumulates. The mobility actually is often expressed in a narrative form that is capable of adapting flexibly to different cultures and different social environments over the course of time, and of coping with the growing complexity of the many, varied, historical, and social situations that the *original word* seeks to dominate.

The material that historians of religion have generated by their research on Christianity and Islam, for instance, enables us to propose a simple theorem: the more mobile the personality of the founder, the more the belief system born as a result is capable of developing an autonomous functioning principle, becoming increasingly *autopoietic*, and capable of fine-tuning a set of media for communications between system and environment sufficient that enable it, as it goes along, to transform the unexpected or novel external complexity (of the environment) into internal complexity. The more the founder demonstrated that he knew how to break through different symbolic boundaries and reconstruct them on a new horizon of sense, the more the belief system referring to him is characterized as a *complexio oppositorum*, articulated and differentiated, just as the personality of the person we have called a virtuoso of improvisation was complex and differentiated, right from the start.

The symbolic boundaries of a belief system that has become established along a line that can be traced back to the mobile personality tend not to be impenetrable because, from the very beginning, they were built up not by erecting impassable barriers, but (to use a hydraulic metaphor) like a system of locks that can be closed or opened according to the intensity of the exchange between the belief system and its environment. Seen in this light, the system is not something that has been built and completed once and for all, an *essence* (a *depositum* subtracted from change), but the outcome of an ongoing adjustment process, a mix of deposition and disruption, of invention and conservation—in a word, a process where mobility, not stasis, reigns.

Generally speaking, stasis is what marks the terminal phase of a religious belief system, before its disappearance, swallowed up by history. Besides, the *complexio oppositorum* alludes to this very process that converts the constantly changeable, unexpected and multiple, external differentiation into internal complexity so as to better withstand the countless challenges that systems of belief must constantly cope with in the permanent effort (and this is the objective permanence of which we can rightfully speak in sociological terms when we refer to religions) that religions make, as more or less structured organizations, to reduce the contingency of the environment in which they operate. Faced with a changing environment, the belief system's capacity to stand the test of social changes that *happen* beyond its range of action depends on how well it has retained the capacity for improvisation of its founder. The system is constantly obliged to reinvent or readjust the repertoire of its traditional symbols in order to reduce the unedited or uncontrolled "variations on the theme" that risk casting doubts on the symbolic boundaries of its orderly universe of beliefs.

The Given Word and Memory

In prophetic religions, because the power of communication is initially *pure word* (a living experience communicated by an individual to a group of people who subsequently become the bud from which the community of believers grows), it is subsequently the object of a systematic work of interpretation. This begins immediately after the prophet's death and can be seen as a mnemonic exercise (*do this in memory of me*) on what the leader actually said and did during their life. Memory thus involves not only transmitting a symbolic capital (and an authoritative transmission at that, as Hervieu-Léger [1993] rightly reminds us), but also constantly working on the group's identity, continuously negotiating the extension of the symbolic boundaries of the belief (to what degree other beliefs or marginal beliefs can be included, where the line is to be drawn between liturgies and paraliturgies, between canonical rituals and tendentially anarchical ritualities), always fine-adjusting the languages and the symbolic repertoires to communicate to suit different social and historical situations.

In this setting, the brief but important contributions written by Pierre Bourdieu in 1971 on the concept of religious field (Bourdieu 1971a, 1971b; Guizzardi 1979) contain some useful indications that partly coincide with what we are trying to say here. For Bourdieu, the concept of field gives the idea of forces that interact, often in conflict, to control religious know-how and power, which are unevenly distributed between the specialists of the sacred and the "laymen." The religious conflict is often apparent right at the start of the *system-building* process, when different positions are compared, and one gains a supremacy over the others. This generally marks the emergence of a group, which imposes its own point of view as *the true point of view*, downgrading the others to the rank of heresy or intolerable deviations.

To take an example, the name of Christ was attributed to Jehoshua/ Jesus at a point in time after his preaching, passion, and death. In fact, Christ (and Christian) refer to a theological interpretation that translates the Greek concept of Messiah. While the first witnesses and the early disciples were convinced that God himself was manifest in Jesus, the early communities that began to take shape after Jesus' death used different *titles* or sacred credentials to give a name to the sovereignty of the Lord (Lupieri 1997; Stroumsa 1999; Pesce 2004). There were those who identified him by the title of Messiah (or Christ in Greek), progressively distinguishing themselves from the Jewish stock (Mark 8: 29); and there were those who preferred to call him the Son of man (Luke 12: 8), a name progressively abandoned in favor of a third title: the Son of God (Mark 15: 39; Matthew 14: 33). These are just three of the best-known ways, from among the many that were adopted over the subsequent centuries and that were a cause of continuous doctrinal and cultural conflict up until the Councils of Constantinople I (533 AD) and II (680–81 AD). I am not interested here in retracing the history of the socio-religious conflicts underlying the Christological and soteriological disputes that continued up until modern times; I wish to draw attention to the process of choosing *words* to communicate concepts and ideas that were the fruit of a symbolic transaction between different hermeneutic currents that existed right from the origins of Christianity (Theissen 1987, 1998).

The match played in the Christian religious socio-linguistic field revolved around the issue of how to delineate the symbolic boundaries that had to establish once and for all (according to those institutionally responsible for unitarily governing a salvation organization such as the Church, at least) which words could be used to express in what *all believers had to believe* (Christian believers, that is, in the example we are using here). But the sense attributed to the word "Jesus" proved refractory to all attempts to reduce the variety of meanings that it evokes: it is God and man, or only God, or only man, one of a Trinity or the hypostasis of a unique substance. The sense attributed to the word was always open to other potential meanings. It sometimes became necessary, for instance, for the Catholic Church to resort to coercion to oblige its members to respect its socio-linguistic constraints.

The *word Jesus* and *Jesus' words* become the object of communication, and then of the communication of the communication, in a hermeneutic circuit that is often increasingly abstract and sophisticated, in an attempt to construct a coherent system of meaning capable of reducing the redundancy of sense. The definition of the *name* thus becomes the functioning principle of a belief system that historically has sought to dominate the external turbulence represented by groups that *interpret the name differently* and, in so doing, they mark *their identity* and they select the *right memory*. The differentiation that emerges, with time, in the reference socio-religious environment for the Christian belief system will be impossible to pin down within orthodox, uniform, and unequivocal frameworks. Communication generates power struggles for which a compromise cannot always be found, at which point other powers gain a place as autonomous principles for the construction of parallel, alternative belief systems.

We can likewise see that the passage from *Koranic discourse* to the definition of the *official closed body* of the written Koran (Arkoun 1991) is marked by a study on the *word* spoken by Muhammad to his disciples and the definition of the sense attributable thereto, starting from the premise that the Koran enables an understanding of: (a) the social process of announcing the contents of the text; (b) the social antagonisms emerging in it; (c) the dialectic between emerging social groups and those being excluded (with the consequent considerations on the dynamics of power), and finally (d) the dialectic between different social and religious positions that give rise to a hierarchy of meanings that establishes the rules of orthopraxis (behaving properly) and ortholalia (speaking properly) (Arkoun, 1991: 24). Now, in the light of systems theory applied to religions, speaking properly means attempting to set up a boundary between a belief system (especially in the early stages of *work in progress*) and its environment, where there is naturally an excess of sense that the system seeks to contain within limits and symbolic boundaries that must be as uniform and shared as possible.

We might wonder, therefore, if there is any reason why all this should happen in religions generated by a *mobile personality*, born of the unrepeatable interior experiences of an individual. We are inclined to believe that the social effects of the mobile personality are destined to remain in the long-term history of a belief system. In this setting, for instance, it may be easier for us to see if, and to what degree the original prophetic energy tends to be transmitted to the system if we draw a comparison between Christianity and Islam, leaving aside the differences between Jesus and Muhammad—partly because particular historical circumstances obliged the latter to serve as the governor of a city (Medina), while the former flatly refused to be seen as the head of a political liberation movement, and consequently as a potential King of the Jews.

This original energy may remain in a latent state or become fully apparent; it may prompt the arrival on the scene of other mobile personalities, or trigger controversies over issues that seemed to have already been decided once and for all, prompt internal renewal, or support a defensive entrenchment. In principle, we might say that, when a belief system seeks to reduce its internal differentiation (which is by no means an easy matter), it condemns itself to immobility vis-à-vis the environment. When, on the other hand, it accepts the idea that its internal boundaries can bend a little in order to contain diverse positions (up until it becomes that *complexio oppositorum* that not only contemplates a variety of "believers," but that also places them along an ideal axis where believers may diverge on far from negligible points of faith), then it can be said to preserve the original mobility of its founder.

This mobility also affects another aspect. If, as we have seen, the virtuoso was a person who *went beyond the boundaries* of previous belief systems operating as lifeworlds for whole populations, and he drew a new belief map (which in turn became a system of belief), then a religious message has an all the more universal vocation, the greater the *mobility* of the personality of the virtuoso. From the sociological standpoint, universality can be intended as an unavoidable dilation of the symbolic boundaries of believing that the virtuoso enables people to imagine when he *moves the mountains* of the well-established traditional beliefs. It matters little that he might have to give a new sense to gestures, notions, sentiments (the symbolic materials already existing in the environment) in order to *move the mountains*; what counts is the orientation of the sense that he impresses on these materials.

Universality may exist at the baseline in a belief system and be threatened and restricted later on, when the belief system becomes an *ethnic religion*, which is limited by definition to a given people living in a given territory, so its symbolic boundaries tend to coincide with its territorial borders. Conceptions such as India is Hindu, or the Promised Land belongs to the people of Israel, or Sri Lanka is the island of the Dharma (Buddha), allude to this process in which a belief system becomes established as the guardian of a collective identity, of a whole population.

Example and Mission

Max Weber outlined two ideal types, when he spoke of the prophet or charismatic leader, in reference to which we could define one as exemplary and the other as "missionary." The abstract (not real) difference between the two ideal types is easy to explain: the former offers his ascetic or mystical experience as an example to follow; the latter sees himself as a special envoy with a mission to perform, which involves questioning a society in its fundamental values. While the former has no inclination to change society, the latter is distinctly cast in the role of the ethical and (indirectly) social reformer.

Not only the prophets of ancient Israel, but also more modern figures such as Martin Luther more closely resemble this second type. Luther felt it his moral and religious duty to oppose a church (the Roman Catholic Church) that he felt was corrupt and theologically in error. The religious reform that he proposed and that led to him breaking away from Rome later took on a social aspect too, when the German translation of the Bible made it possible for people to read the Gospels themselves, which contributed to the German farmers' realization that they could oppose the aristocratic landowners. The resulting rebellion was guided by two of Luther's followers, Stork and Münzer, in 1521, who took the idea of a church-community with no popes or bishops, where all believers were equally "priestly," to its extreme consequences. Münzer, in particular, behaved like a political-missionary prophet: in addition to wanting to change the structural organization of the Catholic Church, he was convinced that, once the temporal power of the

Church had been destroyed, there would be a call for social justice in the name of the Gospel, and the economic and political power of the feudal system would be overthrown.

When Weber spoke of the exemplary prophet, he was thinking especially of Buddha, who embarked on a spiritual path to enlightenment and apparently did not initially intend to change society. In actual fact, if we look carefully at his life as an ascetic, we discover that his experience originated not only from an interior need to discover the reason for suffering and death, but also from his critical attitude to the dominant belief system of his times, Hinduism, which necessarily implied stepping beyond the symbolic boundaries that traditionally justified the division and discrimination of individuals by caste. The same can be said of another spiritual master such as Nanak, the founder of the Sikh path. He to came to preach against the caste system, after reflecting on the need to cross the frontiers of the worlds of Hinduism and Islam.

When we speak of ideal types, following in Max Weber's footsteps, we are well aware that they cannot be found in real life exactly as they appear from the abstract description. The ideal type can be said to emphasize prevalent or salient traits, but that certainly does not mean that, in practice, a given figure of a prophet cannot reveal elements belonging to another type, as well as the abstract recurrent traits. This means that Weber's typology is useful, but not sufficient, because it is founded on the assumption that the difference between prophecy as an example and prophecy as a mission lies in the type of socio-religious action undertaken by the one or the other. Weber sees the relationship with the world as being central to the action of the latter, but not of the former. Buddha embarks on a spiritual path that is selectively configured as an escape from the world, a condition without which he cannot directly experience the cancellation of all sources of desire (the origin and cause of pain and death), whereas other prophets take action in the world, also to change its economic, social and political order.

It just so happens, however, that even an exemplary prophet like Buddha seems far from indifferent to the particular form of human suffering caused by poverty and social injustice. On the other hand, the whole Gautama experience can be set, as far as we know, within a religious perimeter that was dominated not by any social and political commitment, but by the search for spiritual techniques that could free the mind of all the conditioning influences that cause suffering. The way of the ascetic that he charts, like a mountain guide showing the way along a difficult high route, is potentially accessible to anybody. Although the monastic model was subsequently chosen by only a minority of people, the basic idea intrinsic in Buddha's message is essentially available to every human being, irrespective of caste or social status. Anyone dedicated to seeking enlightenment by following in Gautama's footsteps commits themselves not only to purifying their own mind of anything that might disturb their inner tranquility, but also to helping others embark on the same path. What we are talking about here is the figure of the *bodhisattva*, the enlightened existence capable of loosening the ties of our ego to the passions that generate suffering.

What therefore seems not entirely convincing about Weber's typology is the idea that the exemplary prophet does not "interact" with the world around him (maybe only through his example). He may do so in a more understated and less explicit manner than the missionary prophet, but he does so nonetheless. This being the case, we can say that both of the figures of which Weber speaks question the world to some degree, because they both—with different degrees of awareness—explore new horizons of sense, seeking to select new meanings from among the numerous possible meanings, and daring to go (and this is what seems to our mind to be the most interesting trait of the two prophetic figures) to the limits of the imagination, giving people an impression that "another world is possible." By doing so, both types of prophet establish a difference with respect to the environment in which they operate, tracing mobile, dilatable symbolic boundaries that can expand to incorporate other possible meanings to attribute to the events of human life. From this standpoint, the lifeworld is the environment of the prophet's psychic system. He asks himself or others about the sense of life and of the life-world, marking the difference between himself and others, and giving the idea that reality can be interpreted *another way*.

In conclusion, what possibly distinguishes the two types of prophet is the way in which the symbolic boundaries of belief are traced through differentiation in relation to the environment. A trace of how this takes place subsequently remains in the belief system-building process. The gap separating Buddha from Jesus or Muhammad has little to do with the fact that the first seemed more inclined to embark on a private mystical pathway, while the other two were more involved in preaching in public. In actual fact, both Jesus and Muhammad had their "desert" experience, that is, a more or less lengthy and intense period of withdrawal from the world (in the desert) and meditation—the real difference, if any, lies in the fact that Buddha continued to question himself and to look for an answer by "working on himself," whereas both Jesus and Muhammad went out at some point to question *other people*.

To return to the abstract language of systems theory, we can say that the difference lies in the degree of self-reflexivity that the three personalities express: in the case of Buddha, it takes the form of pure *autopoiesis*, since all the levels of differentiation that Gautama tests on himself before arriving at enlightenment (*nirvana*) lead him to the conviction that "salvation" consists in being free of one's ego, and therefore the operating principle of the belief lies within ourselves. The difference in relation to the environment is removed because the "world" appears for what it is: a changing game of impermanence, a series of fleeting apparitions. We must therefore expect the belief system stemming from this figure to preserve this *autopoietic* principle and, as a general consequence, we should not expect this system to be interested in interacting with other systems, such as politics or the economy. Conversely, the experience of the other two figures— Jesus and Muhammad—lies midway between interior analysis and public life or, in other words, the difference between their "believing" and the environment is the outcome of a direct, critical confrontation with the differences and complexities of the environment with which they interacted.

For instance, when Muhammad became convinced that his preaching was not only not meeting with the success he had expected in his home town of Mecca, it was also arousing a deep and widespread hostility even amongst the members of his own clan, and he felt the time had come to go elsewhere (as he did in 622), he had to face the exponents of the *other religions* existing in the socio-religious environment of the Arabian Peninsula (for example, Judaism and Christianity, and particularly, in the latter case, the Christian communities already condemned by the Church of Rome as heretics). This meant that he had to deal with faiths that he did not see as being in contrast with his search for the one God, whose envoy he claimed to be. Hardly surprisingly, Islam represents itself as a religion that continues the prophetic line that started with the Jewish people, included the figure of Jesus, and ultimately arrived at Muhammad.

In many ways, for the most part of his public preaching, Jesus also did not separate himself from his ancient Israel; it is clear that he wanted to oppose a set of beliefs that he knew well and that did not satisfy him entirely because he was becoming convinced that it was possible to go beyond the boundaries traced by the most influential and hegemonic groups of his time in the Jewish world.

Along the same lines, we can add a final comment, to widen the horizon of our observation, on what are considered (maybe incorrectly) minor figures in the landscape of modern prophets, by taking a look at the Baha'i religion, which emerged in nineteenth-century Persia. Its roots can be traced back a long way, to the Shi'ite Muslim tradition that strongly influenced the area's history, from the sixteenth century onwards, at least. More recent premises can be found, however, in the *bābī* movement (from the Arabic word *bāb*, which means *door*) that sprang up in Persia due to the work of a preacher called 'Ali Muhammad of Shiraz (1819–50). This man took up the idea dear to Islam according to which prophetic manifestations are a recurrent event in history, having begun with Adam, included Moses and Jesus, and reached a new phase with the advent of Muhammad. According to 'Ali Muhammad, the cycle did not end with the death of the Prophet of Islam, however, it continued with a new cycle that began in his own person. So he wrote a new sacred text that aimed to surpass the Koran and all the other revealed scriptures. The essential idea behind his preaching was very simple: all the prophets basically say the same things because they speak in the name and on behalf of the one God. The form may vary, but the substance is the same. So we can expect more prophets, after the many that have already appeared in human history. According to 'Ali, the new cycle that began with his person would be completed after 2031 years. He entered into conflict with Shi'ism when he proclaimed himself the savior they were waiting for, the *mahdi*, an eschatological figure particularly dear to the Shi'ites, who is expected to appear at the end of time to restore justice on earth before the day of judgment. There was a chain of other reasons for dissent too, such as the parity between men and women, the abolition of the veil for women, the limitation of divorce, and the recommendation of monogamy in marriage. The leader of the new sect came to be seen as subversive by the reigning powers in Persia, so he was arrested and condemned to death.

The movement seemed to disperse, only to rise again in other forms and with other intentions, going by the name of Baha'i. The small group that remained of Bāb ʿAli's followers came together again around the figure of Mirza Husayn ʿAli Nuri (1817–92), who claimed to be a new prophet in the cycle begun with the advent of the Bāb. He took the name of Bahā'Allah, "Splendor of God," and was to preach a universalist religion, said to be the ninth religion after the Sabean, Jewish, Hindu, Zoroastrian, Buddhist, Christian, Islamic, and Bābist religions. The numeral 9 is a canonical number in the Baha'i religion: there are nine letters in the name of the founder and nine holy days; nine is the minimum number of people needed to establish a place of worship and there are nine doors to the temple. Like others, the case of the Baha'i confirms the emergence of a type of prophet who strives to go beyond the symbolic boundaries of the different belief systems, making them mobile and interpenetrable.

Chapter 4
Spirit and Order

Putting the Spirit in Order

The passage from the living word of the founder of a religion to the construction of a system of belief can be described, with the aid of a metaphor, as a continuous process for putting the *spirit* in *order*.

In what sense do we mean these two words, spirit and order? We allude not only to the fact that a religion tends to become organized and consequently establish its own internal norms, hierarchies, functions, and capabilities that, combined together, make a religion a type of organization (Guizzardi and Pace 1987; Beckford 1973) that can be studied using the analytical tools typical of the sociology of organizations. Without a minimum of apparatuses and structures, it is not easy to ensure the reproduction of a religious message in time. This means that we can analyze how the relationship between knowledge and power is articulated within a religion, between those who have the authority to preserve and interpret the (founder's) message and those appointed to implement it.

Authority and power are really distinct domains in the context of religions. A prophet may, at some point, be acknowledged as a source of authority even though they may not possess the tools of power needed to impose a certain message, or their interpretation of a message. The head of an institution of salvation may formally have ample powers of coercion within an organization, but discover that he is not seen as an authority on the norms by a more broad-based audience. Authority is exerted in the definition of the symbolic boundaries of belief, and power defends them, stigmatizing and condemning those who arbitrarily go beyond the boundaries, or move too close to them, or come into conflict with them. The authority *says* that he knows *what people are to believe*, while the power watches over what happens.

With the word *order*, therefore, we refer here to the complex relationship between authority and power in the religious setting. The people who believe, or have faith in a given religion tend to consider the founder an undisputed authority, while they may have a contingent and variable attitude to those who, after the founder, are cast in the role of ensuring the proper transmission of the content of the original message. For Shi'ite Muslims, the prophetic cycle did not come to an end in the year 632 of our era with the death of Muhammad, it continued with a series of twelve imams (or seven, according to some groups), the last of whom died in Samara in the ninth century and is expected to return at the end of time, reappearing and ensuring justice is done. For them, it is as if there were a dual authority, that of Muhammad and that of the series of imams who came after him.

Ever since the death of the last of these imams, the Shi'ites have lived in waiting, relying in the meantime on the presence of people capable of reading the signs of God (that is, the ayatollah), who can predict the imam's return. Now, while a genuine Shi'ite believer would never question the authority of the imam, he or she may well choose whether or not to follow one ayatollah rather than another. In the Shi'ite environment, an organization has evolved in this particular belief system over the course of time that bears a resemblance in some ways to the model of the Catholic Church, consisting of an organized hierarchy of experts on holy matters divided by rank and function, a hierarchy in which people are promoted by means of filters and selections, moving progressively from one step to another thanks to lengthy studies, intermediate examinations, and the publication of books. This hierarchy ranges from the lowest level (the simple student, who follows the courses at a faculty of theology, such as the very famous one in Qom, in Iran, or in Najaf, in Iraq) to an intermediate level, passing through a whole series of positions of religious power/knowledge culminating in the figure of the *marj'a al-taqlid* (literally he who is worthy of imitation—for his piety and wisdom, of course), a timid, temporary reflection of the supreme spiritual pole represented by the Hidden Imam, who will one day reappear on this earth. A believer may therefore choose to follow the recommendations of one ayatollah rather than another if he or she thinks the former is more authoritative. This means that, while the central core of belief in the imam, and consequently also the general conception of the world accepted as a result of this belief, remain secure, there is a variability in the relationship between the (power) system of the ayatollahs on the one hand, and the socio-religious environment in which they claim to exercise their power on the other. In other words, a belief system's capacity to ensure that its symbolic boundaries are not trampled over is limited by the very fact that believers are relatively free to accept or question the line of interpretation that a given ayatollah may develop in his conviction that he is protecting the integrity of the doctrine, or of the original message.

Shi'ism is therefore a good example of how a belief system can be constructed *in the absence of a subject*. It is assumed that the imam has hidden and become invisible; he will reappear one day, but nobody knows quite when. It is as if, despite his absence, the system continued to function by relying on its own vitality, continuing to reproduce even though it cannot count on a visible authority or an unquestioned power. There is a paradox here: the ayatollahs are respected and followed, but they are fungible (in the sense that I may swap one for another, or decide not to follow any of them); they have power but, because they lack the authority of the Hidden Imam, their power is somewhat precarious, even though it is legitimate.

For a system of belief, maintaining order therefore means preserving the original spirit of the founder on the one hand, and renewing its differentiation from the environment over the course of time on the other. So what is the difference, for instance, between the experience of a trance that can occur during a session of Candomblé (one of the most important forms of Afro-Brazilian religion) and the experience of being possessed that occurs in the liturgies celebrated at an assembly of the Universal Church of the Kingdom of God (one of the many new charismatic churches born in Brazil in 1977)? Taken in isolation, they are similar in many ways, but placed in the ritual context in which they occur, it is clear that they each fit into a precise, distinct belief system.

The Universal Church condemns the Afro-Brazilian cults, but they are a part of the socio-religious environment in which this church seeks to differentiate itself. At the same time, it strives to transform the external differentiation represented by the cults and their persistent popularity into internal differentiation. The use of the trance by the Candomblé is transferred within the liturgical context of the Universal Church, symbolically reformulated and defined as an articulation of a complex liturgical action (or interaction). For the traditional Afro-Brazilian cults, the new Pentecostal or charismatic churches in turn become an extra element that adds to the complexity of the socio-religious environment. This is not really a question of competition, because up until the arrival of the new churches people tended to go to Catholic Mass, but when they felt the need, they would also consult the mediators on holy matters (the *pai* or *mai do santo*, that is, the fathers or mothers of the saint), who manage the places of worship, or *terreiros*, without feeling any particular inner conflict. This is a sign of an interpenetration between these cults and the culturally dominant Catholic belief system. Where necessary, the Candomblé trance supplemented the canonical liturgies of the Catholic Church. Conversely, with the advent of the charismatic churches, the competition between newcomers on the scene and the Afro-Brazilian cults was explicit because the trance is incorporated in these churches' belief systems and in the narrative rhetoric they use to assert their identity. According to these churches, in fact, only they can offer a genuine trance experience because they define it as being a manifestation of the spirit (the Holy Spirit, presumably), while what happens in the *terreiros* is the work of the devil, where Candomblé or Umbanda rites are celebrated to help people become possessed by the spirits.

Putting in order means both preserving and innovating, succeeding in keeping the founding spirit alive while, at the same time, defining and redefining the symbolic boundaries that make it distinguishable from the environment. We speak deliberately of innovation here to emphasize the fact that the belief system construction process is, by definition, an *ongoing jobsite*, where different viewpoints (as to where to mark the boundaries) are exchanged, sometimes leading to controversies, and where some tend to override others. But there is more to it than that: the increase in the socio-religious complexity outside a belief system obliges the system to review its boundaries and decide whether they need to be adjusted (expanded, or made more impenetrable, for example). The innovation relates not to the creation of new symbolic frontiers that might alter the constitutive principle of the system, but to the fact that it is obliged to come to terms with the *constant novelty* of the environment in which it operates. Unless a system succeeds in reiterating how it differs from the environment, while simultaneously growing in terms of its internal complexity so as to withstand the external complexity, it risks extinction.

So far, the word order (as we defined it earlier on) has given an idea not of stasis, but of a dynamic process in which certainty and risk, stability and instability, the conviction of being in the right and threats from outside that shake this conviction, are all combined. All this may seem paradoxical for belief systems that, in the name of the absolute truth, claim to be able to keep their symbolic boundaries perfectly secure. In point of fact, stability and instability may and do coexist for the very reason that every system tends to preserve the *spirit* of its founder. The act of conservation is actually a transformation of the original *spiritual energy* into a belief system's *autopoietic* operating principle. But because this energy has been set in motion by a virtuoso of improvisation, it tends to preserve some of the typical traits of improvisation. If the founding leader himself experienced, or enabled others to experience the possibility of going beyond relatively new symbolic boundaries, this experience is not entirely cancelled in the passage from the *subject* to the *system*—if for no other reason than because religions generally use a descriptive repertoire that, alongside philosophical and rational speculation, also involves the narration of events. This means that the story they tell is the object of continuous symbolic investments and reinvestments, depending on the social and historical settings in which a religion seeks to become established and flourish. These different ways of narrating the founding event give rise to movements, inside or outside a given religious confession, that each come to enact new interpretations or go back to past interpretations, adopting radical views of the world or coming to a compromise with it

What we learn on this issue from the analysis of Christianity conducted by the German sociologist Troeltsch lies in just this: the same event, that is, the original preaching of Jesus of Nazareth, gave rise to movements, groups, and churches that have taken a different approach to the basic narration of the event (starting from the stories in the Gospels). Christianity has given rise to churches and sects, messianic movements and mystical networks, militaristic groups and solitary spiritual pathways (from the hermits to the recluses). This strong differentiation cannot be explained merely on the basis of historical reasons (responsible, for instance, for the many schisms and fractures within this religion), they must have some sort of link with the original *spirit* of the founder.

The founder's energy is not destroyed with his death, it is preserved—both in the sense that the inspiring force of the virtuoso who give the religion its *incipit* is retained and, at the same time, the thrusts and parries that it may inspire in the course of its expansion and circulation in time and space is contained.

The word "spirit" (here again, it is worth clarifying what we mean) usually brings to mind something that cannot be reduced to mere *matter*. It refers to the idea that there is an interior space in relation to the exterior space, something that lies within us and that we consider a source of sense. Here, we use the word as synonymous with *movement*, intended as the capacity to move beyond the *material*, temporal and social constrictions that objectively influence human experience.

There is a saying that the soul is prisoner of the body and after our death it will be free to fly away. The image that this narration suggests (and that goes back to Plato) is that of a force obliged to stay within certain confines, although these confines are unable to completely restrict its movement.

We speak of religion and of belief systems. So we are talking about sense and its excesses. As we have said more than once already, the virtuoso of improvisation has a mobile personality, in the sense that he is capable of breaking certain constraints, of experiencing and having other people experience other possible meanings to attribute to human actions, and to the relationship between human and superhuman. That is why we believe that the original movement tends to be reproduced whenever a system tries to preserve its force—not only in the sense that it can produce a symbolic conflict (of memory or concerning the power over memory), but also and more importantly in the sense that it can shed a new light on the heritage accumulated with time by a religious belief system.

So the evolution of a system should not be seen as a progression from one point to another, from the simple to the complex. Religious belief systems are not progressive in this sense. Their evolution is not like a straight line along which they advance, nor a sloping plane that they might slide back down until they disappear. I prefer to use another metaphor: that of yeast and dough—an evangelical metaphor that, out of context, seems useful for clarifying a concept. The yeast makes the dough rise, which can then be shaped in various ways to suit personal tastes and expectations. The dough is adaptable to a variety of expectations, but without the yeast it will not rise. The dough can be used to make a number of things, but only the yeast makes it suitable for handling, kneading, and shaping, so that it can be turned into an end-product by different hands, using different methods, and obtaining different results (from sweet to savory). The metaphor should be taken for what it is: it simply lends an image to the concept of the growth and continual adaptation of an original principle—the spirit—that tends, as long as it lives, to reproduce itself in time and in *matter*, in a multiplicity of *things*.

If, simply as a scholastic hypothesis and therefore adopting a purely logical artifice, we were to focus for a moment on Protestantism as a specific belief system that became established in a certain historical period (the sixteenth century) in the heart of the German-speaking area of Europe, we can monitor its evolution by looking at the social and religious differentiation that came afterwards. It is as if we were to imagine a system that continues to grow inside because the operating principle inspiring it is the *precarious nature of its center* (Willaime 1993), the absence of a center that can track down and reduce the differences. Free churches are just that, free of any authoritative constraint governing their lives. In principle, each of them can be self-governing, becoming a sub-system within the macrosystem of belief called Protestantism, and establishing lightweight relationships with one another (since they recognize none as taking pride of place), from the more democratic (as in the Congregationalist model, according to which each community has a degree of independence) to the more structured with a hierarchy of functionaries (as in the Anglican Church). The only center is the Bible but, because it is a text that is freely and variously analyzed, the way in which this is done can give rise to models of socio-religious aggregation that can range from types founded on mechanical solidarity (typical of a sect organized in a hierarchy, at the top of which there is an authority who imposes a uniform interpretation of the text) to those inspired more by a sense of organic solidarity (typical of all the churches of the Protestant world that become organized internally according to different responsibilities and functions, based on a simple logic of sharing the socio-religious workload).

The Power of Holy Language

Putting the spirit in order is a job well done when, through the holy scriptures, the fluidity and vitality of the word (of a prophet or virtuoso of improvisation) is contained and regulated by the language in which it is written in a document that is considered sacred. Even before we wonder who wrote it, why, in what context, and for whom, we need to pause briefly to ask ourselves about the *autopoietic* value of the language that becomes the material and symbolic vehicle of the *spirit* (in the sense explained a few paragraphs earlier).

A good test for moving towards an understanding of the problem that we are dealing with is represented by Sanskrit. When we look at the most ancient layer of the Vedas (the set of holy books of Hinduism), consisting of a collection of hymns and prayers called Ṛgiveda, that delineates and justifies the distribution of society into four castes, we need to remember what the scholars have brought to light: that the symbolic legitimization of the caste system came about thanks to the persuasive force of the Sanskrit language, or rather—as suggested by Witzel (Jaminson and Witzel, 1992), among others—thanks to the process of *Sanskritization*. We are dealing here with the times of the reign of the Kuru dynasty in the fourteenth century BC, one of the various kingdoms created by the white, Indo-European Ārya peoples, who became settled in the Indus Valley, ruling over the black, Asian local populations already living there. This *Sanskritization* process would seem to have consisted in the construction of a barrier that was linguistic, religious, and ritual, erected by order of the Kuru kings, who appointed for this task a class of specialists (the *Brahmin*), allies of the noble class of warriors. The domination of the Kuru over the non-Aryan populations took shape and drew strength from this work performed on the language and its sacralization. The socio-linguistic studies conducted by Deshpande (1979) on the Sanskrit language have demonstrated, in fact, that this sacralization meant establishing the primacy of one language over all the others, and particularly over those of the subject populations. A proper speech was set against the improper manner of speaking: the former was only accessible to the elite peoples, the latter belonged to those who were to be called *dasyu* (Barbarians) or *mleccha* (non-Aryans), who came to form the indistinct layer of outcasts or untouchables. Those who knew the language controlled its power, and used it especially in the ritual and liturgical space, occupying a socially privileged position. Squarcini made the point that:

> The ability of the word thus becomes a sort of *natural* primacy and those who possess it must consequently be seen as privileged. The fact that being privileged in this way gives them power, and that this *savoir faire* is considered a weapon, is emphasized later on (towards the end of the 2nd century BC) … in the *Mānavadharmaśāstra,* where the synthesis between language and power is attenuated and the word is equated to a weapon, the weapon of the Brahmin. (Squarcini 2006: 111–12)

The language that is elevated as a result to a holy rank, Sanskrit (from a root that seems to mean "combine together, compose, make perfect, decorate"), is placed in opposition to the *prakrta*, that is, all the other languages, that are vulgar and barbaric by definition.

Now, once the language skills have been thus defined (as the ancient texts of the Vedas demonstrate) and recognized as belonging in particular to the priestly class (the *Brahmin*), its sacralization is no abstract construction, prepared at the desks of grammarians or language experts, it is the result of the *concrete formulation of the ritual action*, and particularly of the very fundamental action of the sacrifice. The formula for the action must therefore have a strong symbolic value, subtracted from the ordinary commerce of spoken languages; it must have a semantic wrapping that immediately signifies the distance between the spoken (common) language and the other (divine) word that only the priests know and can "handle with care," the secret of which they alone possess, so that it can be used without risk, for the benefit of the community. The holy language—Sanskrit, in this case—separates, differentiates, and distinguishes on several levels (that is, the symbolic, the ritual, and the social). In one of the Vedic texts, we find the following words: "everything is founded on the word: the word is their way; and they proceed from the word." When the sacred language subsequently comes to imply the identity of a people, it lends itself—right up until our modern times (Pace 2004b)—to being used as a powerful tool for identifying a population with *their territory*: the sacralization of the language leads to the sacralization of the land where its users live. The language contributes to the construction of the myth of foundation, and of the origins of the *natural* link between a people and *their land.* This applies not only to the ancient Ārya, but also to the Jews and the Promised Land, or to the Serbs and Kosovo, which they consider as the heart of Serbian Orthodox identity according to the nationalist rhetoric. It is easy to see how the very notion of *dharma*, so central to the construction of the belief system that was first ancient Vedic and subsequently Hindu, appears as a *distinguishing concept.* The definition and the contents of the *dharma* were elaborated and consolidated in the Brahminic literature, and therefore by the Brahmin, who passed on the sacred power and knowledge from one generation to the next, within their own caste. The word *dharma* itself alludes to the idea of *putting in order, sustaining, possessing*, and it corresponds, as Squarcini reminds us (2003: 79), to a long list of synonyms: " … nature of things, something that has been established, order, norm, support, religion, statute, law, character, particular condition, specific property, habit, custom, prescribed conduct, straight, righteous, duty, morality, justice, good deed … ."

This is a polysemy typical of a notion that is circulated and that makes sense according to the social settings and needs consistent with the balance of power.

When, as happens in many other religions too, a certain notion is said to be difficult to translate (into other languages maybe), we are not really dealing with some arcane meaning concealed in a word with a core meaning that is beyond our grasp, but with a very normal case of an excess of sense. When a discourse—possibly contained in a text—becomes a means of communication, it acquires meanings that do not necessarily coincide with those attributed to it by the speaker or writer. Sense has its own, uncontrollable way of circulating, so the polysemy of a word is structural. There is no way a religious authority can ever succeed in promptly governing the many directions in which the sense of a word may carry. Sacred language traces a precise symbolic boundary that enables a belief system to perceive the difference while enabling the difference to become the system's operating principle, irrespective of who actually inhabits it, adheres to it, controls or transmits it. The lines that this language traces are therefore not reserved for the expert eyes of the priests alone, who can see them in the scriptures—they are also available in some form for viewing by those who are not priests. The short-range visibility of the former opens onto another, more far-reaching visibility.

From this point of view, the ritual or liturgical action is a symbolic transaction that the priests establish to have other people understand several things; their particular, privileged status derives from the ability they are acknowledged as having to manipulate the holy word, to interpret the possible sense of the content of the religious message, to awaken in the minds of the non-priests a sense of belonging to a community that is different from other human communities and, finally, to confirm the existence in a structured form of the holy power that distinguishes those who have access to the word in the ritual action from those who must only act as spectators.

The abundant production of judicial texts in the Hindu world is related to the fact that, even before defining any moral standards of conduct and explaining the requirements sanctioned by punishments, the various priestly schools elaborate a literary genre that has to do mainly with the complex norms dictated for the ritual sacrifice. I'm speaking of the so-called *dharmasûtra*, that the different schools have produced at local level mainly for a liturgical purpose. The derivation from this type of action of parameters suitable for defining conceptual pairs of the type legal/illicit, just/unjust, right/deviant, has been a socio-logical consequence. According to the Brahmin tradition, human beings are born burdened with debts that they must pay during their life. It is as if each of us, simply by being born, had contracted five debts. In order to honor these debts, we have to make a corresponding number of sacrifices. The world of the spirits is also one of our most demanding creditors. So each individual has to pay their debts by performing daily sacrificial gestures that generally consist in offering the spirits that populate the world small bowls of rice wetted with water (to make it symbolically pure) and then scattered over the ground.

Alongside these forms of rituality, both individual and domestic—the majority of which have been abandoned nowadays—there are still, even today, acts of faith taking place in Hindu temples, where the faithful go to pay homage to their deities in the three principal liturgical moments of the day, at dawn, midday and dusk, officiated by a priest who, before undertaking any of the specific actions allotted to each occasion, performs a whole series of ablutions and acts of purification (on himself, on the object that is to be used in the ritual, on the place, on the formula that will be read, and on the image of the deity concerned). The officiating priest is purified through sexual abstinence and libations of water, and the place is cleansed with cow dung (since cows are the ultimate sacred animal in the Hindu belief system). The objects are pure if they have just been collected from the plants and trees (in the case of fruit or flowers) and have not touched the ground nor been touched by human hands other than those of the priest. But what most interests us is the way in which the purity of the prayer formulas (the mantra) is also assured: this is done by pronouncing the words perfectly, which is an indication of the remarkable effort of inner concentration needed to do so. If something goes wrong and the rite is contaminated, it becomes necessary to resort to five products that are considered a sort of natural vaccine against impurity, that is, milk, curd, butter, cow's urine, and cow dung (Piano 1996: 175).

The example that I have given here and the comments on the topic of the holy scriptures serve to illustrate two of the greatest devices for *putting the spirit in order* that we find in systems of religious belief once they have become established and consolidated as such. In the process of their construction, the two devices represented by the sacred texts and the sacrificial rites are used as symbolically generalized *communication media* that enable the system's difference vis-à-vis the environment to be reiterated (this is the way we are, and no other way will do, because this is the way we pray, and no other way will do). They also enable a specialist know-how to be developed, that generally becomes a part of the credentials boasted by a particular class of specialists, not an abstract conception, but a practical skill that demonstrates the understanding of the liturgical gestures performed in the places of worship at specifically ordained times on the calendar of religious festivities and, importantly, in the fundamental moments of a human being's life-cycle.

Thanks to these two devices, the process of putting in order enables a system to fix its symbolic boundaries, in which to disseminate a *minimum* sense that is conventionally accepted within the system, but that cannot be absolutely certain because it may be misunderstood at any time, and individuals (who, by definition, constitute the environment for a religious belief system) may attribute a variety of meanings to the *guaranteed minimum sense*. In the communication process between religious belief system and socio-religious environment, scriptures and liturgy are seen as doubts that have been settled: it is written (in the sacred texts) because it is prescribed, and a given action must be taken in a particular (ritual) way in order to get results. What has been prescribed has also been enacted—and it is generally in this that the *autopoietic* strength of a religious belief lies.

The two devices form a continuum. Both are orphans of the first bearer of the word (the spirit) and they are both faced with the problem of seeking to revive it using languages that differ from the living word. Barring rare exceptions (for example, the case of the prophet Mani), the scriptures generally do not directly reiterate the intentions of the prophet or spiritual master who began to preach a religious message. It is *somebody's* orphan. Likewise, there are no longer the first listeners for whom the sacred texts were probably intended, and that is why the scriptures can be the object of more or less extensively variable interpretations, depending on the environments in which it comes to be read.

On the other hand, if scriptures were not read, they would be dead. Different versions can thus be found of the same scriptures, and several meanings can therefore be attributed to the written word. The link that is created between this first device (scripture) and the second (liturgy) is structural: the liturgical action repeats gestures, words, body postures, and so on, thereby instilling a stability that the sacred texts are unable to fully guarantee. That is why many holy texts are clearly in the form of liturgical manuals, public protocols for governing collective and individual rituals. The liturgy is basically the word revived time and again in the ritual action, a word that would otherwise remain a *dead letter*, even if it were deposited in scripture.

There is a fundamental difference, however, inasmuch as concerns their scriptures, between belief systems that attribute their claimed nucleus and heritage of truth to a holy language and the systems that have not become attached, as it were, to any particular language and have thus exposed themselves to a greater risk of the free circulation of sense.

It is now time to look more closely at the meaning of rite and liturgy from the perspective of religious belief systems theory.

The Service Order

At the heart of Christian liturgy there is the Eucharist. This is a ritual action that refers back to the narration of Jesus' last supper, referring to the moment when he says, "Do this in memory of me." Not everybody interprets his meaning in the same way, however. The line of distinction has been drawn relating to how to *preserve the memory*. Some have seen the passage as a recommendation to remember Christ's sacrifice, while others have read into it a prescription to conduct a ritual repetition of his sacrifice every time it is celebrated. There are those who celebrate it using two species, bread and wine (as was probably the case in the early Christian communities), and those who restricted themselves, for various historical reasons, to using real wine but replacing the bread with a consecrated host. What counts, whether these people are Catholic or Orthodox, Anglican or Calvinist, and so on, is the significance attributed to the Eucharist according to the point of view adopted as regards the *memory* of Christ's sacrifice on the cross. In other words, faced with the conflicting memories of Jesus that have come to light, as we know, in the history of Christianity, our attention must be focused on the purpose of the Christian liturgy to protect the sense of the event within reliable symbolic and material boundaries. An uncertain memory, because it is divided and disputed, only has a good chance of being reproduced and withstanding the shock of change and conflict if the related liturgy can be used as a *safe place* for preserving and protecting the sense against the risk of oblivion and misunderstanding. Its security consequently relies on the repetition of formulas and gestures, on a complex balance of discipline and self-discipline that cannot be readily disrupted because otherwise there may be unexpected or perverse effects for those who have an evident interest in ensuring the continuity of the delicate mechanisms governing said balance.

To give an example, Pope Benedict XVI (who was appointed to the office of pope of the Catholic Church in the spring of 2005) took steps to call a religious movement to order. The movement involved was that of the Neo-Catechumenals, which has been widespread in the Catholic Church for nearly thirty years now and it has tested and fine-adjusted its own liturgies, basically coherent with the teachings of the Church but presented in quite a different format. They tend to celebrate Mass on Saturdays, not Sundays, following up readings from biblical texts with lengthy spontaneous comments from the congregation, who contribute to the celebrating priest's classic sermon. They remain seated when they take communion and they literally break proper bread, that they then distribute, together with the wine. They shake hands as a peace-making sign before the offertory (as in the Ambrosian rite) and they do not recite the Apostles' Creed or the Gloria. In short, they have introduced in their ritual practices several gestures that they see as better interpreting the original sense of the phrase "Do this in memory of me." Early in December 2005, the Congregation for Divine Worship that governs and keeps vigil over official Catholic liturgy had sent a note to the founder of the Neo-Catechumenal movement to urge its members to comply more precisely with the rules that apply to all Eucharistic celebrations—what we might call a service order that attempts to restore order where, in the eyes of those governing the Congregation for Divine Worship, it was threatened in several ways. If we read this note from the point of view of the outside observer, we can see that the author had set himself a far from easy task, that is, that of making up the difference that the Neo-Catechumenal movement had created by experimenting with its own liturgies, even though they are certainly not radically alternative to those established by the authority of the Catholic Church. The note can be interpreted as a sort of negotiation concerning the symbolic boundaries of the system: it identifies what lies outside (or might find itself outside) these boundaries and it explains how to return within these confines without entirely surrendering the position already reached by the movement as a result of its several decades of experience.

Generally speaking, the rite very often (and not only in the case of Christianity) has to do with memory. In Judaism, many liturgical actions are conducted specifically to commemorate fundamental occurrences in the history of the people of Israel. Much the same happens in Buddhism, in the case of the *vaisakha-puja* celebrations (so called because it falls on the day of the full moon in the month of Vaisakha, that is, when the astronomical spring is in full swing between April and May), which recall Buddha's final passage from this world (his death, which in actual fact occurred sometime around 543 BC) to a state of reawakening, of the enlightenment that in Buddhist terminology is called *nirvana*.

Similarly, the Pesach celebrations of the Jews are an opportunity to recall an epic event, that is, their flight from Egypt, and their liberation from oppression and slavery. The text that is read during the rite is called the *haggadah* (which literally means "narration"), and it is accompanied by a ritual meal loaded with symbolism called the *seder*, that literally (and by no accident) means "order."

This handful of minimal examples would suffice to highlight an extraordinary sequence of words that we have just mentioned: *memory, narration, order*. The essence of rituals is therefore contained in the link existing between these three words. Put differently, the narration relies on a text that is analyzed time and again, according to a previously established, precise sequentiality that is used to fix the memory (of individuals and, more importantly, of communities), renewing every time the pact that binds us through the memory. A community of believers seeks to keep the memory alive because it believes that, in so doing, it can renew the pact of faith in the *word given* once and for all by the virtuoso of improvisation who is no longer with us, while the traces of his passage are preserved in the scriptures. To be more precise, the sequence is illustrated in Figure 4.1.

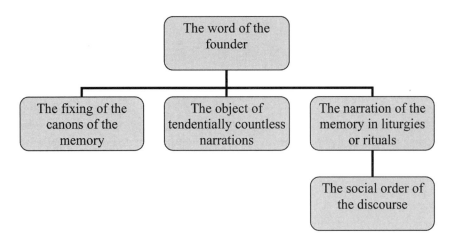

Figure 4.1   Memory, narrative, and social order

Given all that we have said so far, liturgy consequently needs a service order to follow. Changing its rules is always a risk, because every change can be interpreted as a new way of interpreting the memory and the narrations deposited in the scriptures and in the comments recorded on the sacred texts that have been the object of study, reflection, meditation, and prayer.

The holy texts of the great religions often contain the ritual patterns to follow in order to conduct liturgical actions successfully, be it when they are accomplished in periodical or occasional acts of worship, or when they are used to establish a relationship with an extra-human force, or when they propose to produce an immediate benefit (against a wicked spell), or a modified state of consciousness (a trance or ecstasy), that gives those who succeed in entering into it a particular holy status as well as a number of exceptional powers (of prophecy, healing, chasing evil spirits away, and so on).

The terms that we have used—liturgy, rite, worship—can be considered as synonyms in the economics of our present considerations, but in the language of the social sciences, the rite is seen as the broadest possible genre in which we can include both the various forms of worship of a deity and all the *performances* designed to acquire extra-ordinary (magical, divining, therapeutic, …) powers; whereas by liturgy, we generally mean a public religious service conducted and officiated by dedicated experts. In other words, liturgy is a sequence of ritual actions that can serve various purposes. But, going back to the terminology of systems theory, be it a rite or a liturgical action, we are always looking at communication media. Liturgy, in particular, is an effective communication medium for marking the symbolic boundaries of a belief system: if it has charted its boundaries, the sense communicated (reduced and selected) by the liturgical action tends to be *covered* by the differentiation of the rites.

It is sometimes said that the pivotal element in liturgical actions is mystery. In the general theory of religious belief systems, the mystery is the excess of sense that the liturgies strive to contain within preset, predictable boundaries that guarantee the endless repeatability of the action concerned. The gestures are always the same, and yet the sense that they convey is not necessarily the same—if for no other reason than because those taking part in the action are free to attribute other meanings to what is happening.

Every belief system consequently feels the need to elaborate communication media that can function in practical terms as markers of its symbolic boundaries, while at the same time presenting and representing the essence of a religious message and underlining its specificity in relation both to other messages and to unofficial (para-liturgical or extra-liturgical) formats that are usually produced just inside or outside the borders of a religious belief system. The moment a religious system incorporates something from outside, drawing from the variety of existing and pre-existing beliefs in an environment, the conversion process substantially consists in inventing a medium that gives the *right to speak* to the deities or superhuman powers with which it intends to enter into contact, but this medium should not be confused with other means or tools of human communication.

Liturgy places *words* in an orderly sequence and the different ritual actions enable a belief system to reduce the external complexity. The *voice* that speaks in the liturgical action is imagined as an emanation of the voice of the divine or superhuman power. It is no chance that some of the most recurrent rituals in religions are the oracle, the prophecy, the reciting of mysterious formulas that should give us access to the sphere of the superhuman. Liturgies express the power of the word detached from its human source, a word that is in origin impersonal; in fact, in ritual actions, people tend to imagine a deity taking action directly or indirectly through the mediation of the officiating priest.

Reflecting on the significance of the rite, Emile Durkheim emphasized that the important aspect, from the sociological standpoint, is not so much its content or the exterior form that it may take, but rather the *compulsory* characteristic that it acquires for those involved in it. In addition, the linguist Emile Benveniste, when analyzing the origin of the Latin word *fas*, connected it to the verb *fari* on the one hand, which means "to speak," and on the other hand to the compound form *fas est*, used by the Roman *pontifex* to say that a certain decision was *the will of the gods*, that therefore had an unquestionable normative content because it was a manifestation of divine will. Besides this, that a sacred genealogy of the law exists is a well-known theory. As Benveniste wrote:

> … we can reconstruct, right from the Indo-European stage, an extremely important concept, that of *order*. It is represented by the vedic *ṛta*, it. *arta* (avesta *aša,* due to a particular phonetic evolution). This is a cardinal notion in the judicial, religious and moral universe of Indo-Europeans: it is the *Order* that governs the universe, the movement of the celestial bodies, the periodicity of the seasons and the years, the relationships between human beings and the gods, and ultimately of human beings with one another. Nothing that has to do with mankind can escape the empire of *Order*. (Benveniste 1976: 357)

Law and Order

The concept of order is often associated with that of the *law* in many religions, and priests are assigned a combination of religious and judicial functions. In Hinduism, this corresponds to the notion of *dharma*, which in Sanskrit means that which is in the right place, stable and ordered, concatenated series of norms to follow in order to be in harmony with the cosmos and its mysterious architecture. In Greek, the same concept is contained in the word *themis*, which indicates the foundations or grounds, but also family law, which is considered to be of divine inspiration. The juxtaposition of religion and law can be used to explain how liturgy functions like a code, with its own norms and procedural formulas. The cases may vary, but the form must remain faithful unto itself in order to communicate stability, continuity, and order.

Many formulas and liturgical practices have been fine-tuned by the specialists in holy things in whom the community of believers has placed its trust, not only as concerns the public celebration of the deities, but also in relation to the principal moments in an individual's life-cycle, as in the case of the rites of passage when a child becomes a member of the adult world, with all the rights and duties deriving from this status (Van Gennep 1909).

If a sacrifice is made (of an animal, for instance) according to precise procedures, it will be attributed a precise meaning depending on the purpose of the sacrifice, be it to obtain the favor of the gods, to save the world from impurity and evil, to obtain hoped-for benefits in the here and now, to give someone special powers in order to reinforce a group's sense of identity, to exorcise and dominate the violence inherent in society (Girard 1972), and so on—a plurality of meanings that the liturgical formula governing the various possible ritual actions seeks to reduce, selecting the authentic, primary sense to attribute to the action in a given situation.

Connecting does not mean annexing, however. In other words, the liturgical formulas and procedures strive to establish binding connections between sense and action, but they are never able to completely control whether this connection is retained and repeated without those taking part in the ritual action coming up against any misunderstandings or overlaps. In the Catholic environment, carrying a statue in a procession is an action by means of which a person wishes to transmit the *material* presence of a holy figure in a given reality (in a village that has a chosen patron saint, for instance, or in a broader-based community of believers who visit places where the Madonna is said to have appeared). But it can be interpreted in other ways too, that is, as a way of bringing good luck (people go to visit a statue and attach banknotes to its clothing in the hope of economic prosperity, or they see propitiatory signs in the statue tilting to one side or the other during the procession if it is being carried at a run by a group of devout bearers), or as a gesture of collective identification, of belonging to an ideological and political formation. For example, in the case of Italy immediately before the political elections of 1948, the Catholic Church (which had taken a very definite stand alongside the Christian Democrat Party and against the Communist Party) organized processions that had a dual, religious and political meaning, that is, to save the soul and also to save Italy from communism.

In one of the most important rituals in the Shinto religion, the *matsuri*, for instance, the deity that is being celebrated—according to a complex ritual of offers (generally grains of rice and sake, the popular Japanese rice wine)—is raised up on a platform right in the middle of the festivities and carried on the shoulders of its bearers along the roads of the village or district so that its beneficial effect can descend over all and sundry. It is worth noting that the young men who carry the dais on their shoulders are usually intoxicated because they have drunk too much sake (as a ritual sign of homage) so the statue often leans over, giving rise to outbursts of laughter and a sensation of precariousness. As Raveri pointed out (1993: 636), the contrast between "the controlled, solemn and calm gestures of the religious and social authorities" on the one hand, and "the unruly, amusing, violent or provocative behavior of the young men" on the other is basically a device foreseen in the formula of the liturgical contingency that, in the *matsuri*, correlates the order of things with the creative and potentially transgressive gesture that it should symbolically regenerate.

Therapeutic rituals are still widespread even today in many African realities, and are performed to deal with the various diseases affecting the body and mind of human beings. Disease, be it physical or mental, is seen as a sign of disorder that comes from a poor relationship with the deity or the ancestors. As a result, healers must wear both the white coat of the (generally homoeopathic) physician and the colorful garb of the witch doctor or shaman capable of entering into contact with the invisible spiritual forces that can be entreated to help the patient be cured of the disease that afflicts him or her. So there can be no healing of the body unless the mind is purified of the negative influx arriving from some evil force. The whole therapeutic process is governed by precise ritual norms ranging from the color of the participants' clothes to the magical circle in which the rite must take place, from the sacrifice of particular animals (depending on the disease to combat) to the use of natural elements that take on a symbolic value in relation to the disease to heal, right up to the recourse to dancing, singing, and musical rhythms capable of arousing strong emotions, even to the point of achieving a state of trance or possession.

In the traditional African religions, but also in the Afro-Brazilian cults (which draw to some degree from the ancient Yoruba beliefs, for instance), becoming possessed actually represents the culminating moment in the ritual because it is seen as "the god entering the head of a human being" so that, by taking possession of the patient's mind, he can *speak*, and the words that he pronounces through the mouth of the possessed are considered as if they were spoken directly by the deity, as if the deity were using the human voice to express himself and explain why the person has become ill, for instance, and what must be done to overcome his or her infirmity. The theatricality that generally accompanies the *performances* of those who enter into a trance suggests the idea that the ritual action evokes a drama, a representation with a carefully studied choreography, handed down and learnt, with songs and dances, fainting, shouting, and weird gestures that communicate surprise, stupor, terror, joy, and so on. In this case, the body of the possessed communicates something extraordinary, his body immediately becomes a communication medium, a form of liturgical contingency that somatizes the sense selected for acting out an event (in the case in point, the disease of a person who has come to ask for help) for those who are capable of possessing or being possessed by the gods. It is as if the possessed were saying, "This is no longer me; in my place there is a god who is using my body and my head to speak." Order is thus restored and the disease, the very essence of disorder, disappears (Prandi 1991; Pierucci and Prandi 1996).

It is worth noting, to switch to another example that refers to the case of African Islam—from the Maghreb to the sub-Saharan nations—that underneath the skin of canonical and official Muslim beliefs, ritual practices continue to exist that incorporate rites of possession and trances typical of the traditional African religions. It is as if a previous symbolic layer had been absorbed within the dominant belief system (Islam in this case), facilitating a process of differentiation within the system. We can take as an example the Gnawa groups, which are still widespread in Morocco. Descendants of the black slaves who were rounded up and deported by the Arabs, from 1591 onwards, from Mauritania, Senegal, Mali, Niger, and Guinea, the Gnawa groups were converted to Islam, but they preferred to adhere to the mystical (Sufi) ways that had spread all over Morocco during the ninth and tenth centuries AD. This gave rise to a confraternity (*tariqa*) that referred to Bilal, an early companion of the Prophet Muhammad, a black slave who had been freed by the Prophet himself and, according to tradition, had become the first *muadhdhin* (the person responsible for calling people to prayer) because of his stentorian voice.

The characteristic feature of this confraternity lies in the use of dance and music in their liturgies, which focus on a dramatic narration and representation of the primordial sacrifice behind the genesis of the universe. Focusing on the magical number 7, the dancers invoke the seven original divine emanations (*mluk*), represented by seven different colors and seven different musical themes (with different melodies and rhythmic tones, each of which gives rise to seven variations on the theme, and the set composes a suite, or *makam*. At each stage, seven different types of incense are burned, and the dancers wear seven differently colored veils. Each of the seven *mulk*, moreover, evokes the presence (*hadara*) of symbolic figures that refer to a corresponding number of states of mind or spirit, as well as to physical conditions that serve the purpose of restoring the inner equilibrium and reawakening the deepest energies of body and mind, that belong to the divine creator principle. So, here too, we have a liturgy of ecstatic type that aims to produce an altered state of consciousness, an extra-ordinary experience of mystical fusion with the deity (Lapassade 1976; Fumarola 1997).

The liturgy takes place at night, during a meeting (called *lila*, which means night in Arabic) that lasts until the first light of dawn, the symbol of a rebirth of the profound spiritual energies. Entering into contact with the divine ancestral forces can produce physical and spiritual benefits. The names of Allah and the Prophet Muhammad are invoked in the course of a long liturgical performance, that also involves a woman associated with the confraternity dancing to show how to achieve the state of trance, rather like what happens elsewhere (for example, in the Tunisian confraternity that looks after the mausoleum of Saida Lalla Manoubiyya, a woman who lived in the sixteenth century and is venerated as a saint [Treppete 1999]).

In the example that we have given, it is clear that—set against the sobriety that traditionally characterizes the collective prayer in the mosque (and even more the individual prayer that can be conducted anywhere), which is disciplined in its gestures and in the recital of the liturgical formulas—the *performances* of a Gnawa (like those of any other Sufi confraternity practicing the dance of possession or trance) can come as something of a surprise. But, leaving aside the marginalization that they have suffered over the course of time and the fact that, despite everything, they continue to resist, the important aspect to note is that we are looking at practices and beliefs that are *tolerated*, at a layer of belief that certainly cannot be afforded full citizenship, but that nonetheless *speaks in the name of Islam*.

While music, song, and dance are banished from the Moslem canonical liturgy, here they are practiced with such conviction as to be functional to the achievement of a state of ecstasy. While in the former setting what counts is to pay homage to God, here the purpose is to *be possessed* by divine forces in order to combat evil presences and thereby gain an immediate physical and spiritual benefit. These two methods in apparent contradiction actually represent two aspects of the coexistence of opposites that a belief system, by becoming differentiated from the environment, accepts as being a part of itself in order to function better in relation to an otherwise uncontrollable environment.

It is worth sparing another thought for the origins of the Gnawa: when the first black slaves were forcefully deported, they took with them their culture and religion, including their particular way of entering into contact with the sphere of the sacred and divine. Later on, when they were converted to Islam, willingly or not, their earlier spiritual baggage was not discarded, but went to nourish a type of religiosity that could coexist with the official Islam (Geertz 1971), without entering into open conflict with it. It is tolerated as a religiosity suited to the typical mentality of a particular (non-Arabic) segment of Muslim believers. Seen in abstract terms, through the eyes of an observer of how a belief system functions, the ethical, religious, and cultural difference that the Gnawa of sub-Saharan Africa brought with them was transferred from the outside into the system called Islam, as one of its allowable expressions of the various *ways of being Muslim*, and—we might add—as proof of the pluralism that has always characterized Islam from its very origins.

In the great belief systems, the liturgical field can be seen as a set of rituals with a variable geometry: from the official rites to the para-liturgical rituals, from those that are tolerated to those that are banned, but still show the signs of belonging to a given symbolic and religious system. If we imagine a pyramid, then working from the top downwards, it is as if the control exerted by an ideal, all-knowing and all-seeing authority over the manifestations of the body and spirit progressively diminishes. At the hour of trance at Lalla Manoubiyya's sanctuary in the suburbs of Tunis, the liturgical space is occupied entirely (even in the sense of the juxtaposed continuity of bodies) by the women officiating at the ceremony, who dance in a circle and beat drums to facilitate the trance. The men and the heads of the confraternity that manage the sanctuary are nowhere to be seen, because they consider that particular *time* and *space* (that they normally occupy at other times) as a special liturgical *place*, not only because it is reserved for the women, but also because it is dominated by a form of ritual that they essentially can only tolerate ("it is women's business," as we were once told by the guardian of the sanctuary when we asked if we could attend the liturgy of the *hadra*, where the trance occurs). The body loses control: when the women go into a trance, they remove the veils on their heads and let their hair down, rotating their heads while their whole body leans back, a sign of their imminent fall to the ground in the final act of being possessed. The bread and water that are ingested at the end of the session and distributed to all those who attend is a sign of communion with the divine that someone has achieved on our behalf, through the intercession of the saint buried at the sanctuary (Amri 2008; Boissevain 2006).

In this case, it is difficult not to think that there is a *gender-related* differentiation in *the ways of being Muslim* in the Islamic religious belief system. The difference in gender is taken for granted and gives rise to a typology of liturgical actions often seen by the men as *borderline*, on the margins of the belief that is recognized as canonical and official. Although it is only tolerated, this *female* version of the liturgy is nonetheless acknowledged. There is a boundary inside the belief system that reproduces the difference (of gender, in this case, but the same could be said of *ethnic* diversities) and enables it to be exhibited, shown, and managed in ritual spaces and forms that are different, but accurately circumscribed. Thus, conflict is reduced and religion is the communication medium that reduces the external complexity.

The Order of the Discourse

A belief system can become differentiated by creating sub-systems. For instance, a religion is often not presented simply as a set of truths of faith relating to a deity or to the final destiny of mankind, but also as an economic doctrine, a theory of political power, and an apparatus of legal norms. Law, politics, economics— as soon as these spheres of human and social action become incorporated in a religious belief system, it is as if the religious system had become organized internally in a number of sub-systems, each of which can claim a certain degree of autonomy and a differentiation in relation to the others. When this autonomy of the sub-systems develops into a full-blown capacity to organize themselves and to govern their spheres of social life, then religions usually begin to lose control over those most crucial aspects of society—the law, politics, the economy, or the mass communication media.

This process began in Europe starting with the Renaissance and is better known as "secularization." From the macro-social point of view (Dobbelaere 2002), this process has not so far given rise to any decline in interest or clearly visible loss of the sense of religion or the sentiment of belonging to a church, nor will it necessarily do so in the future. What has been lost, however, is religion's capacity for integration by comparison with other great "provinces" of meaning that define the framework of relationships between individuals in society, that is, the economy, which tends to function on the strength of its own rules (the utility of human actions); the law, which has detached itself from the original influence of the sacred, and politics, which functions on the basis of a friend/enemy logic and is certainly not inspired by any ethics of brotherhood, the search for peace, or the like. So there are ample territories from which the religions have been dispossessed, though they have sought to control them by interweaving the multiple aspects of social life in a divine and holy order. This is what we generally mean by *doctrine*, that is, a set of social rules deductively seen as deriving from an interpretation of primary principles that are perceived as being divine and absolute.

Having said as much, let us adopt the viewpoint of systems theory to see how we can interpret the role of a *doctrine* that a religion usually seeks to acquire. We have deliberately examined liturgy and rites in the previous pages, because analyzing these objects so dear to all the social sciences of religion (rites for the anthropologists, religious practices for the sociologist) has shown us that they are really the visible signs of those symbolic boundaries that a belief system tries to construct so as to distinguish itself from the outside environment.

The historians of religion (and the biblical exegetes too) have taught us, for instance, that there are numerous similarities between Christian and Jewish liturgy. But the continuous efforts made by the Christian churches over the centuries to distinguish themselves from Judaism has erased (or effectively concealed, at least) the features of this analogy. The various liturgies are like mirrors that enable an impersonal belief system to see its own image reflected and to reflect about itself. Leaving the metaphor aside, liturgy provides an opportunity for a system to observe itself, to report what happens in the liturgical space and time, according to the rhythm of the *repetition* of gestures, formulas and codes of conduct, as *something that is and will always be identical to itself* and, as a consequence, to confirm its difference vis-à-vis its environment. This is a case of self-referentiality. When we use this word, we need to remember that in the terminology of systems theory it does not necessarily refer to a subject. As Luhmann explained:

> ... many verbs, that we neither can nor wish to avoid using, refer in their daily usage to a conscious author of the operation. Take, for instance, verbs such as: observe, describe, recognize, explain, expect, act, distinguish, attribute ... It has been necessary for us to eliminate, for precise theoretical reasons, the premise that links the reference to the (linguistic) subject of these verbs, to consciousness. They should be interpreted ... so as to refer them to an author describable as a self-referential system that, not being necessarily a psychic system, does not necessarily perform its operations in the form of consciousness. (Luhmann 1995: 439)

When these comments are attributed to religion, at first glance they might seem incomprehensible. In the critical approach to systems theory that we have adopted, it is one thing to speak of the founder of a religion, emphasizing the subjective components of his actions, quite another for the observer to focus on how the belief system that developed from his preaching operates. It is on this second aspect that it seems appropriate to apply Luhmann's above line of reasoning.

Religion can be seen as a self-referential system too, if we consider not how it is perceived in the experience of single believers, but how it has historically become solidified in an organized form with more or less extensive degrees of bureaucratization, so that it is obliged to function *as if individuals and their consciousness were the external environment for the belief system*. For instance, practicing Catholics go to Mass on Sundays and this is a liturgy that reflects the fundamental principles of the specific Catholic belief, and the Christian faith in general. So, from the *point of view* of those taking part in this rite, this is a shared action that is experienced in the first person together with the celebrant. This particular event, happening at a precise moment in time, with the participation of people in flesh and blood, is repeated (apart from a few shades of meaning due to national languages and local customs) using the same symbolic construction everywhere and all the time. This example shows that it is not only and primarily the individuals who, the world over, attend this same ritual every Sunday, but also the system of liturgical signs that classifies and differentiates, distinguishes and unites believers, wherever they may be and irrespective of where they are. It is as if the belief system were observing itself in the liturgy, and particularly its capacity to function as a self-regulating system of signs. Liturgy is the dramaturgy of a religious doctrine.

In point of fact, the real force of religions lies less in their capacity to impose a doctrine by resorting to forms of coercion or authoritative control over people's minds and more in its people's more or less convinced compliance. If a religion is obliged to use coercion, it generally risks losing authority, or *face*. The successful religions rely on a delicate balance between discipline and self-discipline. When conviction is based on self-discipline and not on mere custom, or a *habitus* instilled by the authorities, then a belief system's authority gains in ideological vigor and social efficacy, because all the individual psychic systems are able to observe themselves, reflect on themselves, and imagine that what they do as an act of faith is really the fruit of their own decision, of a free individual choice rather than a supine, passive adhesion to an authority (or orthodoxy), or to a tradition that has become consolidated as a shared behavior (orthopraxy).

We must consequently assume that belief systems can also develop a self-referencing principle that enables them to connect its constitutive elements *as if they were* an organic and consistent whole with a degree of internal cohesion sufficient to preserve them from the constant risk of being questioned. In particular, religious belief systems are founded on the claim (which is legitimate from their point of view) to possess the truth and to be obliged to deal both with other systems making the same claim, and with the variable socio-religious attitudes and behavior characterizing the social environment. Introspection and self-referentiality consequently represent the means by which a system demonstrates that it is not only capable of self reflection, it is also able to use this as a *debating strategy* in dealing with what lies inside and outside the system: when looking inwards, to support the dual contingency of preservation and change; and when looking outwards, to be immunized against the changes taking place in the environment that can determine an increase in its complexity that is not always readily convertible into internal complexity.

Self-referentiality is therefore an operating principle of belief systems once they have become settled and have defined their symbolic boundaries. Self-referencing identifies and differentiates: the system's identity becomes the constant object of reflection when the system is functioning so as to better distinguish itself—or emphasize its difference—with respect to the environment. Another example may be useful here to better explain this concept.

The self-referentiality thus consists in the capacity of a given community of believers to *remain within the complexity*, keeping one foot in the old and the other in the new or, in plain words, to remain *in between* identity and difference. In response to the question that some people asked, in the Christian communities of the religion's origins, about whether it was possible to believe as Christians while remaining faithful to certain precepts of Hebrew law, the answer was yes, that it was possible, so people retained the practice of circumcision and continued to belong symbolically to the Jewish community. There is ample evidence in the great mass of writings and fragments considered by the official church as the apocryphal texts (Ehrman, 2003) to demonstrate that this was a cause of conflict and tension in the newborn Christian communities. In fact, Paul of Tarsus found himself faced with no easy dilemma: did the Gentiles or pagans adhering to the faith in Jesus have to become Jews in order to be Christians, given that Jesus had always been, from start to end, a Jew who observed the Law (as we can see clearly from reading Matthew, the most "Jewish" of the Gospels), even though he interpreted that law in a new way? Should they too observe the Law? Ehrman made the point (2003: 129) that "we might imagine that the question was particularly pressing, especially for the male Gentiles, the majority of whom were not circumcised." There are very obvious traces of this by no means negligible hermeneutic controversy between Paul and the Christian communities remaining attached to their Jewish roots in his Epistle to the Galatians, for instance (2: 11–14).

All this weighs in favor of the idea previously mentioned several times of religion as a system that does not fear internal contradictions, because they are the means by which the system tends to be self-referential. The rationality applicable to religious systems differs from the scientific concept of "where there is A, there cannot be B." For the great clusters of religious belief, contradiction constitutes a way to deal with conflict and checkmates without being defeated. The contradiction can thus be seen as a sign of the way in which a system reacts to the increasing complexity of its external environment.

As soon as a belief system designates itself as being different from the environment, it begins to function as a self-referential system. A religious belief system can consequently be defined as a *closed system*—not in the sense that it has barricaded itself behind solid walls to protect itself from a disorderly and changing environment, but because of its capacity (learned at some point in the process of the system's construction) to function with a relative degree of autonomy. The term "autonomy" indicates the ability to produce as a unit everything that is used as a unit (Luhmann 1995: 506), to produce an *all-round* discourse that connects the elements, or the constituent parts of them, without having to continuously negotiate the sense attributable to *all that there is* outside the system. As soon as it becomes self-generating, the system is thus able to control by itself the possibilities of denial (which are theoretically endless for every single element in the religious discourse) that are continually being presented. But every element of the discourse communicated by a belief system can be accepted or rejected by a potential believer, or by someone who does not believe at all. It is important to allow for incomprehension or denial. Hence the need to develop a specific knowledge within a system that can govern the predictable negativity (rejection, incomprehension, doubt) that may be triggered by its proposal of a dogmatic formula or religious content.

Basically, it is a matter of being skilled in debating and communication, a communication of the communication, expressed by means of codes that are generalized on a symbolic level, the interpretation of which is a job for specifically selected and qualified specialists, that is, theologians, experts in religious law, exegetes, and scholars of the scriptures. In the division of the socio-religious workload in a given belief system, these experts have a role strategically different from that, for instance, of other figures of religious functionaries (those officiating at rites, those responsible for missionary work, the expert preachers, and so on).

The various figures just mentioned are complementary because they all help to cope with the system's need to develop an apparatus for managing the communication codes that enable the risk of rejection to be reduced, and, in positive terms, to keep its doors open to the highest possible number of understandings, acknowledgements, and identifications with the object of its discourse and of its religious communication, on the part not only of those who are already *faithful*, but also of those who might become so.

All these socio-religious figures communicate on the communication; they produce a more complex symbolic discourse, starting from the fundamental symbols that lie at the very heart of the basic communication that a belief system has made the object of its original investment. They seek to safeguard the *validity of the communication* that would otherwise be submitted to the risk of continuous and recurrent denials and misunderstandings. The self-referencing of a religious system is therefore assured by the work of its specialists in religious communication. While some of them defend the boundaries of the doctrine, others scrupulously monitor compliance with its rituals and liturgies.

This guarantees that a system is both closed and open to the environment at one and the same time: it must be closed in order to be able to withstand the impact of a changeable environment that is much more fluid than the system can be. We must not underestimate the fact that, where there is a class of people dedicated full-time to reflecting on and studying the content of a religious message (be they Catholic or Protestant theologians, Buddhist monks, Hindu masters, or ʿ*ulama*, that is, experts in the Koranic sciences), we shall see an imposing body of knowledge developing that, at some point, tends to grow with a force of its own, becoming a sophisticated web of know-how and a rich array of concepts that are useful in various spheres of life—not only the strictly religious, but also the social and cultural (from law to politics, from science to art). The work that these groups do consists partly in making the system introspective (this is what we call self-referentiality, a closed system), and partly in relating to something outside the system (in what we have called its environment, a feature of the open system). When the balance between these two functions is broken, the belief system generally no longer succeeds in communicating effectively. Then all the various types of religious conflict that we have historically learned to know and recognize take place. If the system can balance its closure and openness, then it can receive precious information from the environment and convert this information into resources to use in its communication.

From what has been said so far, it is easy to perceive the importance of studying what in religions is conventionally called doctrine in one sense, and theology or, more generically, knowledge focusing on the search for the sense of a religious or spiritual message on the other. Between these two concepts, there is a degree of differentiation in the socio-religious workload within a belief system: doctrine is a set of works containing the fundamentals of a religious belief, while theology is a continuous reflection on the way of intending, interpreting, and communicating the doctrine, that the same theologians have contributed to delineating in its fundamental elements. To put it differently, doctrine is basically the summary of an extensive effort of excavation and reflection done by theologians, or other such scholars, given that not all religions have figures corresponding to the theologian with which we are familiar.

The efficacy of the rite as a means of communication lies in the very fact that it puts a stop to the question, "Why do we do things this way and not in any other way?", whereas theology or similar disciplines are introspective forms of communication, that reflect on themselves as an articulation of the belief system. So it seems a good idea to take a closer look at how the two levels—doctrine and theology—function in the processes of construction and evolution of religious systems.

Fine-tuning and Communicating the Discourse

Religions live in a sort of perennial circle: from the living word of the founder, they move on to the construction of a body of doctrine that becomes the object of constant reflection, not as an end in itself, but with a view to renewing the communicability in time and space of what remains of the originally given word. Thus we have a circle of communication that unwinds like a spiral. Combined together, doctrine and theology constitute what can be called "tradition." In religions, the transmission from one generation to the next of the (founder's) *given word* concerns the contents that are handed down through time and also the act of transmitting them. It is on this second aspect that we wish to draw the reader's attention now.

When the contents of a religion are represented as a nucleus of fundamental beliefs that are assumed to be unchangeable and unquestionable, the act of transmission indicates a continuous movement in time. In the passage from one generation to the other, however, not only do the outside conditions change, there are also different shades of meaning and interpretations of the contents of the belief being transmitted that alternate and are compared. The word "doctrine," in the singular, consequently needs to be explained: behind the definition of a nucleus of beliefs considered fundamental and consequently unchangeable, there has really always been an exchange of opinions (sometimes harsh and a cause of controversies, schisms, and excommunications) the object of which is the sense of the original message.

I have already mentioned this problem in speaking about memory and of the process of recalling the founder's words. Now, *traditio* follows two laws, that is, of accumulation and selection. On the one hand, it is like a river that, as it flows further away from its source, it grows wider and wider; on the other it is like a filter (and it could not be otherwise), that relies on a mechanism of selective memory: some things are constantly preserved, others are left by the wayside or even deliberately cast out. All this depends little, or not only, on any decision made by a religious authority, and much more on a problem of sense: some parts of the tradition are expunged because the range of possible meanings to lend to a religious message becomes broader. This association of stability (preserving the definition of the symbolic boundaries delimiting and designating the fundamental nucleus of the original message as far as possible) and flexibility (in conducting a long-term battle against the risk of a plurality of possible interpretations of the sense of that message) is further proof of the *complexity* of characteristic of religions. The doctrine seeks to consign to memory the perennial contents of a religious belief, just as the canon seeks to fix the living word in a written text. But no act of fixing will suffice to escape the risk of a displacement in the transmission of the message: just as a passage in the scriptures can be read in different ways at different times, so too can a doctrine be interpreted selectively or critically, even to the point of questioning certain aspects that were previously considered unquestionable. The movement inherent in *tradere* alludes to the fact that, in practice, this action takes place between individuals living an objectively different religious experience, if for no other reason than because the historical conditions change, sometimes even radically (Prandi 1983; Guolo 1996; Goody 2000).

If we look at the dating of the Christian Gospels, we see that the first, probably written in Rome and attributed to Mark, dates back to 65–70 AD; the second, Matthew, was written in Palestine and dates from 80–90 AD. The third, the Gospel of St Luke, can be dated around the same time as St. Matthew's, and it was clearly written in an environment still dominated by pagan religion; the fourth, the Gospel of St. John would seem to have been written towards the end of 90 AD in a cultural and religious setting strongly influenced by Gnosticism. The first texts of a Christian matrix are actually the Epistles to the Thessalonians, dating from around 51 AD and written by St. Paul, where among other things we read:

... our gospel has not been unto you *in word* only, but in power also and in the Holy Ghost, and in much fullness; as you know what manner of men we have been among you for your sakes. And you became followers of us and of the Lord, *receiving the word* in much tribulation, with joy of the Holy Ghost. So that you were made a pattern to all that believe in Macedonia and in Achaia. (1 Thess.: 5–7, emphasis added)

Paul is really the person responsible for the construction of a network of solidarity between the various Christian communities, and he urges them to see themselves as sharing the same heritage of faith. According to Paul, receiving the word is the fundamental act of acknowledging a shared line of belief, that equates to becoming imitators of the Lord and an example to all. The sense of this line of belief lies in a shared spiritual experience. It is common knowledge, however, that the canonization of what would subsequently be called the New Testament in the Christian environment (consisting of the above-mentioned four Gospels, the Acts of the Apostles, the Epistles of St. Paul, the Epistle to the Hebrews, those of Peter, John, James, and Judas, and finally the Apocalypse of St. John) came about by degrees and the texts that ultimately came to be seen as canonical did not count for much in other Christian communities. Moreover, some of these texts, such as the Epistle to the Hebrews, were generally accepted only after bitter internal controversies. All these documents, even those among them that were not the object of hermeneutic debate, reflect the particular experience of people representing the variety and specificity of the Christian communities beginning to take shape between Palestine and the Hellenist world, and later on in the Roman world as well. The transmission was no simple passing of the baton from a first generation of Jesus' followers to the next; it was filtered through experiences of the meaning of being and feeling Christian that, in the absence of a central authority, was open to a plurality of interpretations and convictions, to such a marked degree as to give rise to genuine cognitive divergences and dissonances of faith.

If this was the case for the preparation of the body of scriptures that came to be considered as canonical, we must expect similar and even stronger controversies of sense to extend to the definition of the dogma and ethical norms that, together with the scriptures, constitute the two load-bearing columns of the doctrinal apparatus of a religious belief system.

In some religions, the device that has theoretically been fine-tuned to reduce the risk of accidents along the way, in the transmission and subsequent elaboration of the doctrine, is represented by the *chain of transmission*. The most interesting example is provided in this case by Islam, which explicitly mentions the *isnad*, or chain of faithful transmitters. Alongside the written source (the Koran), Islam acknowledges the existence of the oral source, relating the words and deeds (*hadith*) attributed to the Prophet Muhammad. These words and deeds were collected and their authenticity assessed, ultimately proclaiming them a source of moral, religious, and legal norms, by a long line of authoritative Koranic scholars over a period of time that went from the year 800 to 1000 of our era. The criterion used to decide whether a saying could be traced back to the Prophet was the presence or absence of an uninterrupted chain of witnesses who had reported a given word or deed. Starting from the latest, it was necessary to go right back to Muhammad, verifying whether each link in the chain—each witness—was trustworthy (if the person existed historically and was known, and particularly if the person concerned could be considered an authority, and so on). At the end of this backtracking process, the first witness was a person who was on the scene when Mohammed said or did something, or who heard something about a particular issue from the Prophet's own lips; in other words, the witness was one of the early companions or belonged to the circle of the first converts.

The following example gives an idea of the complexity of the criterion that the scholars of the Koranic sciences elaborated. One collection of words and deeds, edited by Ibn Hanbal, the leader of a school of law that was well established in Baghdad (in the *Abbaside* period) in the ninth century, mentions six witnesses who would have transmitted the sense of words and deeds attributed to Muhammad to the author of the collection. Working backwards from the sixth witness to the first, at the end of the chain we meet one Abu Hurayra, the so-called "man with a dog" (a nickname apparently attributed to him because he was a goatherd and he was assisted in his work by a small, intelligent dog). He was apparently converted in Medina (and therefore not during the early period of Muhammad's preaching at Mecca) and, according to Muslim tradition, he became a faithful witness of the Prophet's words and deeds. Other collections trace their chain back to him too, as a sort of top of the league of transmission (Chabbi 1997: 1349). The interest of this example lies in the fact that, after a lengthy and meticulous assessment of a huge collection of words and deeds (approximately 60,000 instances!), such learned Muslims as al-Bukhari, for instance, demonstrated that only a minority could be considered reliable because either some of the characters involved in the process of transmission were not to be trusted, or they did not even exist. If we look carefully, the chain is really a sort of self-referencing procedure: everything must be traced back to the figure of Muhammad so that it is as if a word of truth had come from his very lips, recorded by a witness and handed on to another—a stamp of authenticity based on the chance to preserve the *given word* of the Prophet. The communication taking place in the passages from one witness to the next cannot guarantee, however, that the sense of the given word has reached the ears of the last link in the chain intact, and proof of this lies in the fact that even the most convincing of the Prophet's words and deeds in the *isnad* have always been debated and interpreted in various ways. Since the *hadith* have become a source of moral and legal norms in Islam (together with the Koran, they form the load-bearing structure of Koranic law), the moral and judicial doctrine founded on them cannot be presented as a closed, compact, and coherent body of doctrines. Quite the reverse, it exhibits a marked degree of differentiation, if for no other reason than because, within the belief system called Islam, there are at least two sub-systems, the Sunni and the Shi'ite, and they each contain further distinctions, based on different schools of law, theological branches, and philosophical currents.

Doctrine can be defined as the way in which a belief system seeks to understand itself and to communicate with the environment as a result. Communicating here does not mean "listening and giving a suitable response" (based on the old stimulus/ response pattern), but selecting the elements (and the links between them) of the doctrine that can reduce external complexity. The doctrine is therefore not a stock of dogma and precepts that are always applicable, systematized and organized once and for all, but the way in which the system's comprehension of itself and self-referencing operates.

For a belief system, doctrine cannot be something given and established once and for all. People mistake for fixity the legitimate claim of a belief system to represent itself as being well founded, sure of its principles, and always coherent and compact in time.

Communicating the One–Multiple Relationship

The real frontier passes between belief systems based on the idea of a revelation and those referring instead to a wisdom transmitted by a master to a disciple, who in turn becomes a master, and so on. In the latter case, the doctrine is elaborated *in initere*, in the sense that it can expand or be continuously revisited in the passage from one sage to the next, from one guru to another. Even when there is a written text on the founding principles, the doctrine's evolution echoes the continuous shifting induced by each master's personal interpretation as a result of his own experience and of the community relationships that he creates around him.

It is a different story if there is a revelation that is presented as a Word from on high, expressed through a special envoy, because we refer in this case to a memory of the extraordinary experience of a founder, and of a spiritual lineage that departs from him and arrives at the belief system. Such a system will have a formidable self-referencing mechanism in its constitutive principle. It will comprehend itself and organize itself by referring to those first, legitimate founding principles. In all the so-called religions of revelation, the religious doctrine or wise theological reflections are bound to rely on those primary founding principles.

In referring to their constituent principle, religions develop different forms of belief in a god or a superhuman being. The belief (in a god or superhuman being, transcendent or imminent as the case may be) is the object of the revelation or of the transmission of a spiritual understanding. A sacred text records what human mediators said they learned directly from a deity or as an interior revelation resulting from a profound meditation on the mysteries of human life. The text is consequently a communication of the communication: God communicates his message to an envoy, or an interior light speaks to the soul of a person who then becomes convinced that he is a bearer of the truth, but we—as recipients—only know what that envoy or spiritual master announces and relates to us.

If I use the conceptual tools of systems theory to examine, for instance, the controversial question of monotheism vis-à-vis polytheism and animism, that was first raised at various times by the father of the anthropology of religion, Edward Burnett Tylor (1832–1917), we soon realize that the difficulty, brought to light by many scholars, of clearly and distinctly defining what distinguishes the former from the latter two ways of intending the deity stems from the fact that they are assumed to be intrinsically different, while they are really three outcomes of the process of internal differentiation that a belief system implements in relation to an external (natural or social) environment. To say it with a paradox, even a religion that claims to be strictly monotheistic may contain elements typical of both animism and polytheism, since its monotheism would simply be the result of a belief system's "border wars" proving victorious over other existing beliefs in the environment, and the vanquished will very often have been absorbed and converted into other symbolic forms.

We are therefore far from conceiving—as Tylor and another anthropologist, James Frazer, did—the three forms of belief in a deity like a number of steps in the evolution of human religious thinking: from animism (considered the more primitive) to polytheism, and from there to monotheism; or from magic to religion, to science, as Frazer suggested, partially reiterating the rule of the three stages of social evolution suggested by Auguste Comte. There have even been some, like the learned Catholic priest Wilhelm Schmidt (1868–1954), who have sought to demonstrate—on the strength of a rich ethnographic documentation— that monotheism is the very core of religious thinking: an original thought on the uniqueness of a supreme Being, a sort of great God that has yet to acquire the many physiognomies that religions have subsequently attributed to it. Now, although Schmidt's hypothesis cannot be demonstrated (given the difficulty of documenting the symbolic-religious universe of the first human beings), according to some anthropologists, it nonetheless contains an idea that warrants further analysis.

For instance, if we take a careful look at the belief system of populations such as the Sioux Indians (the majority of which were exterminated by colonialism), or the Bambara of the African savannah (annihilated by advancing urbanization), we can see that the representation of the deity is articulated as illustrated in Figures 4.2 and 4.3.

The idea lying behind the belief system of the Bambara, the people of the middle Niger (though similar traits can also be seen among the Dogon, and among the Yoruba too), is that of a supreme God, who created the world from the Void (*fu*), through the work of *gla*, an uncreated principle that in turn creates that the whole cosmos. The creation begins when God produces *a voice from the void*, that generates his duplicate, *dya*, or the vital energy, from which the other principles and complementary spiritual forces such as Pemba or Faro descended. We can see that both approaches conceive of a one god, but this deity becomes manifest through a plurality of gods or a multiplicity of spirits. Marcel Griaule (1898– 1956) was an anthropologist who contributed decisively to our understanding of the symbolic universe of the Dogon people living to the south of Timbuktu, collecting their stories and detailed accounts of their cosmology from the elders of

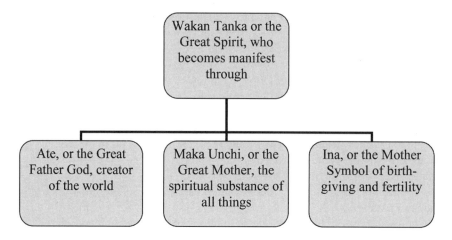

Figure 4.2   Conception of the deity, according to the Sioux

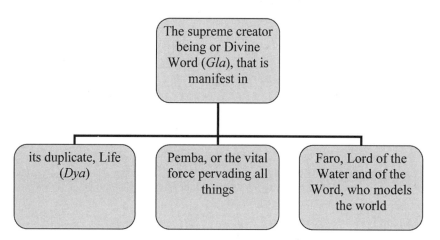

Figure 4.3   Conception of the deity among the Bambara populations of the African savannah

the villages. He reported that the most widespread belief among these populations focuses on supreme being (Amma) who becomes incarnate and manifest through Nummo, conceived here again as Water and Word (vital symbols *par excellence*), from which all living things originate, including the first ancestors and mankind. Commenting on this system of belief, Griaule (1966) cannot help but say that it revealed "an internal coherence, a secret wisdom and a perception of reality ultimately corresponding to those that we Europeans believe to have achieved."

What particularly impressed Griaule was the idea that Ogotemmeli (a wise man that he interviewed in a village), when he sought to explain the Dogon cosmological universe, resorted to a synthetic formula of undeniable efficacy to explain the complexity of their belief system: *the word is divine and consequently good, because it serves the purpose of classifying and organizing the world, of putting it in order*. Surely, putting the world in order is tantamount to developing a belief system capable of distinguishing itself from something perceived as a source of disorder, and thereby of restoring the multiple to the one?

The word, as the symbol of communication, is thus the *medium* that classifies and puts in order, seeking to dominate the external disorder without succeeding (and here lies the interesting aspect of the Dogon cosmogony) in eliminating it altogether ("but, right from the start, the word left space for disorder"). The Dogon people's faith in their system (of belief) guarantees a social control over the disorder always lying in wait. As Davidson reminds us (1972: 156), we can see why a member of the Ijo tribe, when asked by a Christian missionary to abandon his gods, answered, "Does your god really want us to climb to the top of another palm tree and then let go and allow ourselves to fall?" The stability of the order of things guaranteed by a belief system would have been jeopardized, just as an earthquake shakes the domestic walls within which we live.

The above considerations show that belief systems can become differentiated internally by composing a set of interrelated elements that include elements closely related to what we conventionally call monotheism, polytheism, and animism. If we rid ourselves of the mental classification that tends to place monotheism on one side and polytheism on the other, as if they were two irreconcilable systems, and if we consequently abandon the binary logical approach, then we can embrace the view of religious belief systems theory and say that, because it must continually differentiate itself from its environment, a system of beliefs needs to develop internally both a principle of unity and identity, and a principle of difference and controlled multiplicity. Faced with a multiple, variable, and unpredictable environment, a religion tends to claim a unique foundation of sense but, at the same time, it needs to find a communication medium capable of keeping within certain limits the variety and mutability of the "forces" in the outside environment.

Similarly, if we consider the religions that define themselves as monotheistic, we see—here again—that their efforts to proclaim the supremacy of the one God does not really cancel the problem of how to consider the multiplicity of forms in which he becomes manifest as soon as he is imagined as a supreme Being speaking to finite beings. A historian of religions who has reflected more than most on the topic of monotheism, starting from the pre-Socratic philosophical tradition, Raffaele Pettazzoni (1957), has demonstrated that a close correlation exists between the claim to monotheism and the idea of a powerful and sovereign God presiding over the creation and the ultimate destiny of the universe. But this one, sovereign, and transcendent God is revealed and speaks through his prophets, he makes his Word comprehensible to human ears and, in so doing, he lovingly comes closer to human beings instead of hiding after creating the world.

It is from taking this view of the Word that we can understand how the best-known monotheisms have dealt with the philosophical and theological problem of the relationship between One and multiple. Even the systems that most vociferously claim to believe in the one, absolute, and unique God, such as Judaism and Islam, must accept the idea that God becomes manifest through visible signs that enable human intelligence, inspired by faith, to understand the sense to attribute to *the world in all its multiple aspects* in the light of said faith.

A practicing Jew who observes God's law must follow 613 precepts, that evidently cover various types of behavior, from prayer to nutritional rules, from requirements relating to purity to ethical norms. It is as if the divine oneness could be separated into an articulated semantics of religiously oriented actions: it is not enough to acknowledge and adore this one God; we have to encounter him, as it were, in a variety of practical manifestations of our individual and social life. The development of the mystical in the Jewish setting seems to confirm the idea that a strict monotheism does not prevent a conception according to which God can be known through a communication medium that is accessible to human intelligence. As we see from a passage in one of the most important texts of the Jewish *qabbalah* (literally "tradition"), the *Sefer ha-zohar* (the Book of Splendor, published at the end of 1200 in Castile, Spain), when God decided to create the world, he consulted the Torah, "*word for word,*" and he created the world on the strength of what he found there, since "all the words and all the deeds of all the worlds are written in the Torah." The Lord becomes manifest, word for word, through the holy text (the Torah), and creates all things. In the end, his gaze falls on his last masterpiece, the human being, whom he asks to gaze on him in return. So we come full circle, starting from God, arriving at man, and returning from here to the absolute. In this mystical view of the Jewish *qabbalah*, human beings are asked to "retrace their steps and, from the shadows of this earthly world, to aim towards that veil through which they can see the supreme light: just as God looked to the Torah to create man, so man turns to the Torah to seek God, and do his bidding" (Busi 1995: viii).

As Scholem (1986) and Idel (2000), two interpreters of Jewish mysticism, have effectively demonstrated, the *qabbalah* invents a method for analyzing the scriptures that is mainly concerned with the power of the word, or of the language in which the Torah is written. In fact, the *qabbalah* has developed a complete doctrine of the alphabet that aims to become a genuine cognitive scheme. It was Busi again who explained that the doctrine of the alphabet becomes "a dynamic method for explaining the flow of experience and the endless composition and decomposition of individual realities" (1995: xxii). A single letter or a word become a key for interpreting the mysterious sense concealed between the pages of the holy book. The alphabet is seen not only as a basic communication tool but also as a powerful mechanism for revealing the sense of reality—and if it is understood, then it can be dominated. This brings us very close to the magical and apotropaic conception of language dear to many ancient cultures of the Mediterranean basin. It is no chance that this idea should be found not only in the world of the Jewish mystics, but also among Sufi Muslims, as is clearly illustrated by the great Andalusian mystic Ibn 'Arabi.

Jewish mysticism goes so far, for instance, as to give an esoteric interpretation of the Tetragrammaton (the four letters indicating the otherwise unpronounceable name of the Lord). The four letters in the word "Yahwe" (*yod, he, waw, he*), according to the sixteenth-century mystic Yishaq Luria, are simply the four levels of reality through which God becomes manifest, from the original level where the light of primeval man shone, from which comes the first divine emanation, the created world, and so on, down to the other two, lower levels. A descending ladder on which God's splendor "comes down." a ladder that man is called upon to climb, allowing himself to be guided by the numerous signs coming from God himself. In this setting, we cannot avoid our minds going back to Plotinus' philosophy of the One.

A similar alpha-numeric framework for a mystical approach is used in the Muslim world to demonstrate the fact that, even in strict Islamic monotheism, the concept of a God revealed entails the need to develop a doctrine of God's signs (hardly surprisingly, the verses of the Koran are called *ayat*, meaning signs, and the Muslim interpreters and scholars in the Shi'ite world are thus called *ayatollah*, or experts on God's signs). Finally, in both these monotheistic religions, the fact of adoring the one God has certainly not prevented the widespread worship of saints, spiritual masters, or mystics (more in Islam than in Judaism, in point of fact), who are venerated even today in tombs dotted all over the Islamic world, from the Maghreb to India and even in Pakistan. Saints are a further demonstration of the combination of oneness and multiplicity in religious thinking, a combination that, with the aid of system theory, we can interpret as the dialectic within a belief system between identity and difference, between self-reflection on its founding or constituent principle and the simultaneous attempt to transform the variety and complexity of the external environment into internal differentiation. It is easy to see that the characteristic trait of Christianity is another matter: in the passage from Christ's word to the elaboration of Christian doctrine and theology, the dominant concept became the dogma of the Trinity, of one God who is one and three at the same time, a relational God, who can thus incorporate *ab imis* the one and the multiple, making the development of the belief systems deriving from the Christian matrix much more flexible in incorporating the identity-difference combination.

The Authenticity of the Truth

A system of belief can evolve and face the changes coming from the environment not only because it succeeds, as we have just seen, in developing an internal communication medium that makes it relatively independent and capable of self-referentiality and *autopoiesis*, but also because there is an authority that guarantees the *authenticity of the truth* in various ways. This wording is used not to allude mainly to the specialists in holy matters or the priests who produce and control the religious know-how (to return to Bourdieu's theory [1971a]), but rather to the abstract form that the principle of authority takes in the functioning of a religious type of belief system. To explain this better, we are not thinking first and foremost of figures such as the pope in the Catholic Church or a rabbi in a Jewish community, or a *faqih* (Muslim law scholar), or a Hindu *Brahmin*, or other people of their ilk. An example may help us to understand what we are driving at with the *incipit* of our reasoning.

Let us consider the ancient texts of the Vedic religion (including the Upanishad, which dates back to 500 BC, and the Bhagavad-Gita, dating from the early first century AD). These are the holy scriptures acknowledged by all Hindus as an undeniable authority. But what is the meaning of the authority of these texts in the absence of any founding figures who announced the word subsequently transcribed in the text and transmitted from one generation to another?

Hervieu-Léger (1993) advanced the hypotheses that every religion needs to establish itself as an authoritative descendant of a given belief (*"lignée croyante"*): a memory shared one generation after another and transmitted with authority. So it is not always necessary to postulate a physical and visible power imposing this line of belief in the course of time. It can penetrate time and withstand the wear and tear of the centuries, possibly thanks to a powerful structure founded on an organic alliance and on the functional division of the social and political workload between king and priest, or between temporal and spiritual power. As a belief system, a religion can also place the will of the subjects under its religious and political command in brackets. The system can even reproduce itself on the sole strength of the authority attributed, for instance, to a holy text, without necessarily having a person standing guard over its authenticity. This is what characterizes the Sikhs, for instance. Their religious memory has needed no physical authority since the seventeenth century. It is entrusted to a holy text; it has become been objectivized, and thus impersonal; the force of the original message has thus lain in its faithful transmission from one generation to the next.

The job of guaranteeing the authenticity of the truth can also be entrusted to an *impersonal* communication medium, to a given word that has become a holy scripture. To remain with the example of Hinduism, the idea that animates all of religious Hindu thinking is that the revelation is none other than a descent of the divine that becomes manifest in multiple forms (the *avatara*). So it implicitly contains the idea that this revelation has an original nucleus (in the Vedas) that has subsequently developed, expanded, and been interpreted and reinterpreted in later texts, as in the case of both the Upanishad and the Bhagavad-Gita. According to the Hindu conception, the deity never really stops revealing itself, when the time is ripe, sending new signs to show that other ways to salvation are possible. Every existence is a manifestation of the divine, so if I know myself—as a tiny particle in an infinite universe subject to the eternal law of return—then I know God, since there is no difference between the divine universal principle (*brahman*) animating and governing the universe and the sacred spark (*atman*) existing in every living being. The ideal therefore is not a matter of placing one's trust in an outside authority, but rather of freeing oneself, of gaining salvation through one's own efforts (possibly following the recommendations of a master, who has no power unless the disciple commits themselves to the way to salvation that the master reveals). The criterion for ascertaining the validity and authenticity of the truth is ultimately the individual himself, enlightened by the authority of the revelation contained in the holy text (Squarcini and Bartoli 1997).

It is only with the advent of the new interpretation of the Vedic texts proposed by the Bhagavad-Gita—focusing entirely on the idea of devotion (*bakhti*) to a unique deity such as Vishnu (who became manifest through incarnation in the figure of Krishna) or Shiva, according to a mental scheme of belief that someone has said resembles monotheism—that the principle of an "incarnate" authority begins to take shape, integrating and sometimes replacing the abstract authority of the scriptures. Krishna is thus conceived as the eighth revelation of God (Vishnu), who will be followed by others. This makes us understand why, in modern times, some neo-Hindu spiritual masters have had no difficulty in conceiving Jesus as an *avatar* of the god Vishnu. A contemporary case is represented by Sai Baba, who believes he is the *avatar* of a multiplicity of divine forces, including the figure of Christ.

This means that there is no need to see authority in religions exclusively as a visible power of control over orthodoxy; it is more a *fiduciary communication* established between the believer and the person he acknowledges the role of *trustee* of a truth here on earth. In other words, religion allows us to imagine that the world has sense and that the indeterminate or infinite are within reach of the human, finite and determinate. We therefore rely on those who demonstrate (by their virtue or because they belong to an institution that appoints them to this function) that they know how to mediate between the determinate and the indeterminate, including a holy text, a word objectivized by being written.

Taking an oversimplified approach, it is sometimes suggested that anthropomorphic representations of the deities are rough forms of belief. If we look more closely, however, they are the way in which human beings come closer to their deities. They can communicate more easily with a god, the more the latter takes on human or similar features (even to the point of imagining the god can eat, drink, and make love, engage in intrigue to gain favor, go to war, and so on). In religions, the job of mediating between human beings and the kingdom of the sacred and divine has been entrusted to a great variety of figures, but they can always be brought down to the idea that they are *vicarious* of something that is not visible, determinate, and finite, because this is the only for them to be able to speak on behalf of the deity and give us to understand what the deity wants human beings to do in order to be acceptable—in various ways—in his eyes.

These *vicarious* figures can be divided into three main groups or ideal types:

- those who say they receive the *live* divine word and therefore claim that, through their own voices, it is the voice of the deity himself that is making itself heard;
- those who perform ritual functions by order of a religious institution or

recognized by a royal power, and

- those who say they have particular skills to enable a believer to access an extra-ordinary dimension.

We have actually described three types of charisma: one personal, one belonging to a function, and one specific. In fact, a person can be accepted as a *trustee of the truth* either because we assign that person the status of prophet, or because he or she is part of an institution or class of specialists to whom we assign a priestly function, as mediators in the rituals between the divine world and the human world, or because they show that they know how to act as guides on the spiritual path to perfection, in the particular relationship created between master and disciple. But that is not to say that, in practice, the three we have mentioned cannot overlap or be rolled into one.

What it is ultimately important to emphasize here is the recurrence in religions of figures who are perceived by believers as *special*, extraordinary, different from themselves because they are particularly dedicated to a task that is considered of great symbolic value, that is, to make us imagine the feasibility of a unity between determinate and indeterminate. It is up to a body of people who cannot, by definition, be confused with the rest of the population to produce effective images of this type. Their authority stems from a process of internal differentiation within a religious belief system: religious power as communication demands that, for religious sense, the balance between supply and demand must always derive from choosing from among the many possible meanings that are selected and imposed, indicated and proposed, at some point in the evolution of the system, depending on how authoritarian a given religion has decided to be in order to better establish itself in the social environment.

Those who have religious knowledge and power will seek to keep it firmly within their own hands (Bourdieu 1971a) and they will try to instill in the faithful a mental *habitus* resembling obedience and submission. But this is not enough to explain the function of authority in the religious field. It is a good idea, moreover, to bear in mind the political effects of exercising religious power, though in that case we risk grasping only the exterior aspects of authority.

What we mean to say is that this authority has to do with the process of choosing the sense (or communication) governing the relationship between those who have the power (of communication) and those who do not, and must consequently rely on somebody they acknowledge as being capable of selecting one of a number of possible meanings, the one(s) most likely to enable us to imagine as united what would otherwise really be mysteriously differentiated. Mystery inhabits not the world of the divine or sacred (where it is possible to imagine an origin for everything, a unity of the sense and purpose of human history), but the real world in its changeability, variety, and elusiveness. Religions classify everything that moves in the world and in history, enabling us to attribute a sense to things that would otherwise have no sense.

The truth of religion lies not only in the content, but also in the binary form that it often takes (true/false, manifest/hidden, illusory/enlightened).

When a system relies on the true/false contingency, it tends to develop an introspective science (theological and philosophical, or metaphysical) that incorporates logic and dialectic. In other cases, based on the illusionary/enlightened principle, the doubts are never overcome; instead, doubting becomes a part of the system's ascetic and meditative methods; this is the case of Buddhism, for instance, and of Zen Buddhism in particular, which gives priority to a form of debate based on endless paradoxes, incorporating contradiction as a technique for destructuring rationality and leading believers to intuitively gauge the impermanence not only of all things, but also of human thought, when we attempt to understand everything that we perceive as the *world* and to put it in order in our own mind.

The certainty that a system of belief transmits anyway—when all doubts have been overcome—can be translated into experience of sense with the aid of the figures that we have called trustees of the truth, that is, the interpreters or mediators who translate the question of true/false, or illusory/enlightened, into gestures, words, actions, works, and rituals accessible to believers without having to resort constantly to the energy or force of reasoning (that belongs to the level of scholarly debate) to be persuasive and make believers behave accordingly—and the latter do so because they accept the reduced complexity of the sense presented to them by the trustees of the truth.

All this distinguishes *mass* religions from *elite* religions: the former must speak to everyone, the latter can permit themselves the luxury of speaking to only a few, because only a few are capable of the climbing "the vertical walls" of the spirit. The two levels have coexisted historically in the same religion—as in the case of Christianity or Islam. In Buddhism too, there is a nucleus of monks conducting an intensely ascetic life and a majority of people who follow much more straightforward devotional practices. In principle, the ideal or model that people should strive to imitate in Buddhism is the Buddha himself, who succeeded in life in breaking the chains of attachment to the world, achieving that emptiness (*nirvana*) that lies beyond good and evil, beyond life and death, or true and false. For those embarking on the path charted by Gautama, it is as if they were adventuring onto a dangerously exposed ridge at a giddy height: not everyone can take that route. It is hardly surprising that modern-day Buddhism has shown a growing tendency, clearly visible nowadays in several neo-Buddhist movements (for example, the Soka Gakkai) to suggest the feasibility of a layman's path to freedom, that is, a path that is accessible to everyone, not exclusive to the monks.

The languages used may vary, sometimes even considerably, but they can still be brought down to the (legitimately wielded) power of the word. The well-worn phrase, "Let the women remain silent" (in the temple) that we find in many religions—from Judaism to Islam, and from Catholicism to Hinduism—effectively synthesizes the idea of the power of the word. When the word is conceived as the medium for communicating something extraordinary, we usually see in religions a sacralization of a language (as in the case mentioned before of Sanskrit in classic

Hinduism, or as in the case of Arabic, the sacred language of the Koran). Because it is sacred, the language cannot be *used by all and sundry*; a particular and special linguistic competence is required. Those who do not have certain acknowledged credentials are not qualified to speak, that is, they cannot demonstrate their competence concerning the holy Word. So there must be somebody superior to the others, in that he knows how to use the word, while the others are not allowed and, *propter hoc*, not able to use it.

The language game in the religious sphere always has to do with authority and an imbalance of power. The more the ritual formulas sound incomprehensible, the more they gain—in the ears of simple believers—the power to evoke a mysterious presence that is revealed and becomes manifest. When Mircea Eliade (1959) coined the effective notion of hierophany, he identified a fundamental mechanism in the communication processes characterizing the function of religion in human societies. Hierophany is a manifestation of the sacred that becomes perceivable and visible because somebody knows the *password* to an otherwise impenetrable world of signs that is accessible only to a chosen few. Control over the holy word in the sacred texts of the Vedas, for example, gives the *Brahmin* not only a particular authority, but also a special force, like a special weapon that other believers and faithful lacked: a weapon for defeating ignorance and evil. The *Brahmin* is pure and must stay that way because he is needed to deal with a perfect, pure word. This may be the object of communication only after special precautions have been taken, and only if it handled by people with "clean hands." It is worth adding here that the dialectic of gender existing in many religions stems specifically from the idea that women are believed to be impure (because of their biological characteristics) and consequently not suitable for "touching" holy things. The male domination that was established in patriarchal societies was thus sublimated by the violence of the sacred.

Authority is therefore expressed as a sovereignty over the word, which becomes manifest in the form of a holy language with a code that is controlled by a class of acknowledged specialists who act as if they had received a divine mandate for their power. Believing consequently also entails being convinced of the need to trust in those who can communicate with the deity and enable communication therewith. The authenticity of the truth is a phrase that indicates the whole process that we have described: the truth becomes authentic by means of a fiduciary communication between individual believers on the one hand, and those who, for various reasons, wield the power of communication on the other.

Conclusion

The Notion of System in Clifford Geertz

In his *The Interpretation of Cultures*, Clifford Geertz wrote:

> Two characteristics of anthropological work on religion accomplished since the second world war strike me as curious when such work is placed against that carried out just before and just after the first. One is that it has made no theoretical advances of major importance. It is living off the conceptual capital of its ancestors, adding very little, save a certain empirical enrichment, to it. The second is that it draws what concepts it does use from a very narrowly defined intellectual tradition. There is Durkheim, Weber, Freud, or Malinowski, and in any particular work the approach of one or two of these transcendent figures is followed, with but a few marginal corrections necessitated by the natural tendency to excess of seminal minds or by the expanded body of reliable descriptive data. (Geertz 1973: 87)

Based on these critical considerations, the author first recalls the starting points that withstand time, which come from the four classics that he mentioned, respectively: Durkheim's notion of the sacred, Weber's comprehending methodology, personal and collective rituals according to Freud's psychoanalytical approach and, finally, Malinowski's distinction between religion and common sense. He then presents his theory on the cultural dimension of religion, referring explicitly to Parsons and Shils. In a handful of pages dense with meaning, Geertz arrives at a proposed definition:

> A religion is: (1) a system of symbols, which acts to (2) establish powerful, pervasive, and long-lasting moods and motivations in men by (3) formulating conceptions of a general order of existence and (4) clothing these conceptions with such an aura of factuality that (5) the moods and motivations seem uniquely realistic. (Geertz 1973: 90)

Geertz's notion of system resembles that of Talcott Parsons (1951), for whom religion is a belief system that *ultimately* serves the purpose of integrating the social norms with the practical actions of individuals, providing non-negotiable grounds for the ethical and religious values to which those norms refer. Like Parsons, Geertz also sees religion as contributing to representing the world and the order that reigns therein as an "actual state of affairs," a social order that is also of the mental and emotional at the same time (Geertz 1973: 90). It makes people see as orderly, sensible, and united a world that would otherwise not seem so, which is why our author can claim that very often "sacred symbols function to synthesize a people's ethos" (ibid.: 97).

Religion as a cultural system is thus a source of information that individuals draw from (either because they are trained to do so, or because they are driven by the urge to explore the meaning of human experience) in order to lend meaning not only to their own lives as individuals, but also to their life together in society. Religious symbols model the world and, by doing so, they provide those adhering to them with conviction with emotional dress codes, lifestyles, norms of conduct, passions, and inclinations—in a word, the symbolic resources they need to act. Adhering to such a universe of symbols could be more rightly called believing. For Geertz, people believe primarily in an authority, on which they rely to understand or explain the world and the mysterious and profound order governing it. "He who would know," writes Geertz, "must first believe" (ibid.: 110).

Before they can be interiorized, social norms need to be based on a higher order, a service order that is not going to be constantly questioned because it is basically considered transcendent, eternal, and absolute. The term "uniquely realistic" that Geertz uses in his proposed definition refers to the absolutely abstract. In the terminology of systems theory, this concept is contained in the pair of terms "determinate/indeterminate."

In the light of his fieldwork, conducted in places as wide apart as Indonesia and Morocco, Geertz was aware, however, that religion as a cultural system is not a compact and unchangeable symbolic universe; it evolves and changes in relation to changes taking place outside (and sometimes despite) the boundaries that religions, or religious traditions, are actually able to control. In fact, they tend to represent themselves as the depositaries of an immutable truth, which enables them to emerge unscathed from the storms of history and social turbulence that often induce radical changes in entire human societies.

In actual fact, as we have tried to demonstrate so far, religions as systems of symbols and sets of rituals interact with the social environment, so they suffer the backlashes of changes taking place in the society where they operate, but possibly only in the longer term. As an example, an analysis of how the syncretic rituals typical of rural and village society on the island of Java have progressively been disrupted by advancing urbanization illustrates, according to Geertz, that the short-range solidarities that kept the little farming communities relatively close-knit have withered and crumbled, giving rise to new social tensions that contribute to emptying of meaning all the syncretic religious rituals (such as the funerals that the village community held when one of its members died, regardless of whether they were Hindu, Muslim, or animist). Up until the eve of these social changes, the villagers combined the symbolic elements of all three cultural worlds, but when many of them moved more recently from the country to the towns, they started to cling to their original religious identity, emphasizing their respective differences and consequently abandoning any practices that we might call inter-communitarian and inter-religious.

In such cases, the structure of a cultural system on a religious basis is no longer able to serve its purpose of furthering social cohesion as it did in the past, so either it goes into decline or it is largely reshaped: instead of integrating, the religious symbol begins to separate, accentuating the differences between Hindus, Muslims, and animists. This goes to show that the conservative function of religion can by no means be taken for granted—the idea that culture is a set of symbols learnt once and for all, capable of forging immutable collective identities is naive and unacceptable, as many have effectively illustrated (Gallissot, Kilani, and Rivera 1998; Mantovani 2004; Sen 2006).

Social changes are sometimes so deep that they are not registered by the cultural systems with the same speed and intensity at which they occur (and religion can be included among the cultural systems). When this happens, as history has often shown, the change affecting the social structure as a whole may not necessarily be fully reflected in the system of (cultural and religious) meanings shared by the society's members. Social structures—and cultural structures in particular—as Geertz made plain (1973), are not simply reflections of one another, but independent variables, even though they are interdependent. So, through interaction with the social environment, a cultural system changes and becomes reorganized (if it is able), but it does not necessarily reflect—as a certain naive and abstract functionalism would sometimes have given us to believe—the changes that have taken place in the social structure. In its interaction with a changing environment, a cultural system may be defeated (when individuals no longer experience the sense in the set of symbols that it has produced and transmitted over time), or it may initially fall apart, but subsequently succeed in reassembling itself in a new way of imagining and believing, of *religiously* thinking the order of things in another way.

The above considerations drawn from Geertz's writings demonstrate that a cultural system, called religion, can be observed as if it were a living organism that, by adapting to the environment, can serve a plurality of functions: not only to engender solidarity and social cohesion, but also to elaborate conflict. The idea that religion means the preservation of the social balance cannot stand the test of the social sciences if the latter critically adopt the systemic paradigm. Religions as systems are susceptible, by definition, to the pressures of a changing environment, so they tend to measure themselves with what changes in the latter (exogenous change), sometimes autonomously making changes to their own internal layout (endogenous change) in order to adjust somehow to the social changes underway. Just as the hypothesis of a linear decline of the sacred in modern society was hardly very convincing, the assumption that religion invariably serves the purpose of social integration and preservation is likewise open to question.

The Systems Theory of Religion

The difference between Geertz's approach and systems theory applied to the analysis of the religious phenomenon can be identified in two crucial aspects.

The first concerns the idea that religion can be seen as a cultural system and therefore in much the same way as any other ideology configured as a complete, all-round view of the world. Geertz is aware of this too, since he dedicates a whole chapter to the topic of ideology (1973: 247–94). This means that not only do we question the supposed relative autonomy of religion vis-à-vis other collective belief systems (of which the all-round ideologies, and political ideologies in particular, are an important example), we also and more importantly risk conceptually separating the structure of religion from its function. In fact, Geertz basically continues to wonder about the function of religion (or, broadly speaking, of culture or ideology) in relation to the social order, be it stable or in the throes of change.

The approach of belief systems theory that we have adopted departs instead from the assumption that it is more fruitful in cognitive terms to consider religion as a structure that has a specific function that cannot be readily absorbed by or reduced to other functions characterizing other structures or systems. This particular function has little to do with the relationship between religion and social order (religion guaranteeing order), but rather with the highly specific way in which a system of religious belief *functions* internally in order to interact with the outside social environment. The difference between Geertz's idea of system and what we have attempted to demonstrate here by taking a systemic approach (albeit with all the critical precautions that we have mentioned) thus lies essentially in a word: *autopoiesis*.

Secondly, religious belief systems appear to be capable of self-reproduction, not only because "society changes," but also because they function as systems required primarily to make sense of their characteristic internal complexity. This is the only way for a system of religious belief to withstand time despite profound and radical changes taking place outside in society, beyond its control (in the sense that it can neither determine them, nor prevent them), from economics to science, from politics to communication media. To withstand time, they must develop their own internal complexity, not just the capacity to filter external complexity. A system of religious belief may be efficient (in terms of performance) not because it knows how to weather the storm of social change, but rather because it succeeds in creating its own internal elements and corresponding relationships between them, so as to be able to tolerate the external complexity—with a relative degree of autonomy in relation to the social environment and other social systems or sub-systems—without necessarily having to undergo radical changes or any definitive replacement of the elements comprising its network of links (be they symbolic, ritual, mythological, or whatever). This is what—in the second phase of Luhmann's thinking, which took shape in the 1980s—was also called *self-referentiality*.

To switch from wondering "what is the purpose of religion" (taking the classical structural-functionalist approach) to wondering how a religious belief system functions, as seen from the inside, as it were (taking a systemic approach), enables us to overcome several paradoxes that have become apparent both in the secularization theories and, to some degree and more recently, in the theories that focus on *rational choice* or the religious economy. The former made the mistake of taking a linear, and consequently causal approach to studying the relationship (stated in a nutshell) between modernization on the one hand and the decline of the sacred, or of religiosity on the other. The latter, although they restored value to the organizational autonomy of religious institutions in relation to the demand for sense of potential "customers," who move freely in an abstract religious market, have proved unable to grasp the particular operating principle of (religious) belief systems, because they have limited themselves to making the point that the strictest organizations on the market, the most conservative in defending their doctrines, have better chances of success nowadays than their more relaxed and liberal competitors. In other words, they reduce the complexity of a belief system to its *entrepreneurial* capabilities. Among the proponents of rational choice, in fact, there are those who speak explicitly of a religious *portfolio*, imagining a customer demanding a *faith* policy on the one hand, and a series of able *faith promoters* on the other. The theoretical assumption here is that of a free market, where religious supply and demand meet and strike the right balance, establishing a causal relationship between a growth in the *membership* of a religious organization and its presentation of a "reliable" product (clear and distinctive in its doctrinal principles, strict in fixing the boundaries between what is allowable and what is not, precise in distinguishing between good and evil, and so on) and, vice versa, between a loss of consent and a liberal attitude to the promotion of symbolic-religious goods (Pace 2006).

In both cases, the problem for a theory aiming to deal with the *question*, stubborn as a stone, facing the social sciences, lies in the more or less explicit assumption that we can only understand religion if we establish a link of cause and effect between religion and something else, that is, with human beings' structural tendency to calculate the costs and benefits of their actions (including those of a religious type), or with the dependence of religion on the socio-economic variables of a social system, meaning that it varies with changes in the latter. We therefore cannot answer the question of why religions persist. We might claim, as many have done before, that they intercept an anthropological need (for sense, to transcend ordinary life, and so on) or a genetically programmed need (but, that being the case, it is hard to see why individuals believe differently, or even not at all), or a deep-seated layer of our neural structure. All these approaches seek to find a place from a point of observation that is no longer mainly social, but biological, neurological, psychological, or economic, as the case may be. From the methodological standpoint, this operation is in some ways rather bizarre for anyone wishing to analyze the religious phenomenon socially. It is as if we were to depart from our own discipline, not to see the other's cards (that is, to learn how the same thing is considered by an ecologist, a neuroscientist, or a cognitive psychologist), but to steal their job, transposing the patterns, methods, and concepts from one field to another, generating the illusion that, once sociology has gained possession of a language that is seemingly strictly scientific, or more scientific than the one it normally uses at least, it can finally rise to the ranks of the exact and hard sciences, thereby renewing the nineteenth-century dream of positivism imagined by the father of sociology, Auguste Comte.

Religions as Expert Systems

When social scientists study the phenomenon of religion, they cannot avoid taking the point of view of individuals who wonder about the sense of life, asking questions that human beings have recurrently asked themselves—presumably while looking empirically at the force that religions have always had in the past and present. In so doing, sociologists deduce that, if religions persist and remain alive, it is because they (and probably only they) manage to specialize in providing reassuring answers to fears of death and hopes of immortality. With this, we grasp only a part of the truth, as anthropological and sociological research, as well as comparative studies on the history of religions have demonstrated, but we do not give sufficient emphasis to the specialized function of this particular knowledge that religion, in its broadest sense, itself generates and represents. In other words, religions are expert systems, organized on the strength of their specific ability to develop an understanding of the final destiny of human beings and humanity. This expertise boasted by religions is something that other cultural systems do not have to the same degree, or with the same level of complexity.

If I acknowledge religion this structure, then I can take another step and ask ourselves whether this very structure is the autonomous principle of religious belief systems. This means that, even before I study a religion's social performance—its manifest and latent functions, to return to a known distinction drawn by Bryan Wilson (1985)—I need to start, from a methodological standpoint, by assuming that:

a. Religion is a system that has continued to build and rebuild its relationship with the social environment, which changes with time; unless we focus on this inseparable relationship, we risk failing to understand the dynamics of the religious phenomenon.

b. The process that constructs and defines the symbolic boundaries of a system of religious belief takes place in an environment *crowded* with religious symbols and other belief systems (religious and otherwise); in defining itself, a religion has the problem of distinguishing itself from this environment and of increasing its internal complexity in the process. It consequently tends to withdraw within itself, emphasizing its own identity specifically in order to better interact with, and be open to, changing and multiple environments.

c. Differentiation lies at the very origin of a belief system because, before the system exists, there is a *virtuoso of improvisation*, a mobile personality who shifts the boundaries of the historically dominant beliefs in a given environment and, by means of variations on the earlier symbolic themes, invents a new way of interpreting them. From this point of view, every system of religious belief contains *variation* and *mobility*, and the more these two characteristics are present in the beginnings of the system, *before* the system existed, the more we must expect these characteristics to be transferred in the *system building* process. Much more than Weber, Troeltsch has given us an exemplary demonstration that we can study Christianity, for instance, from a historical and sociological standpoint, as a generative grammar of both spiritual and organizational models that are highly differentiated, not only in relation to the different settings in which a religion has been successful, but also by virtue of its original charge as a religion *in motion*, designed as if it had *moving partitions*.

d. The differences between systems of religious belief depend not only on the environment where they are born and gradually become established, but also on their *genealogy*, on the relationships of interdependence that they have known historically and socially since the dawn of their existence and in the course of their diachronic evolution and territorial expansion. Religious syncretism is not a particular species of religion, but a characteristic structural feature of systems of religious belief: syncretism is the name we conventionally give to complexity; systems based on religion are complex by definition, because they have to learn to distinguish themselves from the environment in order to *survive or resist*, they must learn how to reduce the complexity they encounter in the environment, internalizing it to some degree. We have always seen that the battles conducted, with limited success, by all the zealous and zealots of all times to purify and reclaim religion from its supposedly spurious elements, superstitions, magic, borrowings from other faiths and devotions, are proof in themselves that it is impossible for a belief system to reduce its own internal complexity. This is so because the list of the impurities to eliminate is really a list of elements that a system has learnt to handle and correlate in order to withstand and contain the external complexity of the many environments with which it has entered into a vital and stable relationship in the course of time.

The above considerations bring me, in conclusion, round to a definition, not of religion per se, but of the purposes it serves as a *belief system*. What I proposed to demonstrate is that it is more useful for the analysis of the religious phenomenon to shift our attention from the *social function* of religion to its *systemic function*, which implies studying not only its role in *social integration*, but also and more importantly its role in *interpretation*. By this latter formula, I mean the ability of a religious belief system to function as such, with a relative degree of autonomy, drawing on its own internal forces to establish relationships with an unstable environment and represent itself as a set of self-sufficient symbols and rituals, in opposition to those proposed by other belief systems and to the free circulation of these same symbols and rituals in time and in human societies.

The Interpretative Function of Religions

For a more or less elaborate belief system, interpreting primarily means using a self-reflective capacity: for it to be able to interpret the world, a belief system must be capable of introspection and the more it nurtures this capacity, the better it is able to distinguish itself from the environment. This is the only way for it to withstand time and escape the buffeting of social changes. History is a veritable graveyard of deities, but also a river of symbols that continue to circulate freely even after the gods have fallen. To return to a geological metaphor again, a system of religious belief is often rather like a cliff, built in layers—not mechanically, one on top of the other, but held together so that they seem more or less harmoniously arranged, in an orderly and disciplined hierarchy. Nothing has been left to chance. This is the result of the work of interpretation that belief systems are obliged to undertake in their relations with the environment in which they are born and continue to live and thrive, and even more so when they spread elsewhere, reaching faraway places and different peoples, with distinctive cultural characteristics that may be very different from those of the religion's origins. The most effective means of communication with such remote, different cultural and religious worlds lies in the use of rites and rituals, which are generally an excellent vehicle for enabling communications between different layers of symbols and beliefs, establishing the right hierarchy between dominant, official beliefs and others that are merely tolerated or made partially compatible with the former.

Applying the systemic approach to religion thus enables us to evade at least two dilemmas. The first concerns the topic of secularization, or the decline versus the revival of the sacred, both of which are probably partially true.

If we consider a religion as a system of relationships with an environment, it is easier to see that the religion suffers a relative loss of social weight, or a declining consent, during certain evolutionary periods of its relationships with the environment, while at other times it revives. In other words, if we translate decline and revival as an increasing and decreasing social complexity, or cycles of socio-religious inflation and deflation, and if we measure a belief system's capacity to distinguish itself in order to stand the test of a changing environment, then we can legitimately say that a religion may go through all the phases of *social success*, depending on its ability to absorb the new excesses of sense generated in a given environment in its own interpretative categories. Like Diotallevi (2001), we will then gain a better understanding of the tenacity of Catholicism in Italy, for instance, by taking a historically long-term perspective and analyzing the various cycles that the religion has experienced, bearing in mind how the evolution of society has correlated with the evolution of the church system. Research done by Garelli

(2006, 2007) induces us to think twice before we assume that the organizational and spiritual force of the Italian Catholic Church is declining irretrievably: the indicators that were used 20 or 30 years ago to measure its decline appear distinctly unsuitable nowadays, if we examine them critically, to explain the vitality of Catholicism in society and the renewed capacity of the institutional church to take an active part in public life.

Besides, how else can we explain the contemporary expansion of Christianity in Africa, Asia, and Latin America (Jenkins 2002), in forms that are relatively novel and, more importantly, that lie outside and parallel to the historical Catholic or Protestant churches?

In fact, the organizational format adopted by the new charismatic and Pentecostal churches, or by the charismatic movements born within Catholicism (like the Italian *Renewal in the Spirit*, with approximately 250,000 people forming a system based on a network of small communities, that now amount to more than 1,700), seems to indicate that the religious belief system that we call Christianity has become flexibly differentiated to suit the various socio-cultural environments that it has encountered in the course of its history, and particularly around the end of the twentieth and the start of the twenty-first centuries. In the eyes of an outside observer, Christianity can be seen as a living *system* in the world today, because it has demonstrated its capacity to absorb the differences in the environments of its inculturation and thus extend the symbolic boundaries of the sense to attribute to "being Christian." How many ways are there today for a person to be a Christian? It is hard to say, and nobody has yet succeeded in repeating Troeltsch's exercise of social and religious imagination to construct a historical typology of Christianity (Troeltsch 1990), from ancient times up until the present day. How many social doctrines of the Christian groups and churches would the German sociologist have to examine nowadays in order to classify them in his classic church/sect/ mysticism typology? In attempting to do so, he would probably discover the need to invent other ideal types, reflecting a social and religious reality that is becoming increasingly diversified, its symbolic boundaries much dilated, where symbols *marked as Christian* circulate with considerable degrees of freedom, to such an extent that they may be adopted by new *religious entrepreneurs* and even by new prophets, reformers, and preachers wandering around the World Wide Web, that is, cyber-religion (Pace and Giordan 2010). Faced with such a dilated panorama, we must avoid making the mistake of only considering the great historical churches that have drawn life and legitimization from Christianity; we should look at everything moving, with a marked degree of turbulence and effervescence, just outside or along their borders. Christianity is a world-system which, like Islam or Buddhism, is highly differentiated historically as well as in the multiple, diverse relationships that it continues to weave with a great variety of social environments.

So I can still speak of secularization, providing I clearly understand what I mean by the word. It is not a measure of a declining interest in holy things, or of religion's loss of social plausibility, but rather a *process that describes the increasing differentiation* experienced by an evolving religious belief system at certain times in history.

Such systems have a life cycle: *they are born* (thanks to a capacity for improvisation), not out of nothing, but within an environment already inhabited by symbols; *they grow* (establishing their symbolic boundaries, on the strength of which they expand through identity and difference) and *they become mature*, developing the capacity to reduce the external complexity and, *in so doing, they succeed in standing the test of time and reproducing. If they fail to develop this capacity, they perish*. Systems can cope with the risk of decline and disappearance if they are able to preserve the original spirit of mobility that animated them at the start, thanks to their founder's capacity for improvisation.

Neither Muhammad nor Buddha, nor Christ, nor anyone else, could have imagined such a abundance of movements, groups, sects, schools of thought, spiritual pathways, types of churches, and other organized forms of belief as we have seen branch off from these great world religions. A detailed analysis and classification of all these forms (impossible to achieve using the limited cognitive tools of one discipline alone, such as sociology) might be a useful empirical exercise, not only to demonstrate the degree of differentiation that these religions soon came to experience, often in the crossfire of recurrent (sometimes harsh and violent) conflicts, but also to illustrate how the driving force of these religions' respective founders—which extended beyond the symbolic confines of pre-existing and previous beliefs and traditions to imagine other possible worlds of sense and action—remains alive, generating continuous upheavals in the evolution of the belief system.

Releasing and Binding

The founding act both *releases* and *binds*, it releases from the bonds of ancient beliefs and it binds people to new ways of believing. But because, from the very beginning, it challenges the dominant symbolic boundaries in a given environment, we can expect this spirit of mobility not to fizzle out, but to be preserved in the process of building a belief system, also becoming a part of the organizational apparatus that the system ultimately adopts in order to better function as such.

The organizational element is consequently fundamental to the strength of a system of religious belief, both when the chosen organizational model is relatively independent of other social systems (and of the forms of political power in particular), and when it is more or less directly indebted in its organizational aspects to a political power, and especially if emperors and sovereigns have decided to adopt a given religious confession as the state religion. Belief systems that become the cultural and ideological regulators of such organized systems as states (from state religions to political theologies functional to the theories and practices of the powers that be) naturally acquire a greater organizational strength than belief systems that are not lucky enough to pervade the political system. There is clearly a huge difference between Christianity, which has become a church, and Gnosticism, which has remained an organizational nebula with countless clusters that have never succeeded in adopting a precise structural configuration: in the former case, the belief system construction and consolidation process could rely on an organizational format that enabled the system to define its contours and acquire a level of self-referentiality that the Gnostic groups and networks never achieved (Filoramo 1983). At a certain point in its historical evolution, Christianity found in the Emperor Constantine the political and institutional support it needed to stake its claim to being a belief system that enables belief to coincide with belonging to two cities—one political and the other religious—that are functionally connected to one another, but each with a relatively independent organizational model (Stroumsa 2005).

Gnosticism, meanwhile, has become a set of symbols that have continued to circulate in the history of Christianity, interacting within the Christian churches and outside of them. It has entered into relations with a plurality of cultures in the course of its history. In particular for the historically established Christian churches, Gnosticism has represented the excess of sense that could not otherwise be absorbed in the canonical and orthodox vernacular imposed at some point by the various churches. Those symbols have consequently continued to circulate freely and be available to whichever *first bidder* sought to adopt, interpret, and revive them at various times in the course of history, right up until the present day.

The second dilemma that the systemic approach enables us to overcome concerns the question of whether religion is a finite province of meanings (to return to the term used by Schütz), or a superstructure that depends on something else—be it the economy or the genetic code, the neurological structure of our minds, or disorders of our psyche. Even classic functionalism tends to see religion as a geometry of symbols whose center lies elsewhere, in the collective need for social cohesion, in a society's need to represent the fundamental foundations of its social order, and so on. Systems theory, on the other hand, helps to clarify that a religion—being a system—must first develop an independent, internal capacity to function for the very reason that it is founded on differentiation vis-à-vis the environment and, secondly, the more it becomes self-referenced, the better it succeeds in reducing the complexity of the environment. Belief systems thus evolve and mature when they see themselves (and are seen by others) as functionally specialized, expert systems distinguishable from other social systems or sub-systems (politics, economics, law, science, and so on).

They evolve, not from simple to complex in the classic functionalist sense, but from segmented to differentiated. To be part of a *local* history, adhering to a given social and historical segment, linking their future to a population, or to a given social organization (be it a tribal society or nationalist ideology), or to become a system suited to *different, differentiated environments*: that is the question—a tightrope on which a religion must constantly strive to keep its balance. A tightrope because it may unexpectedly meet with accidents along the way: a religion may become the ethnic emblem of a nation, it may be adopted as a symbolic shield against another religious belief system, it may find itself integrated in a society where it becomes the dominant cultural regulator, and consequently incapable of acknowledging the pluralism of faiths that it had previously housed; or it may succeed in retaining its universalistic vocation and avoid being imprisoned in political-ideological or ethnic frameworks.

The great religions' universality (or their claim to it) is basically a measure of how successfully a belief system has gone beyond the limited horizons of the environment where it was born, from where it started out, and thus escaped the risk of being wholly identified with the culture of a given population or nation. Peoples and nations tend to build their collective memory along the lines of one religion or another, but that does not mean that all this obeys a rule. As Weber says, there are world religions claiming that they are able to speak to the heart of all human beings, everywhere and for all time, so—in principle—there is no need for them to become tied to the destinies of one civilization rather than another.

Finally, our proposed systemic approach may help us to put the sociology of religion back on its feet because, with the admirable intention of becoming specialized, this discipline has placed the problem of the theoretical statute or explanatory paradigms needed to analyze the phenomenon of religion between brackets, as it were. Many of us feel the need (and Jim Beckford (2003]) recently returned to this topic) for a social theory in which to frame our analysis of religion and methods for studying the related social phenomena. We therefore hope to have demonstrated that this can be done by exploring new lines of research, instead of having to restrict ourselves to retracing the steps of the classics of sociology, as Geertz rightly said in the passage we quoted at the beginning of this chapter.

The fathers of our science have taught us a great deal, but it is time to look around and take stock of what has been done in other disciplines, such as systems theory, the neurosciences, and the cognitive sciences, with a view to constructing theoretical approaches suited to the complexity of religious phenomena.

Bibliography

Abu Zayd, N.(2002), *Islam e storia*, Torino: Bollati Boringhieri.

—— (2004), *Una vita con l'Islam*, Bologna: Il Mulino.

Acquaviva, S. (1990), *La strategia del gene*, Bari-Roma: Laterza.

—— and R. Stella (1989), *Fine di una ideologia: la secolarizzazione*, Roma: Borla.

Alberoni, F. (1977), *Movimento e istituzione*, Bologna: Il Mulino.

Amri, N. (2008), *La Sainte de Tunis. Présentation et traduction de l'hagiographie de 'Aisha al-Mannūbiyya*, Paris: Sindbad.

Arkoun, M. (1991), *Lectures du Coran*, Tunis: Alif.

Asad, T. (1993), *Genealogies of Religion*, Baltimore, MD: John Hopkins University Press.

Augé, M. (1982), *Génie du paganisme*, Paris: Gallimard.

Balandier, G. (1955), *Sociologie actuelle de l'Afrique noire*, Paris: PUF.

Bastide, R. (1972), *Le sacré sauvage*, Paris: Payot.

—— (1960), *Les religions africaines au Brésil*, Paris: PUF.

Bayly, S. (1999) *Caste, Society and Politics in India from the Eighteenth Century to the Modern Age*, Cambridge: Cambridge University Press.

Beckford, J. (1973), "Religious Organizations. A Trend Report and Bibliography," *Current Sociology*, 2: 1–172.

—— (2003), *Social Theory and Religion*, Cambridge: Cambridge University Press.

Bellah, R. (1967), "Civil Religion in America," *Daedalus*, 96: 1–21.

Benveniste, E. (1969), *Le vocaboulaire des institutions indo-européennes*, Paris: Les Editions de Minuit.

Blasi, J.A., P.A. Turcotte, and J. Duhaime (eds) (2002), *Handbook of Early Christianity*, Walnut Creek, CA: AltaMira Press.

Boissevain, K. (2006), *Sainte parmi les saints*, Paris: Maisonneuve et Larose.

Bourdieu, P. (1971a), "Génèse et structure du champ religieux," *Revue Française de Sociologie*, 3: 295–334.

—— (1971b), "Une interprétation de la théorie de la religion selon Max Weber," *Archives Européennes de Sociologie*, 1: 3–21.

Bova, E. (2003), *Solidarność*, Soveria Mannelli: Rubbettino.

Busi, G. (1995), *Introduzione* in G. Busi and E. Loewenthal (eds), *Mistica ebraica*, Torino: Einaudi.

Canetti, E. (1962), *Crowds and Power*, New York: Farrar, Strauss and Giroux.

Casanova, J. (1994), *Public Religion in the Modern World*, Chicago, IL: University of Chicago Press.

Castaneda, C. (1968), *The Teaching of Don Juan*, Berkeley: University of California Press.

—— (1999), *Pases Magicos*, Buenos Aires, Mexico, Santiago de Chile: Editorial Atlantida.

Cesareo, V. et al (1995) (ed.), *La religiosità in Italia*, Milano: Mondadori.

Chabbi, J. (1997), "Une tradition prophétique: l'homme au petit chat," in F. Lenoir and Y.T. Masquelier (sous la direction), *Encyclopédie des religions*, Paris: Bayard, pp. 1349–52.

Cole, W.O. and P.S. Sambhi (1978), *The Sikhs. Their Religious Beliefs and Practices*, London: Routledge.

Cook, D. (2005), *Understanding Jihad*, Berkeley: University of California Press.

Copley, A (ed.) (2000), *Gurus and Their Followers*, Delhi: Oxford University Press.

Corbin, H. (1971), *En Islam iranien*, Paris: Gallimard.

Cròs, C.R. (1997), *La civilisation afro-brésilienne*, Paris: PUF.

Culianu, I.P. (1991), *I viaggi dell'anima*, Milano: Adelphi.

Davie, G. (2000), *Religion in Modern Europe*, Oxford: Oxford University Press.

—— (2001), "The Persistence of Institutional Religion in Modern Europe," in L. Woodhead (ed.), *Peter Berger and the Study of Religion*, London: Routledge, pp. 101–21

Davidson, B. (1972), *African Civilization*, Trenton, NJ: African World Press.

de Certeau, M. (1987), *La faiblesse de croire*, Paris: Seuil.

Deconchy, J.P. (1971), *L'orthodoxie religieuse*, Paris: Editions Ouvrières.

Deshpande, M. (1979), *Sociolinguistic Attitudes in India*, Ann Arbor, MI: Karoma

Destro, A. and M. Pesce (2004), *Antropologia delle origini cristiane*, Roma-Bari: Laterza.

Diotallevi, L. (2001), *Il rompicapo della secolarizzazione*, Soveria Mannelli: Rubbettino.

Dirks, N. (2001), *Castes of Mind*, Princeton, NJ: Princeton University Press.

Dobbelaere, K. (2002), *Secularization: an Analysys at Three Levels*, Bruxelles: Peter Lang.

Dumézil, G. (1952), *Les dieux des Indo-Européens*, Paris: PUF.

—— (1958), *L'idéologie tripartite des Indo-Européens*, Bruxlles: Latomus.

—— (1995), *Le Roman de jumeaux*, Paris: Gallimard.

Dumont, L. (1966), *Homo hierachicus*, Milano: Adelphi.

Durkheim, E. (1912), *Les formes élémentaires de la vie religieuse*, Paris: Colin.

—— (1996), *Per una definizione dei fenomeni religiosi*, Roma: Armando.

Ehrman, B. (2003), *Lost Christianities*, Oxford: Oxford University Press.

Eliade, M. (1951), *Le chamanisme et les techniques archaïques*, Paris: Payot.

—— (1959), *Cosmos and History*, New York: Harper.

Esposito, E. (1992), *L'operazione di osservazione*, Milano: Franco Angeli.

Filoramo, G. (1993), *L'attesa della fine*, Bari: Laterza.

—— (1997), "Alla ricerca di un'identità cristiana," in G. Filoramo and D. Menozzi (eds), *Storia del cristianesimo*, Roma-Bari: Laterza, Vol. I.

—— (a cura di) (2002), *Maestro e discepolo*, Brescia: Morcelliana.

—— (2004), *Che cos'è la religione*, Torino: Einaudi.

—— and C. Prandi (1987), *Le scienze delle religioni*, Brescia: Morcelliana.

Flusser, D. (1997), *Jesus*, Brescia: Morcelliana

Foerster, H. (1960), "On Self-Organizing System and their Environment," in C. Marshall Yovitis and S. Cameron (eds), *Self-Organizing System*, Oxford: Oxford University Press.

—— (1987), *Sistemi che osservano*, Roma: Astrolabio.

—— (1996), *Attraverso gli occhi dell'altro*, Milano: Guerini e Associati.

—— and R. Porksen (2001), *La verità è l'invenzione di un bugiardo*, Roma: Meltemi.

Foucault, M. (1998), *Taccuino persiano*, Milano: Guerini e Associati.

Fumarola, P. (1997), "Per una sociologia delle transe estatiche," in D. De Nigris (ed.), *Musica, rito e aspetti terapeutici nella cultura mediterranea*, Genova: Erga.

Gallissot, R., M. Kilani, and A.M. Rivera (1998), *L'imbroglio etnico*, Bari: Dedalo.

Garelli, F. (2006), *L'Italia cattolica nell'epoca del pluralismo*, Bologna: Il Mulino.

—— (2007), *La Chiesa cattolica in Italia*, Bologna: Il Mulino.

——, G. Guizzardi, and E. Pace (eds) (2003), *Un singolare pluralismo*, Bologna: Il Mulino.

Geertz, C. (1971), *Islam Observed*, Chicago, IL: Chicago University Press.

—— (1973), *The Interpretation of Cultures*, New York: Basic Books.

Gira, D. (1997), *Les chrétiens et les grandes religions*, Paris: Draguet et Ardaut.

Girard, R. (1972) *La violence et le sacré*, Paris: Grasset.

Goody, J. (2000), *The Power of Written Tradition*, Washington, DC: Smithsonian Institute Press.

Griaule, M. (1966), *Dieu d'eau*, Paris: Fayard.

Guizzardi, G. (ed.), (1983) *La narrazione del carisma*, Roma: ERI.

—— (1979), *Le religione della crisi*, Milano: Edizioni di Comunità.

—— and E. Pace (1987), "La chiesa e le altre organizzazioni religiose," in D. De Masi and A. Bonzanini (eds), *Trattato di sociologia del lavoro e dell'organizzazione. Le tipologie*, Milano: Franco Angeli, pp. 493–533.

Guolo, R. (ed.) (1996), *Il paradosso della tradizione*, Milano: Guerini e Associati.

—— (2007), *La via dell'Imam*, Roma-Bari: Laterza.

Hérail, F. (1986), *Histoire du Japon*, Paris: Publications Orientalistes de France.

Hervieu-Léger, D. (1993), *La religion pour mémoire*, Paris: Cerf.

—— (1999), *Le pèlerin et le converti*, Paris: Flammarion.

Hinde, R. (1999), *Why Gods Persist*, London: Routledge.

Hubert, H. and M. Mauss (1929), *Essai sur la nature et la fonction du sacrifice*, Paris: Felix Alcan (first edn 1899).

Huntington, S. (1996), *The Clash of Civilisation and the Remaking of World Order*, New York: Simon and Schuster.

Hurbon, L. (1972), *Dieu dans le vaudou haïtienne*, Paris: Payot.

—— (1993), *Les mystères du vaudou*, Paris: Gallimard.

——— (ed.) (2000), *Le phénomène religieux dans le Caraïbe*, Paris: Khartala.

Idel, M. (1998), *Messianic Mystics*, New Haven, CT: Yale University Press.

Jamison, S.W. and M. Witzel (1992), *Vedic Hinduism* <www.people.fas.harvard. edu/-witzel/vedic.pdf>.

Jenkins, P. (2002), *The Next Christendom*, Oxford: Oxford University Press.

Khosrokhawar, F. and P. Vieille (1990), *Le discourse populaire de la révolution iranienne*, Paris: Contemporaneité.

Kilani, M. (1994), *Antropologia: un'introduzione*, Bari: Dedalo.

Lagerwey, J. (1987), *Taoist Ritual en Chinese Society and History*, New York, McMillan Press.

——— (1991), *Le continent des esprits: la Chine dans le miroir du taoïsme*, Bruxelles: La Renaissance du Livre.

——— (2007), "Ritual, Pantheons and Techniques : A History of Chinese Religion before the Tang," *Iias Newsletter*, 44, 23.

Lambert, Y. (1991), "La tour de Babel des définitions de la religion," in *Social Compass*, 1: 73–85.

Lapassade, G. (1976), *Saggio sulla transe*, Milano: Feltrinelli.

Lévy-Bruhl, L. (1922), *La mentalité primitive*, Paris: Les Presses Universitaires de France.

Lévi-Strauss, C. (1966), *The Savage Mind*, Chicago, IL: Chicago University Press.

——— (1969), *The Elementary Structures of Kinship*, New York: Beacon Press.

Libson, G. (2003), *Jewish and Islamic Law: A Comparative Study of Custom During the Geonic Period*, Cambridge, MA: Harvard University Press.

Luhmann, N. (1977), *Funktion der religion*, Frankfurt a.M: Suhrkamp Verlag.

——— (1985), "Society, Meaning, Religion Based on Self-Reference," *Sociological Analysis*, 46: 5–20.

——— (1986), *Religious Dogmatic and the Evolution of Societies*, New York: Edwin Mellen Press (introduction by Peter Beyer).

——— (1995), *Social Systems*, Stanford, CA: Stanford University Press (1st edn 1984).

——— (2000), *Die Religion der Geselschaft*, Frankfurt a.M.: Suhrkamp Verlag.

Lupieri, E. (1997), "Fra Gesù e Cristo," in G. Filoramo and D. Menozzi (eds), *Storia del cristianesimo*, Roma-Bari: Laterza, Vol. I.

McLeod, W.H. (1968), *Guru Nanak and Sikh Religion*, Oxford: Oxford University Press.

Maccarinelli, M. (ed.) (2001), *Un padre per vivere*, Padova: Il Polografo.

Madan, T.N. (ed.) (1991), *Religion in India*, Delhi: Oxford University Press.

——— (ed.) (2004), *India's Religions*, Delhi: Oxford University Press.

Mantovani, G. (2004), *Intercultura*, Bologna: Il Mulino.

Martelli, S. (1990), *La religione nella società moderna fra secolarizzazione e desecolarizzazione*, Bologna: Dehoniane.

Mary, A. (1999), *Le défi du syncrétisme*, Paris: Editions de l'Ecole des Hautes Etudes en Sciences Sociales (EHESS).

——— (2000), *Le bricolage africain des héros chrétiens*, Paris: Cerf.

—— (2005), "Métissage et Bricolage in the Making African Christian Identity," *Social Compass*, 3: 281–94.

—— and J.P. Laurent (eds), (2001), "Prophètes, visionnaires et guérisseurs de l'Afrique subsaharienne contemporaine," *Social Compass*, 3.

Maturana, H.R. and F. Varela (1980) *Autopoiesis and Cognition*, Boston, MA: Kluwer.

Mauss, M. (1923–24), "Essais sur le don," *Année Sociologique*, II séries.

Michel, P. (1989), *La société rétrouvée,* Paris: Fayard

—— (1994), *Religion et politique: la grande mutation*, Paris: Albin Michel.

Nesti, A. (2003), "L'ashura e i giorni del Muharram: da una religione della giustizia ad una religione del lamento?," in A. Nesti (ed.) (2003), *Laboratorio Iran*, Milano: Franco Angeli, pp. 106–12.

Ortiz, F. (1943), *Los cabildos y la fiesta afrocubana*, La Habana: Editorial de Ciencias Sociales.

Pace, E. (ed.) (1984), *La società parallela. Religione, resistenza e opposizione nella Polonia contemporanea*, Milano: Franco Angeli.

—— (1986), "La funzione della religione nella teoria dei sistemi di Niklas Luhmann," *Rassegna Italiana di Sociologia*, 3: 44–61.

—— (2003), "Politics of Paradise," *Rassegna Italiana di Sociologia*, 1: 25–42.

—— (2004a), *Sociologia dell'islam*, Roma: Carocci.

—— (2004b), *Perchè le religioni scendono in guerra*, Roma-Bari: Laterza.

—— (2006), "Salvation Goods, the Gift Ecomony and Charismatic Concern," *Social Compass*, 53: 49–64.

—— and G. Giordan (2010), "La religione come comunicazione nell'era digitale," *Humanitas*, 5–6: 2–24.

Parsons, T. (1951), *Social System*, New York: Routledge.

Patel, S.K. (1992), *Hinduism in India*, Delhi: South Asia Books.

Pesce, M. (2004), *La parole dimenticate di Gesù*, Milano: Mondadori.

Pettazzoni, R. (1957), *L'essere supremo nelle religioni primitive*, Torino: Einaudi.

Piano, S. (1996), "Il Sikh Panth," in G. Filoramo (ed.), *Storia delle religioni*, Roma-Bari: Laterza, Vol. IV, pp. 249–76.

—— (1996), "Lo Hinduismo. La prassi religiosa," in G. Filoramo (ed.), *Storia delle religioni*, Roma-Bari: Laterza, Vol. IV, pp. 133–94.

Piantelli, M. (1996), "Religione e religioni nel mondo indiano," in G. Filoramo (ed.) *Storia delle religioni*, Roma-Bari: Laterza, Vol. IV, pp. 4–48.

Pierucci, F. and R. Prandi (1996), *A realidade social das religiões no Brasil*, São Paulo: Hucitec

Piette, A. (1993), *Les religiosités séculières*, Paris: Puf.

Poggi, G. (1984), *Calvinismo e spirito del capitalismo*, Bologna: Il Mulino.

Prandi, C. (1983), *Per una sociologia della tradizione religiosa*, Milano: Franco Angeli

Prandi, R. (1991), *Os candomblé de São Paulo: a velha magia na metropoli nova São Paulo*, São Paulo: Hucitec & Edusp.

Raveri, M. (1984), *Itinerari del sacro*, Venezia: Cafoscarina.

—— (1993), "Riti shintoisti," in G. Filoramo (ed.), *Dizionario delle religioni*, Torino: Einaudi, pp. 633–6.

—— (1998), *Il corpo e il paradiso*, Venezia: Marsilio.

Rokeach, M. (1960), *The Open and Closed Mind*, New York: Basic Books.

Rosati, M. (2009), *Ritual and the Sacred*, Farnham: Ashgate.

Scholem, G. (1946), *Major Trends in Jewish Mysticism*, New York: Schocken Books.

—— (1986), *Le grandi correnti della mistica ebraica*, Genova: Il Melangolo.

Schütz, A. (1967), *The Phenomenology of the Social World*, Evanston, IL: Northwestern University Press.

Séguy, J. (1972), "Max Weber et la sociologie historique des religions," *Archives de Sociologie des Religions*, 33: 71–105.

—— (1980), *Christianisme et société*, Paris: Cerf.

Sen, A. (2006), *Identity and Violence*, New York: Norton and Co.

Shah, G. (ed.) (2001), *Dalit Identity and Politics*, New Delhi: Sage.

Squarcini, F. (2003), "Violenza, norma, immaginativa politica," PhD dissertation in Religious Studies, University of Bologna.

—— (2006), *Ex Oriente Lux*, Firenze: Società Editrice Fiorentina.

—— and C. Bartoli (1997), *Il monoteismo hindū*, Pisa: Pacini.

Stark, R. and W.S. Bainbridge (1987), *Theory of Religion*, New Brunswick, NJ: Rutgers University Press.

—— and R. Finke (2000), *Acts of Faith*, Berkeley: University of California Press.

Stefani, P. (1997), *Gli ebrei*, Bologna: Il Mulino.

Stroumsa, G. (1999), *La formazione dell'identità cristiana*, Brescia: Morcelliana.

—— (2005), *La fin du sacrifice*, Paris: Odile Jacob.

Terrin, A.N. (1991), *Introduzione allo studio comparato delle religioni*, Brescia: Morcelliana

Theissen, G. (1987), *Sociologia del cristianesimo primitivo*, Genova: Marietti.

—— (1998), *The Historical Jesus*, Minneapolis, MN: Fortress Press.

Todorov, T. (1982), *La conquête de l'Amérique*, Paris: Seuil.

Treppete, M. (1999), "La religiosità popolare femminile in Tunisia fra tradizione e modernità," *Religioni e Società*, 35: 14–26.

Trigano, S. (2001), *Qu'est-ce que la religion*, Paris: Flammarion.

Troeltsch, E. (1990), *The Social Teaching of the Christian Churches*, Louisville, KY: Westminster John Knox Press.

Turina, I. (2006), "Aspetti cognitivi della fuga dal mondo: il caso dell'eremitismo," *Rassegna Italiana di Sociologia*, 2: 297–328.

Van Gennep, A. (1909), *Les rites de passage*, Paris: Picard.

Walzer, M. (1985), *Exodus and Revolution*, New York: Basic Books.

Weber, M. (1993), *The Sociology of Religion*, New York: Beacon Press.

Weil, S. (1951), *Lettre à un religieux*, Paris: Gallimard.

Willaime, J.P. (1993), *La precarité protestante*, Genève: Labor et Fides.

Wilson, B. (1982), *Religion in Sociological Perspective*, Oxford: Oxford University Press.

—— (1985), *La religione nel mondo contemporaneo*, Bologna: Il Mulino.

Yang, F. and J. Tamney, "Conversion to Christianity among Chinese," *Sociology of Religion*, 62, 2: 125–9.

Zürcher, E. (1996), "Il buddismo in Cina," in G. Filoramo (ed.), *Storia delle religioni*, Vol. IV, Roma-Bari: Laterza, pp. 364–411.

Index

Abbas the Great 3
Abu Hurayra 123
African religions 6–8, 10, 12–13, 112–13
Afro-Brazilian cults 99, 112
Alberoni, F. 26
'Ali Muhammad of Shiraz 95–6
alphabet, use of 129
animism 125
anomia 51
anthropomorphic representations of deities
  131
Asad, Talal 13, 67
ascetic practices 15
Ashoka, King 39
Aspromonte 56
authenticity of the truth 129–34
authority, religious 97, 132
autonomy
  of individuals 14
  of religions 51–2, 115, 118–19, 138
autopoiesis 34–6, 59, 63, 68–9, 72, 88, 94,
  100, 102, 106, 138
  and belief systems 54–7
ayatollahs 98, 129
Aztec religion 9

Baha'i religion 95–6
Balandier, G. 10
Bambara people 125–6
Bastide, R. 10
Beckford, Jim 146
belief systems 22, 26–34, 43
  and *autopoiesis* 54–7
  construction of 99
  core themes of 58–9
  evolution of 62, 84
  genesis of 67, 69
  hegemonic 81
  internal differentiation of 91
  interpenetration between 80

power of believers in 98
religious 18, 32–4, 48, 50–55, 61, 66,
  89, 109, 117, 122, 130, 138–9
restoration of 77
and risk-reduction 59
and ritual 114–15
role of experts in 119–20
of states 144
see also founders of religions
  and belief systems
believing 52, 57–9, 134, 136
Benedict XVI, Pope 107
Benveniste, Emile 59, 110
Bhagavad-gita, the 23, 28, 130–31
bodhisattva figure 93
boundaries between religions and belief
  systems 8–12, 17, 22, 27, 116
Bourdieu, Pierre 89, 129–30
Buddha and Buddhism 15, 28, 39–41,
  54, 72–80, 92–4, 108, 133
al-Bukhari 123
Busi, G. 128

Calvinism 52–3
Candomblé 98–9
Canetti, E. 4
canonical texts 122
capitalism 52–3
Castaneda, Carlos 75
caste system 56–7, 71–2, 86, 93, 102
Catholic Church 1, 5, 7, 9, 38, 56, 58,
  90–93, 98–9, 107, 111, 117, 142–3
chain of transmission 122–3
charismatic churches 99, 143
charismatic leaders 41–3, 65, 67, 83, 87–8,
  92
China 77–81
Christianity 8–9, 42–3, 58, 82, 90–91, 116,
  118, 122, 129, 141, 143, 145
the church as a system 38, 44

Church Fathers 30
civil religions 50–51
clash of civilizations 17
cognitive maps 17
collective consciousness 51
communication
    between religions 38–42
    concept of 18
    as dominion 27
    power of 15, 27, 29, 31, 46, 59, 74,
        83, 89
    in relation to action 49–50
    as a selective process of sense 48–9
    see also religion as communication
communication media 105, 109
communicative action 83
communism 50–51
communitas principle 38
comparative religion 15–16
comprehending 16
Comte, Auguste 125, 140
Confucius and Confucianism 76–80
Congregation for Divine Worship 107
conquistadores 9
Constantine, Emperor 145
Corbin, H. 48
Cortés, Hernán 9
Culianu, I.P. 82
cultural systems 137–8

Davidson, B. 127
death rituals 7–8
Deconchy, J.P. 27–8
Deshpande, M. 102
dharma 103–4, 110
dharmasútra 104
differentiation, socio-religious 42–6, 55,
        57, 68, 70–71, 77, 100, 141, 143–4
Diotallevi, L. 142
doctrine, religious 116–17, 120–21, 124
Dogon people 125–7
double contingency 35–7, 49, 61
doxemes 28–9
Dumézil, G. 10
Durkheim, Emile 10, 16, 32, 38, 51–2, 110,
        135

Ehrman, B. 118

Eliade, Mircea 74, 134
enlightenment project 33
environment, socio-religious 18
environments related to systems 34–6, 43,
        53–4, 59, 69, 77–8, 84, 91, 105–6
Esposito, E. 35
Essene sect 66–7
essentialism regarding religion 33
ethnic religions 69–70, 92
Eucharist 106–7
expansion, virtue of 72–3

faith and faithfulness 25, 84
Fatima, daughter of Muhammad the
        Prophet 44
field, concept of 89
Filoramo, G. 30, 82
Foerster, Heinz von 61
founders of religions and belief systems
        41–2, 65, 67, 97, 100, 116
Francis of Assisi, St 29
Frazer, James 125
Freud, Sigmund 135
functionalism, religious 33, 137, 145
funeral ceremonies 7

Garelli, F. 142–3
Gautama 39, 41, 93–4, 133
Geertz, Clifford 135, 138, 146
gender distinctions 115, 133–4
genealogical method of analysis 13
Gnawa groups 113–14
Gnosticism 145
God, communication with 124–32
Govind Singh 21, 85
Griaule, Marcel 125–7

habitus 28, 132
hadith 122–3
Hebrew scripture and law 30, 47, 118
Hegel, G.W.F. 81
hermeneutic variability 29
Hervieu-Léger, D. 89, 130
hesychasm 60
hierophany 134
Hinde, R. 58
Hinduism 23, 28, 41, 55–6, 60, 70–72, 86,
        92–3, 102, 104–5, 110, 130, 133–4

historiography 16
Hubert, H. 57
Husayn, son of Ali 3–4
husayniyya 3
Husserl, E. 36

Ibn 'Arabi 129
Ibn Hanbal 123
Idel, M. 128
Ijo tribe 127
improvisation, capacity for 67–8, 72, 81,
        84, 86, 89; *see also* virtuoso of
        improvis-ation
'incarnate' authority 131
incest taboo 11
information (Luhmann) 37
interpenetration, concept of 61, 80
Iran 3–5
Islam 50, 60, 86, 95, 113–15, 122–3,
        128–9; *see also* Shi'a Islam;
        Sunni Islam

Japan 72–81
Java 136
Jesus Christ 21–2, 28, 30, 43–4, 65–7,
        87–91, 94–5, 100, 107
John Paul II, Pope 2
John's Gospel 23, 121
Judaism 22, 26, 30, 47, 59, 66–7, 108, 116,
        128–9
Justin Martyr 30, 82

kinship structures 11
Kojiki text 75
Koran, the 24, 48, 91, 123, 129, 133–4
Korea 74
Kuru kings 102

Lagerwey, John 78
Lalla Manoubiyya's sanctuary 113–15
language, holy 102–6
Lao-Tzu 79
Lévi-Bruhl, Lucien 12
Lévi-Strauss, C. 11–12
life-world concept 35, 94
liturgy and liturgical practices 26, 109–17
Luhmann, Niklas 33–9, 48–9, 61, 116, 138
Luke's Gospel 121

Luria, Yishaq 129
Luther, Martin 92

magic 16, 125
Mahabharata, the 23
Malinowski, Bronislaw 135
Mao Zedong 78
Mark's Gospel 21–2, 65–6, 121
marriage practices 11, 72
Marxism 57
matsuri ritual 111–12
Matthew's Gospel 118, 121
Maturana, H.R. 35
Mauss, Marcel 10, 57
Mazdaism 86
Mbuti Pygmies 62
Mecca 24
mind, theory of 35–6
'missionary' prophets 92–4
mobile personality 65, 83, 87–8, 91–2, 101,
        141
monotheism 124–8
Montezuma 9
Moses 25–6, 44
mudang figure 74
Muhammad the Prophet 24, 44–5, 87–8,
        91, 94–5, 97, 113, 122–3
Münzer, Thomas 92–3
myths 12

Nanak, Guru 84–6, 93
Native Americans 74–5
Neo-Catechumenal movement 107

offerings 59
order in a religious setting 97
Orthodox Church 60
orthodoxies 29

paganism 82
paradigm of religious economics 13
Parsons, Talcott 48, 135
Paul, St 118, 121–2
Pentecostal churches 9–10, 143
Pesach celebrations 108
Pettazzoni, Raffaele 127
Pharisees 66–7
Piantelli, M. 39

Plato 101
Plotinus 129
pluralism, religious 43, 68–9
Poland 1–3, 5
polytheism 28, 125, 127
possession, rites of 112–14
primitive thought 12, 15–16
prophets 21, 27, 88, 92–4
propositions, religious 28
Protestantism 101
pure religions 6

qabbalah, the 128

rational choice applied to religion 33,
    68–9, 139
Raveri, M. 111
reciprocity principle 10–11
reincarnation 58
religion
    bureaucratization of 116–17
    as communication 8, 13–15, 18–19,
        25–6, 38–42, 50, 54, 57
    conservative function of 137
    decline and revival of 142
    definition of 14, 34, 135
    link between *narrating* and *acting* 59
    and the social environment 139–42
    as a source of symbols 57–8
    systemic approach to 141–2, 146
    as a type of organization 97
    and the use of coercion 117
    see also comparative religion
religions
    of *accretion* and of *annihilation* 81
    affinities between 17
    communication between 38–42
    of *deposition* 27
    evolution of 101
    as expert systems 140–42
    interpretative function of 142–4
    living and *dead* 68–9
    as living systems 14, 55
    mass and *elite* 133
    of *revelation* 124
    self-images of 17–18
    as systems of belief 46
    universality of 146

respect, principle of 53
resurrection 58
rites of passage 111
rituality and rites 38, 55, 59–62, 72, 74,
    99, 104–12, 115, 120, 136, 142

sabbath observance 65–6
sacralization of language 103–4
sacrifice 57, 105, 111
Safavid dynasty 3
Sai Baba 131
saints 129
Sanskrit 102–3
sant doctrine 85
Saussure, Ferdinand de 11
Schmidt, Wilhelm 125
Scholem, G. 128
Schütz, A. 35, 145
scripture 21–5, 30, 47–8, 106
secular religions 50–51
secularization 1, 5, 19, 115, 139, 142–4
Sefer ha-zohar 128
Séguy, Jean 35
self-referentiality of belief systems 117–19,
    124, 138, 145
self-reproduction by belief systems 138
sense 36–46, 101, 104
    as consciousness 46
    controversies of 41–2
    as a resource 43
    social dimension of 41–2
shamanism 68, 73–8, 112
Shi'a Islam 3–5, 48, 95, 97–8, 123, 129
Shinto 72–8, 81, 111
Shotku Taishi, Prince 76
Sikhism 21, 70, 84–6, 93, 130
Simmel, Georg 19
Sioux Indians 125
slavery 6–7
social systems and social structures 10–11,
    35–7, 61–2, 137
sociology of religion 1, 13–19, 32–3, 46,
    67, 69, 82, 40, 146
Soka Gakkai 133
Solidarność 2
spiritism 8
Squarcini, F. 103–4
Sufism 128–9

Sunni Islam 3, 48, 123
symbolic generalizations 44
symbols, religious 27, 136
syncretism 6–7, 10, 19, 72, 84–5, 141
system, definition of 35
systems theory 18–19, 33–5, 42–4, 49–50,
    58, 62–3, 91, 94, 116, 124–5, 129,
    136–40, 145

Talmud, the 47–8
Taoism 79–80
Ten Commandments 25
themis concept 110
theology 120
Todorov, T. 9
Torah, the 128
tradition, religious 120–21, 128
trance experiences 99, 112–13
Trinity, the 129
Troeltsch, Ernst 34, 100, 141, 143
'trustees of the truth' 132–3
Tylor, Edward Burnett 15–16, 124–5

Universal Church of the Kingdom of God
    99
'universal ethic' 69

vaisakha-puja celebrations 108
Varela, F. 35
Vedic texts 102–3, 130–31, 134
vicarious mediating figures 131–2
virtuoso of improvisation 19, 83–9, 92,
    100–101, 108, 141
Voodoo 7–8

wars
    justification for 24
    of religion 17
Weber, Max 11, 16–17, 31–3, 42, 44, 48,
    52–3, 67, 82–3, 87, 92–4, 135, 146
Weil, Simone 47
Wilson, Bryan 140
Witzel, M. 102
women priests 37–8
world religions 146

'Yahwe', use of term 129
yoga 60

Zen Buddhism 133
Zoroaster 86
Zürcher, E. 80